The One-Minute Motivator

By King Duncan:

Amusing Grace: Humor To Heal Mind, Soul and Body
King's Treasury Of Dynamic Humor
Mule Eggs and Topknots

The One-Minute Motivator

King Duncan with Rebecca Clark

Seven Worlds Corporation
310 Simmons Road
Knoxville, TN 37922

The One-Minute Motivator

Copyright © 1996 by King Duncan with Rebecca Clark. All rights reserved. Printed in the United States of America by Seven Worlds Corporation. First Edition.

ISBN: 0-936497-19-X   Paperback: $14.95

Seven Worlds Corporation
310 Simmons Road
Knoxville, TN 37922

Library of Congress-in-Publication Data

Duncan, King and Rebecca Clark
The One-Minute Motivator/ King Duncan and Rebecca Clark—1st ed.
p.
ISBN: 0-936497-19-X
Library of Congress Catalog Card Number: 96-69014

Canfield, Jack and Mark Victor Hansen. Quote from *Chicken Soup for the Soul*. Copyright 1993 by Jack Canfield and Mark Victor Hansen. Reprinted with permission of Health Communications, Inc.

Canfield, Jack and Mark Victor Hansen. Quote from *A 2nd Helping of Chicken Soup for the Soul*. Copyright 1995 by Jack Canfield and Mark Victor Hansen. Reprinted with permission of Health Communications, Inc.

Campolo, Tony. Quote from Everything You've Heard Is Wrong. Copyright 1992. Reprinted with permission of Word, Inc., Dallas, Texas.

Clower, Jerry. Quote from *Stories from Home*. Copyright 1992. Reprinted with permission of University Press of Mississippi.

Conner, Dennis. Quote from *The Art Of Winning*. Copyright 1988 by Dennis Conner. Reprinted with permission of St. Martin's Press, Inc., New York, NY.

Covey, Stephen R. Quote from *Principled Centered Leadership*. Copyright 1990, 1991 by Stephen R. Covey. Reprinted with permission of Simon & Schuster.

Drucker, Peter F. Quote from *The Effective Executive*. Copyright 1966, 1967 by Peter F. Drucker. Copyright renewed 1994, 1995 by Peter F. Drucker. Reprinted by permission of HarperCollins Publishers, Inc.

Iacocca, Lee. Quote from *Talking Straight*. Copyright 1988 by Lee Iacocca. Reprinted with permission of Bantam Books, a division of Bantam Doubleday Dell Publishing Group, Inc.

Lucado, Max. Quote from And the Angels Were Silent. Copyright 1993. Reprinted with permission of Questar Publishers, Inc.

Maxwell, John C. Quote from *Developing the Leaders Around You*. Copyright 1995. Reprinted with permission of Thomas Nelson Publishers.

Schuller, Robert H. Quote from *The Peak to Peek Principle*. Copyright 1980 by Robert H. Schuller. Reprinted with permission of Doulbeday, a division of Bantam Doubleday Dell Publishing Group, Inc.

Swindoll, Charles R. Quote from *Stress Fractures*. Copyright 1990 by Charles R. Swindoll, Inc. Reprinted with permission of Zondervan Publishing House.

Tournier, Paul. Quote from *A Listening Ear*. Copyright 1987 Augsburg Publishing House. Reprinted with permission of Augsburg Fortress.

To David and Glenda Newton—
colleagues in the speaking profession
and friends without equal.

TABLE OF CONTENTS

Introduction 1

I. ACTION
"It's your dream" 3
Campus Security 3
How to become an Oil Baron ... 4
Gen. Patton Crosses River 4
Don't Just Stand There--Mop! .. 5
Snowbound, Not Stuck 5
Washington Demands Action ... 6
"It's Worth Doing Poorly" 6
An Artist Says Thanks 7
Stopping a Locomotive 7

II. ADVERSITY

Anna M. Moses' Arthritis 11
The Rose in the Diamond 11
Joe Montana's Sore Arm 12
The Twisted Trees 13
A Boy, A Boat and 14
Hondo Runs to Keep Up 14
Al Jolson's Toenail 15
Bargain with God? 15
James E. Jones Stutters 16
Between a Bear and a Bull 16
Bristlecone Pine 17
Marriott's Root Beer 18
A Bee in Her Bonnet 18
The Japanese Zero 19
Locked in the Shower 20
Murphy's Law 21
So You've Got Problems 21
Warning Light 22

III. ASPIRATIONS
Aim High 25
A Little Salary 25
Impossible Dreams 25
Dolly's Dream 26

I'll Be a Horse 26
Big People 27

IV. ATTITUDE
Wisdom from Winnie 29
National Anthem 29
Supposed to Be Dead 30
Enjoy Your Work? 30
Reagan's Attitude 31
It's What's in You 32
Chuck's Philosophy 32
Directing with Enthusiasm ... 33

V. CHANGE
Tradition Bound 37
Change Your Cleats 37
Perceptual Shift 38
Good News Is Bad News 38
Voyager Spacecraft 39
Dr. Baker's Lament 39
Stay Home, Watch TV 40

VI. COMMUNICATION
There Are Parachutes? 43
Watch the Borders 43
Are You Talking to Me? 44
A French Sheepdog 44
Let Them Talk 45
One Secret of Success 45
Oops, That's Embarrassing ... 46
It Pays to Listen 46
An Idea for Congress 47

VII. CONFIDENCE
Like You Own the Place 49
A Dominant Three-Year-Old .. 49
Crack the Whip 50
Custer's Last Mistake 50
Henry's Secret 51
And Then There is No One ... 52

v

Making Good Impressions ... 53

VIII. CONFORMITY
The Caterpillars' Circle 55
You're On Candid Camera ... 55
Princesses Set the Fashion 56
Coolidge's Cat's Coffee 56
Success, Stanley's Style 57
Edison, Turn Out the Light! .. 58
The Right To Be Different 58

IX. CREATIVITY
Creative Criminals 61
Makin' Mayonnaise 61
Grandfather Goes to Prom 62
And So We Have Levis 63
White Shirts, Emergency Pool . 63
Ford Makes Life Easier 64
Making of a "Golden Girl" ... 64
Irving Can't Play 65
Behind the VCR 66

X. CUSTOMER SERVICE
Break the Rupoles 69
QT Markets 69
Burger King Employee 70
Bedside Manner 70
Never Underestimate 71
Why Customers Quit 71
Service on the High Seas 72
Changed His Life 73
Getting the Run-Around 73
Customer Crichton 74
Do You Smile Enough? 75

XI. DECISIONS
Dumb Coach? 77
Joseph's New Shoes 78
Brer Rabbit Can't Decide 78
Decision Made in Concrete ... 79
Sitting on Two Chairs 79

XII. DETERMINATION
A Gold Medal Landing 83
A Tribute to Everest 83
Susan B. Anthony's Life 84
They Had to Shoot Him 85
Yamaguchi's Feet 85
King & Bench 86
No You Wouldn't 86

XIII. ENCOURAGEMENT
Librarian's Transformation ... 89
Halsey's Hell-Raisers 89
Stranglers & The Wranglers .. 90
Eisenhower Learns Respect ... 91
Lombardi's Secret 92

XIV. EXCELLENCE
Michelangelo Wastes Time ... 95
The "It'll Do" Motel 95
His Work is Sterling 96
The "Nurse Bryan Rule" 96
The Price of Excellence 97
The Physician's Wine 97
U.S. Standards 98
Look Like a Winner 99
The Perfect Statue 99
And Then Some 100
O'Brien Gives His Best 100
Rolls Royce Quality 101

XV. FAILURE
Ford's Failures 103
The Strike-Out King 103
Artists' Hall of Failure 104
Failure: "A Total Plus" 104
Lincoln's Lapses 105
Mickey's Dad's Law 105
Van Gogh: Poor Bungler 106
Marconi's Wireless Waves .. 106
Not Crying Over Spilt Milk .. 107
Stewing in His Misery 108
Ann Learns to Listen 109

Johnson: Make Decisions ... 109
Dad: It's OK to Fail 110
A Lesson from Golf 110
Failure Turns to Teflon 111
Rossini's Bomb 111
Minnie's Mom 112
Learn to Fall 112

XVI. FOCUS
"Don't Look Back!" 115
Keep You Eyes on the Stars . 115
Conversation Cures 116
The Most Important Tool ... 116
Going in Circles 117
The Face in the Photograph .. 117
Following the Snowplow 118
Wings Join the Body 118
Advice: Be There 119
No Fish Here! 120
Water in a Lightbulb? 120
The Path Doesn't Matter 121
One Person at a Time 121

XVII. GOALS
The Class of '53 123
Misguided Muscle Man 123
Focus on the Hash Marks ... 124
Walter Gets His House 124
Big Dreams 125
Goddard's Great Goals 125
The Necessity of Pins 126
Plan For Goals & a Poodle .. 127
Tommy Promotes Peace 127
Bicycles and World Records . 128
Obsessed with Sports 129
Carlson, Iacocca, & Wright .. 129
Thatcher's Advice 130

XVIII. INTEGRITY
In Mexico, It Pays Off 133
An Enemy of the People 133
Sierra Club: No Hypocrisy .. 134

To See "My Fair Lady" 134
A Coach's Ethics 135
The Horizontal Imposter 135
Kissing Off a Wad 136

XIX. KINDNESS
Reds Lack of Compassion ... 139
Third World Kindness 139
Tooth for a Tooth 140
Mother of the White Line ... 140
Comforting Pregnant Wife .. 141
Good Intentions 141
I'll Make You Regret This ... 142
Move the Fence 142
Make Them Happy 143
Doing Good 143

XX. KNOWLEDGE
The Best Computers 147
Franklin & Newton 147
Japanese: Education 148
This Settler's Fool's Gold ... 148
Ignorance Is Not Bliss 149
Ignition Trouble 149
Ford Fires Couzens 150
Take Your Diploma & 151
Franklin Listens and Learns . 152
Safes & Log Jams 152
Too Hot to Handle 153

XXI. LEADERSHIP
"Hands-On" Management ... 155
Consultative Style 155
No "Little People" 156
El Cid Was Dead 156
Leadership Starts at Home .. 157
Stanley's Late For Work 158
Alexander: Loud Results 158
S. Walton: Original 159
The Effective Executive 159
Head of the Racket 160
Small Things Count 161

Definitions of Leadership ... 161
The Queen Sits...and Sits 162
The First Lady 162
If You Don't Trust the Pilot . 163
Mark Spitz Delegates 163
See Them as Individuals 164

XXII. LIFESTYLE
Rest is Good 167
On Time and Interruptions .. 167
Important or Not? 168
Check Your Own Chimney .. 168
Balancing Rest & Work 169
Pepsico: Discipline 170
Bad Habits Rule 170
Responsibility - Control 171
Grant's Weakness 171

XXIII. MOTIVATION
Coolidge: No Advancement .. 175
A Reason to Live 175
A Mink Coat 175
Edison's Revenge 176
Misguided Motivation 176
Victor Hugo's Method 177
The Unfinished Scale 177
Napoleon's Eyes 178
No Water's an Incentive 178
Copy Goes to the Queen 179
A Matter of Pride 179
More Money 179
Going to Disneyland 180
On the Light Side 181
Lasorda's White Lie 181
Going to Battle Uninsured ... 182
Ownership & Incentive 182
Apricot Trees Get the Ax ... 183
Hunt's Hunger 183
Atlas: No More Bullies 184
Safety on the Golden Gate ... 184
Surgery at the Plant 185
"I Wanted To Get Caught" .. 186

Twelve Inches = $15,000 ... 186
Paderewski's Dream 187
Energetic Workers 187

XXIV. OPTIMISM
Peale's Waste Paper 191
Three for Fun 191
See It and Do It 192
Vultures and Hummingbirds . 192
What's Your Plan? 193
Nothing But a Home Run ... 193
D-Day Delight 194
License to Fly? 194
Don't, Worry, Be Happy 195
What Time Is It? 196
Half-Full Glass 196

XXV. PERSEVERANCE
Shirer's Big Book 199
I Give Up 199
Inventor of the Telephone? .. 200
Not Dead Yet 200
Art & Academia 201
Bamboo & Mountain 201
Fighting Breast Cancer 202
Flat on His Back 203
Run Daily, Even If 203
If An Ant Can Do It 204
No Delinquent Here 204
Hit a Thousand Golf Balls ... 205
The Perfect Elegy 205
Keep Advancing 206

XXVI. PERSPECTIVE
The Navajo's Gold Mine 209
Weeds or Flowers? 209
Measurements and Time 210
Measuring Yourself 210
An Eskimo tells the Truth ... 211
How You Look At It 212
A Boy, Big & Bored 212
Efficiency Expert 213

Notre Dame's Giants 213
What Do Poor People Do? ... 214

XXVII. PERSUASION
A Hard Sell 217
Nobody Explained It Before . 217
A Clever Old man 218
Duveen Dares to Deal 218
Fish Fireworks 219
Electric & Edible PR 219
You Gotta Love Him 220
Make Me Feel Important 220
The Power of Warmth 221

XXVIII. POTENTIAL
An Eagle Among Chickens .. 223
Balzac's Handwriting 224
Greatness Thrust 225
Ott's Bad Batting 225
They Aren't Always Right ... 226
First Duckist Church 226
Talent is Cheap 227
Diamond in Plain Wrapper .. 227
Capacity = Performance? 228
Not Limited by IQ 228

XXIX. PREPARATION
Knight: Will to Prepare 231
A Wrecked Hotel 231
Staubach's Ready 232
She Finished the Marathon .. 232

XXX. PRIORITY
A $25,000 Idea 235
Dumping the Crown Jewels .. 235
Don't Forget the Best! 236
Missing Old Faithful 237
On Music 237
Problems & Fool's Gold 238
The Business of Business ... 238
An Expensive Doorstop 239
Making a Difference 239

Pilots Change a Lightbulb ... 240
Crossing the Desert 240
Harping on the Obvious 241

XXXI. PURPOSE
Making You Proud 243
Saving Another 243
Digging without Meaning ... 243
Be Ashamed to Die 244

XXXII. RISK
Grandmothers for Peace 247
Trailblazers 247
Fisher's Seedling Miles 248
Rosa Parks & Communism .. 248
Flight, Height, & Dead Rat .. 249
A Big Dog's Fence 249
Courage at the Mint 250
Hans Flew & God Rejoiced .. 251
Britain's Blunder 252
Throwing Away Diamonds .. 252
Swim on Out 253

XXXIII. SACRIFICE
Lincoln & Schweitzer 255
Her Hands Bring Honor 255
Sacrifice the Queen 256
Shaving Half His Head 256

XXXIV. SELF-CENTERED
Of Sailors and Cemeteries ... 259
Angelyne and Margaret 259
Pay Them to Vote 260
A Student's Self-Deceit 260
Bums & Champions 261
Celebrating Elvis' Birthday .. 261

XXXV. SKILL
Use 'Em or Lose 'Em? 265
Competence Counts 265
Focus on Strengths 265
All Dried Up 266

She Got the Part 267

XXXVI. SUCCESS
Milken's Determination 269
Uncle Scrooge's Secret 269
Always Come Back 270
Ireland & Owens 271
Unpromising L. Pasteur 271
Louis XIV's Thorn 272
Success is Relative 273
Heads, We Win 273
Schwab's Chickens 274
An Unhappy Success 274
Granny Gets Last Laugh 275
Learning in Driver's Ed 276

XXXVII. TEAMWORK
Friends at Work 279
Ghost at the Piano 279
Koop Contributes 280
Artists & Infielders 281
Napoleon's Guillotine 281
Teamwork in Combat 282
Working Together 283
Little Lady and the Nazi 283
Taming Animals 284
A Bunch of Little Battles 285
A White-washed Elephant ... 285
Steam Engine Inventors 286
Get Commitment of Others .. 286

XXXVIII. VISION
Hilton Acquires Waldorf 289
Focus on the Good 289
Seeing Success 290
Clearing the Bar 290
Bigger plans 291
Leaders needed 291

Where There Is No Vision ... 292
Great Hunting Dogs 292
One at a Time 293

XXXIX. WINNING
Value in Victory? 295
Focus on Performance 295
It Isn't Everything 296
World Records 296
500 Foul Shots 297
You Need the Opponent 297
Winners Only 298
Winning Ways 298

XXXX. WORK
The Go-Gitter 301
The Duck That Might've ... 301
Quarterback's Basic Skills .. 302
Down in the Doldrums 302
Pareto's 80/20 Rule 303
Tom Cruise at 100% 304
Work a Gift? 304
Achievers Work Harder 305
Committees & Meetings 305
Musically Speaking 306
Re-engineering 306
On Laziness 307
Stuck on an Elevator 307
Hines Loved to Eat 308
Jones Wrote on Tuesdays ... 308
Shortcuts 309
Real Pros Keep Running 309
The Problem with Busyness . 310

APPENDIX
Endnotes 311
Index of Names 323
Index of Topics 327

INTRODUCTION

Tom Peters and Robert Waterman tell a great story in their book, *In Search of Excellence*:

A man asked his large computer, "Do you compute that you will ever think like a human being?" The machine then set to work to analyze its own computational habits. Finally, the machine printed its answer on a piece of paper, as such machines do. The man ran to get the answer and found, neatly typed, the words: "That reminds me of a story."

That is indeed how humans think. We think in stored images complete with smells, sounds, emotions. To be able to evoke a prior experience and to make it real is to involve others in our communication. As a professional speaker I am continually aware of the power of story.

Stories also affect us personally. A good story can help us regain our perspective. It can energize us, give us a good laugh, and "stimulate the little gray cells"—as Agatha Christie's Hercule Poirot is fond of saying.

In the back of this book you will find a list of the more than 200 resources that were consulted in compiling this book. You will also find a complete index by name and by topic. Every effort was made to make this collection as useable as possible. Of course, none of this would have been possible without the help of my co-editor, Rebecca Clark, and my assistant editor, Cassandra Dowd. Their dedication and hard work exemplify the kind of spirit the *One-Minute Motivator* seeks to evoke. I want to particularly salute my wife Selina, president of Seven Worlds Corporation, whose attention to details makes the whole thing work.

I hope you profit from the *One-Minute Motivator* both as a daily energizer and as a resource for presentations, staff meetings, or wherever you are called on "to say a few words." Discover for yourself the power of story.

                King Duncan

ACTION

To reach the port of success we must sail, sometimes with the wind and sometimes against it—but we must sail, not drift or lie at anchor. — Oliver Wendell Holmes

For every person with a spark of genius, there are a hundred with ignition trouble. — Kurt Hanks

The only thing that ever sat its way to success was a hen.

Day 1

A young man was having a terrible dream. A fire-breathing dragon was gaining on him. He could feel its hot breath on his neck. Terrified but exhausted, he could flee no more. Turning to face the dragon he screamed, "What are you going to do with me?" The dragon replied, "I don't know, young man. It's your dream!"

Life is what we make of it, isn't it? Life can be a masterpiece or a mess. God has given us the ability to choose which it shall be. But to make it a masterpiece we must get moving. Columnist Herb Caen wrote in the *San Francisco Chronicle* sometime back: "Every morning in Africa, a gazelle wakes up. It knows it must run faster than the fastest lion or it will be killed. Every morning a lion wakes up. It knows it must outrun the slowest gazelle or it will starve to death. It doesn't matter whether you are a lion or a gazelle; when the sun comes up, you'd better be running."

Day 2

Can one person—or two people—make a difference? Certainly, if they are willing to put their aspirations into action.

Not long after Howard and Connie Clery's 19-year-old daughter left home for college, they received the devastating news that she had been brutally raped and murdered in her own dormitory room. As they began to sort through the incidents leading to the attack, they discovered that the killer was well know to the campus police as a troublemaker, but that little had been done to restrict his actions.

That is when the Clerys turned their grief into action. Without any formal legal training, they set out to lobby Congress for a federal law making it mandatory for colleges to report the number and types of crimes committed on campus. As a result of their efforts, President Bush signed the Student Right to Know and Campus Security Act of 1990. The Act states that if colleges fail to provide accurate crime statistics, they risk the loss of federal funds. Now parents can access information on the true state of campus security, before sending their teenager into a potentially risky setting.

Instead of allowing grief to paralyze them, Howard and Connie Clery took action that may well save the lives of young people all over the country. Who says one person can't make a difference?

Day 3

During the oil shortage of the early 1970s, Steve Prine decided to become an oil broker. He was only in his early 20s, and his only start-up equipment was a working phone.

He started by calling the presidents of medium-sized and small oil companies and inquiring as to whether they had any oil to sell or if they wanted to buy any—and how much. He also told them he was a young man just starting out and asked for their advice on how to succeed as an oil broker.

After calling around a hundred oil company executives, Steve had compiled a very informative list of all who wanted oil and all who had oil to sell. He also had some great expert advice on how to make it in the oil business. Within a few months he had made over a million dollars! He risked talking with the people at the top, and it paid off.

Day 4

The mark of a leader is often the willingness to take action while others stand around and talk.

The leaders of an Allied armor division were stalled near Coutance, France during World War II. They were studying their map and trying to figure out where they could ford the Seine River. While still deep in their discussion, General George Patton came stomping up and demanded to know what was keeping them. When they reported that they hadn't yet discovered a place shallow enough to cross the river, Patton pointed to his wet trousers and calmly informed them that he had personally waded across the river at a point a few hundred yards away. They hurriedly investigated the river and got their unit moving again.

Day 5

Once the eminent philosopher John Dewey found his son in the bathroom. The floor was flooded and he was mopping furiously trying to contain the water and keep the damage to a minimum. The professor began thinking, trying to understand the deeper ramifications of the situation. After a few moments, the son said, "Dad, this is not the time to philosophize. It's time to mop!"

Know the difference between times for action and times for analysis.

Day 6

A snowstorm hit New York City, stalling many of the inbound trains. Passengers later told their harrowing experiences: sitting in cold, immovable trains for 12 hours or more, toilets overflowing, and railroad employees ignoring passengers' questions. Most riders simply accepted their plight as an inevitable consequence of using the train in a snowstorm.

One woman, however, decided not to give up so easily. While the executives in her car sat around playing games without even bothering to find a solution to the problem, this woman took action. After persuading a railroad employee to open the door and let down the steps, she walked out into the snow (followed by the executives!) and found herself only a block from the subway station and a few minutes from work. She was the only person in the entire car who did not accept defeat. The rest of the passengers might as well have been sheep going to the slaughter-house! Don't be afraid to be the first to act.

Day 7

During the Revolutionary War a young man came to George Washington and said, "General Washington, I want you to know that I believe in you and your cause. I fully support you."

General Washington graciously thanked him and asked, "What regiment are you in? Under whose command do you serve? What uniform do you wear?"

"Oh," said the young man, "I'm not in the army, I'm just a civilian."

The General replied, "Young man, if you believe in me and my cause, then you join the army. You put on a uniform. You get yourself a rifle and you fight."

Lip service rarely accomplishes anything. It is easy to back a project when no commitment is required of you. But it is only commitment which gets things done.

Day 8

Business guru Tom Peters tells about a businessman whom he admires whose motto is "anything worth doing is worth doing poorly." "The logic is impeccable," says Peters. He points out that the plane the Wright Brothers flew at Kitty Hawk was nothing to write home about. Alexander Graham Bell's first telephone was not exactly up to Bell Lab standards. Yet if Bell hadn't foisted that piece of junk on the world we wouldn't have a vast communication network that can instantly link anyone on this planet, and if Orville and Wilbur hadn't gone for lift-off with that bucket of bolts down at Kitty Hawk, we wouldn't have 747s.

Peters goes on to say, "I emphasize the point because the number one failing that I see in small and large organizations is the failure to do stuff. . . In an environment where we know nothing for sure, the only antidote is, to quote my old man, 'Don't just stand there. Do Something!'"

Day 9

There is a story of a poor artist who, in one of the high moments in his life, was royally entertained in a castle. Unfortunately, he had nothing with which to show his gratitude to his hosts. Before leaving, however, he shut himself up in his room for some days and locked the door, refusing to come out or to let anyone in. When he finally emerged and bid adieu to his hosts, a servant found the sheets of his bed missing, and thought that he must have stolen them. Searching further, however, they found the missing sheets rolled up in one corner of the room. Unrolling them, they discovered a glorious picture painted upon them. The artist needed to say thank you, and he did it by using the one gift that he had. Impressions are often made better by deeds than by words or money.

For Reflection

Zig Ziglar reminds us that the largest locomotive in the world can be held in its tracks while standing still simply by placing a single one-inch block of wood in front of each of the eight drive wheels. The same locomotive moving at 100 miles per hour can crash through a wall of steel-reinforced concrete five feet thick.

Momentum is everything. If you are standing still, small obstacles become major ones. Once you are moving, though, there is little that you won't be able to get through.

1) What obstacles keep you from doing what you need to do? Fear? Lack of focus? Low energy? Lack of organization? Indecisiveness?

2) Are you "beating around the bush," substituting busy-ness while procrastinating on the really important areas in your life?

3) What stands in the way of your team or organization when it comes to acting on ideas?

4) If you act now, will even the worst-case-scenario be all that bad?

ADVERSITY

Someone once noted that when a hawk is attacked by crows, he does not counter-attack. Instead, he soars higher and higher in ever widening circles until the other birds leave him alone.

Escape upwards. Rise above your problems.

Day 10

Anna Mary Moses loved to do needlework. She had been enjoying it since before she was married. But as she began to get older, she started to lose some of the dexterity in her hands through arthritis. By the time she was eighty, she could no longer perform even the simplest stitches. Therefore she decided to try something different—painting. The brushes were easy enough to handle, even with her arthritis, so she took it up full time, mostly painting farm and country scenes.

One day a traveling art collector stopped for a bite to eat in her town and saw her pictures in a drugstore. He decided that he liked them, and in a very short time the name of Grandma Moses was known throughout the art world. Although Grandma Moses didn't even start painting until she was eighty years old, she was able to create over fifteen hundred works of art in her lifetime. She had an international following, and prominence as a world-class painter.

All this because she was forced to quit her favorite pastime and take up a new one.

Day 11

Once there was an emperor of China who owned a rare and fabulous diamond that he treasured nearly as much as his empire. But one day the diamond became damaged. One facet of the gorgeous object was marred by a thin scratch running down its center. The emperor was deeply distressed by this, and immediately sent word throughout his empire that he would give a chest of gold and one of his daughters to anyone who could repair his precious diamond.

No one came forward, though. The jewelers were all afraid of the emperor's wrath if they should fail. Finally, one minor artisan offered to save the diamond. He took the diamond without a word, and carried it away to his workshop. It was many weeks before anyone saw him again.

When he emerged, the diamond was wrapped in a velvet cloth, and he took it straight to the emperor. As the emperor unfolded the velvet from the diamond, he suddenly gasped in delight and wonder. The artist had turned the hair-like flaw into the stem of a delicate rose carved into the diamond. It was far more beautiful than ever before.

It is a quality of the best of us to be able to take an apparent flaw and turn it into a thing of grace and beauty.

Day 12

Some people believe that Joe Montana is the best quarterback in the history of the National Football League. He is an artist with the short pass. He throws long so rarely that rumors have floated around the league from time to time that he has a sore arm. John Madden once asked Montana about his style of play. The conversation is interesting.

"Are you going to start throwing deep?" asked Madden before a recent Super Bowl.

Montana never batted an eye. "No," he said.

"Why not?" Madden pressed. "Is your arm sore?"

"No, my arm's not sore: I can throw deep," he said. "But we don't have any plays to throw deep. We never practice throwing deep."

"How come?" Madden asked.

"Look at our practice field here," Montana said. "Most teams have two full hundred-yard fields, one grass and one artificial turf. But we only have one field that's half grass and half artificial turf. When it rains in December here, the receivers have to wear either artificial turf shoes or grass shoes, depending on which half of the field we're practicing on. If we practice on the grass half, the receivers don't want to run out on the artificial turf with cleats. If we practice on the artificial turf half, the receivers don't want to risk falling on the wet grass with their artificial turf shoes.

"When we practice plays, we put the ball on what would be the twenty-yard line, so I've got only about thirty yards to work with. You can't throw deep in thirty yards. Even in the pregame warmup, it's the same situation. You only have half the field to work with. That's why I don't throw deep."

Montana only had a short field to work with, so he became a master of the short pass. What would some other people have done? They would sit around complaining that they didn't have two practice fields like other quarterbacks. Montana didn't complain, he conquered. He took his problem and turned it into a profit.

Day 13

Writers Edgar Jackson and Edward Ziegler lived near each other in Corinth, Vermont. Ziegler, a fan of Jackson's writings, decided to confide in Jackson and ask for help with a personal problem. He visited Jackson's farm, and while they were talking, Jackson took Ziegler out to see his pasture.

The former owner of the place had planted maple trees around the entire three-acre perimeter of the pasture in order to avoid having to set posts for a fence. He had allowed the trees to grow and then had strung barbed-wire between them to enclose the area.

Jackson showed Ziegler the result: a number of the trees had simply incorporated the barbed wire and continued to grow strong, but others had become deformed by the intrusion of the wire.

Some people, said Jackson, are like the strong and growing trees—they deal with their problems and move on. But other people allow their problems to rule them. Their lives become smaller and they become bitter.

If we handle our problems wisely, explained Jackson, our lives can continue to grow and flourish, and we can live triumphantly.

Day 14

Psychologist and writer Denis Waitley tells a story about when he was a child: there was an army emplacement near his home during the war. In order to befriend the children in the area, the soldiers would give them little canteens and army helmets and gun belts. In return, the children would run errands for them, bring them candy, and get them some home cooking.

One day a soldier said to young Denis Waitley, "I want to take you fishing in a boat." Denis had never been fishing out in the ocean and was ecstatic at the notion. That night he sneaked out of his bedroom window, got his tackle box, packed himself a lunch and put it in the refrigerator, and at 4 a.m. was ready to go. He sat at the curb, waiting for the soldier to take him to the boat. But the soldier never came.

Instead of telling his Mom and his friends that the soldier never came, though, he got himself a one-man rubber life raft. He took it down to the bay and pretended that he was launching a marvelous fishing boat. He rafted out in the bay, dug some clams, caught some fish, and had what he called the most marvelous day of his life.

Don't rely on others to accomplish your goals for you. While some assistance from others may be invaluable to you, your ultimate goals are your own, and will only be realized when you act on them.

Day 15

John Havlicek, or "Hondo" as he was called, was a basketball player for the Boston Celtics. While he was with them he played in more basketball games than any other player in professional history. And he went full speed in every game. It is estimated that, running about 6 miles per game, Hondo ran the equivalent distance from Houston to San Francisco and then back past St. Louis in his career. So how did he develop such amazing stamina?

When Havlicek was a boy in Ohio, his friends had bicycles while he did not. When they rode their bikes, he had to run to keep up with them. It was a lot of trouble, but he developed a remarkable ability to keep running, an ability that later paid off.

Our greatest strengths often come from challenges that we faced earlier in life. Look for these advantages, and use them.

Day 16

During a long run of the musical "Honeymoon Express," star Al Jolson developed a serious ingrown toenail on one of his feet. It hurt so much Al was hardly able to stand on it. In fact, he came close to dropping out of the show altogether.

But instead, he hit upon the idea of getting down on one knee, which relieved the pain in his toe and allowed him to appear as though the show's sentimental ballads were truly heart-felt.

The one-knee technique worked so well, he later incorporated it into his famous "My Mammy" number. It became his trademark and helped catapult him to stardom.

Adversity may often be an advantage in disguise, if you can figure out how to use it.

Day 17

According to an ancient legend, there was once a certain small village that sought to strike a bargain with God. They had been experiencing many years of poor harvests, so they asked God for permission to plan the weather for the next year's crops. God agreed. So whenever they asked for rain, God sent rain, and whenever they asked for sun, God sent sun. At the end of the year, the corn and the wheat were higher and thicker than ever before.

When they gathered in their harvest, however, the farmers discovered that the tall corn had no ear, and the thick wheat had no head of grain. So they made a complaint to God: "Why is our harvest so poor when the plants are so lush? We gave our crops the best possible weather!" God replied, "True. When you asked for rain, I sent rain. When you asked for sunshine, I gave sunshine. However, you never asked for the harsh north winds. Without the harsh north winds there is no pollination, and with no pollination there is no crop."

We complain because conditions aren't perfect. Yet it is through adversity that some of our most important lessons are learned.

Day 18

One of the most beautiful speaking voices on stage and screen today is that of James Earl Jones. Did you know that Jones has long battled a severe stuttering problem? From age 9 until his mid-teens he had to communicate with teachers and classmates by handwritten notes. A high school English teacher gave him the help he needed, but he still struggles with his problem to this day. Yet there is no finer speaking voice than his. He was listed recently among the ten actors with the most beautiful speaking voice.

Work on your weaknesses, the effort you put into overcoming them may turn out to be one of your greatest strengths.

Day 19

A cowboy out west was running for his life from an enraged bull. Head down and nostrils flaring, it was just about to overtake him when the cowboy noticed a hole in the ground and dove into it. As soon as the bull passed over the hole, the cowboy leaped out. But the bull noticed that its target had disappeared and came back, madder than ever. Just before the bull reached him again, the cowboy ducked back into the hole. And when the bull passed, he popped back out. He did this several times. A passing stranger noticed the interplay and shouted, "Hey cowboy, why don't you just stay in the hole?" Leaping out of the hole again, the cowboy yelled, "Are you kidding? There's a bear in that hole!"

Caught between a bear and a bull. Sometimes it's all we can do to keep from being overwhelmed by the forces opposing us. But keep moving. Patience will eventually get you "out of the hole."

Day 20

Some time ago an article appeared in *Reader's Digest* about an unusually hardy tree called the "Bristlecone Pine." Growing in the western mountain regions, sometimes as high as two or more miles above sea level, these evergreens may live for thousands of years. But considering the habitat of these trees—rocky areas where the soil is poor and precipitation is slight—it seems incredible that they should even survive at all. The environmental adversities, however, seem to actually contribute to their longevity. Tissue cells which grow in these adverse conditions are densely arranged, and many resin canals are formed within the plant. Wood that is structured in this way continues to live for an extremely long period of time.

Author Darwin Lambert says in this article that "Bristlecone Pines in richer conditions grow faster, but die earlier and soon decay." The harshness of their surroundings, then, is a vital factor in making them strong and sturdy.

Adverse conditions in the lives of people also contribute to their resilience. A few setbacks make us sturdier, they help us to see our errors so that they may be corrected, and they make the next problem easier to overcome.

Day 21

Sometimes, problems create opportunity. In the summer of 1918, Washington D.C. was suffering from a stifling heat wave. A young visitor from Utah was practically overwhelmed by the intense sunshine and humidity, so different from his hometown weather.

A few years later the young man was offered the opportunity to purchase an A & W Root Beer franchise in the nation's capital. Remembering his experience as a visitor, he decided that root beer would probably be a hot seller in so steamy a place, so he opened his first stand in the summer of 1927. As he had anticipated, business was great. Everyone loved the cold, frosty root beer on those hot, muggy days.

But November came, and suddenly, few people were buying cold root beer. Undaunted, the stand owner simply changed the name of his stand to the Hot Shoppe and began serving coffee, chili, and hot tamales. Fifty years later, that stand owner, John Willard Marriott, owned cruise ships, 450 restaurants, and 34 hotels. Flexible thinking may be one key to overcoming problems.

Day 22

The Rev. B. T. Richardson of North Royalton, Ohio tells a great story of something that happened to him when he was pastoring a small church in a rural area near Cincinnati, Ohio.

"We had a packed house during a Sunday morning service. A young man named Bill, a brand new convert, had come that morning and had brought his mother. She had never been in a Protestant church before in her life and therefore had many questions as to why 'things' were being done.

"The message was really connecting that morning and we were leading toward an altar service. The congregation was standing, the music was playing softly, several in the congregation were stepping out and heading toward the altar. While all this was going on, the water heater had finally warmed through the concrete block that framed this church. Hibernating in the bloc was a family of flies. Still lethargic and beginning to move around, they came out of the block and started falling down on some in the congregation. Most of the regular attenders in the church were used to the event which seemed to happen seasonally.

"Well, Bill's mother was this upper-crust kind of a lady, beautifully dressed, poised, mannerly. All this changed during the altar service when one of those flies dropped from the ceiling and fell into her hair that was rolled and tied up on her head. This fly started doing his best to escape from this hair-sprayed trap. Bill's mother didn't know that the sound she heard and the moving she felt was just a fly. She thought it was a bee (she was allergic).

"When she felt all this she started whooping and hollering and raising her hands and jumping around all in a panic. Well, her reaction seemed to be similar to the rest of the parishioners' responses except maybe a little more exaggerated. She finally broke out into the aisle with hands still waving.

"When this happened the congregation thought she was getting blessed, and so they (the congregation) started getting more excited. Thinking when she moved out into the aisle that she was headed for the altar, they moved out for the altar too! But instead of going to the altar, Bill's mother turned and ran screaming out our back door. This, of course, left our altar lined with people, three pews deep. My congregation talked about that service for years. By the way, that was the last time that Bill's mother ever went to another Protestant church."

When faced with a problem, do you fly around in a panic? Or do you calmly look for solutions?

Day 23

At the beginning of World War II, the U.S. was utilizing a fighter plane called the P-40. Unfortunately, the P-40 was considered to be inferior to just about every type of enemy fighter against which it had to fly. The Japanese Zero, for example, was much faster in a climb, was more maneuverable in turns and carried more potent firepower, and was infinitely more capable of flying at high altitudes. The common perception was that the U.S. P-40 was a sitting duck against a Zero, and early in the War, that was true.

With experience, however, American commanders learned to capitalize on the plane's strengths. The P-40 could dive fast, her guns could fire rounds rapidly, and she fought well at low altitudes. When U.S. fighters switched their strategy to hit-and-run dives, they ended up eliminating 13 ½ enemy planes for ever P-40 lost.

Instead of envying other people's strengths, take advantage of your own.

Day 24

One time during a sports clinic at Princeton High School in Cincinnati, Ohio, the softball coach, Dan Woodruff, loaned his office to Dave Redding, the "strength" coach for the Cleveland Browns. Dave was scheduled to appear at the clinic, and he needed to use the office shower. Dan showed Dave the facilities, then left while Dave was still in the shower. After his shower, Dave tried to leave the office but discovered he couldn't open the door! He wrote a note explaining his predicament, slipped it under the door, then waited.

It was about an hour before Dan returned to find a note outside his office door and a man yelling inside. He opened the door to a very relieved Dave. "What happened?" Dan asked. Dave explained that he had been locked inside the office for over an hour. But Dan pointed out that the door had not actually been locked, that he only had to push a button on the handle to open it.

"We laughed about it a lot when we walked down the hall," said Dan. "The 230 pound strength coach of a professional football team being trapped behind an unlocked door."

Explore all of your options before setting your course too surely. Look for that little piece of missed information that could save you a lot of time and trouble down the road.

Day 25

Dr. Mark Miller cites a variation of Murphy's Law: "Buttered toast when falling to the floor will always land buttered side down."

"Well, one day," says Dr. Miller, "in a certain kitchen, the toast fell off the table to the floor, and to the amazement of everyone the toast landed buttered side up. Scientists were called in to investigate this wonder. Did it mean that Murphy's law was wrong? The scientists secured the area, brought in their equipment, measured, weighed, and analyzed everything. They created a model of the scene and put it on the computer. They finally concluded that Murphy's law had not been broken. The toast had simply been buttered on the wrong side."

Things do go wrong. Our reaction is the important determinant of our success.

Day 26

Think your problems get in the way of success? Take heart:

*Charles Darwin spent most of his adult life in pain, suffering from one mysterious ailment after another, yet he made immeasurable contributions to the study of the origins of life.

*Born prematurely and left in the care of his grandparents, Sir Isaac Newton was taken out of school early and became an inept farm boy. Now he is considered to be one of the greatest figures in the entire history of science.

*F. Scott Fitzgerald, Cher, and Thomas Edison were all learning disabled, and yet all three went on to achieve success.

*A Jew, Benjamin Disraeli, became Prime Minister of Great Britain during a time when anti-Semitism was rampant. Though rich and powerful people used less than honorable tactics to get him defeated, Disraeli triumphed.

*Although she was blind and deaf from an early age, Helen Keller achieved more than most unimpaired people and dedicated her life to helping the less fortunate.

All of these people overcame the forces arrayed against them to achieve success.

For Reflection

In one of his books, Chuck Swindoll notes that there are several things a person can do if a warning light flashes on the dashboard while driving down the road. One thing you can do if that light comes on is hit it with a hammer and keep driving. This will work for a while, but before too long the car will stop running and you'll look under the hood. Then you will kick yourself for not doing something sooner. Unfortunately, this is how many people deal with problems—hitting the warning signs with a hammer while ignoring the real issue. Ask yourself if what you are dealing with is a part of the problem, or merely a symptom.

1) Think about your usual attitude when faced with a problem. Do you approach the problem positively and with confidence, or do you panic, allowing the problem to rule you?

2) How valid, really, are the excuses you use for failure to complete assignments or to do you best work?

3) Identify a problem you face right now. What are some small steps you can take today in dealing with that problem?

4) What would happen if you simply took adversity in stride, acknowledging that it's a normal part of life?

5) How might you use your own innate creativity to turn your next problem into an advantage?

ASPIRATIONS

Far away there in the sunshine are my highest aspirations. I may not reach them, but I can look up and see their beauty, believe in them and try to follow them where they lead.
— Louisa May Alcott

Day 27

Never worry about aiming too high in life. Page Cooper tells about a champion shot named Ambrosio, who noticed an infinitesimal speck high in the sky one morning. Seizing his ever-ready rifle, he banged away at it. He was incredulous when it appeared that he had missed his target. All was well, however, when a note, written on beautiful parchment, dropped at his feet the next morning. It read, "Please don't shoot my angels," and was signed, "God."

"Shoot for the moon," says Les Brown. "Even if you miss it, you will land among the stars."

Day 28

In Arthur Miller's great play *Death of a Salesman*, Willy Loman's wife cannot understand why he should have committed suicide, especially at the time he did. For the first time in 35 years they were just about free and clear. He only needed a little salary, and he was even finished with the dentist. But a friend says, wisely, "No man only needs a little salary. When a person's dreams and goals and purposes in life are destroyed, that person is destroyed. We not only need something to live on, we need something to live for."

Day 29

John Killinger tells of the time when W. Clement Stone, the Chicago financier and philanthropist, was asked how he had done so much in his lifetime. Stone's reply was this: "I have dreamed. I have turned my mind loose to imagine what I wanted to do. Then I have gone to bed and thought about my dreams. In the night, I have dreamed about them. And when I have arisen in the morning, I have seen the way to get to my dreams. While other people were saying, 'You can't do that, it isn't possible,' I was well on my way to achieving what I wanted."

Day 30

"My high school was small," says Dolly Parton. "So during a graduation event, each of us got a chance to stand up and announce our plans for the future. 'I'm going to junior college,' one boy would say. 'I'm getting married and moving to Maryville,' a girl would follow. When my turn came, I said, 'I'm going to Nashville to become a star.' The entire place erupted in laughter. I was stunned. Somehow, though, that laughter instilled in me an even greater determination to realize my dream. I might have crumbled under the weight of the hardships that were to come had it not been for the response of the crowd that day. Sometimes it's funny the way we find inspiration."

If someone laughs at your dreams, at least you will know your dream is big enough to challenge the best that is in you.

Day 31

Meg F. Quijano relates the following incident that happened upon her return from a meeting of the National Organization for Women. Her five-year-old daughter, Lisa, greeted her with the news that when she grew up she wanted to be a nurse. There was a time when nursing was thought by many to be a "woman's job." Quijano told Lisa she could be anything she wanted to be. "You can be a lawyer, a surgeon, a banker, President of the United States—you can be anything." Lisa looked a little dubious. "Anything? Anything at all?" She thought about it, and then her face lit up with ambition. "All right," she said. "I'll be a horse."

For Reflection

We grow great by dreams. All big men are dreamers. They see things in the soft haze of a spring day, or in the red fire on a long winter's evening. Some of us let these great dreams die, but others nourish and protect them; nourish them through bad days until they bring them to the sunshine and light which comes always to those who sincerely hope that their dreams will come true.
— Woodrow Wilson

1) What kinds of negative self-talk keep you from pursuing your aspirations?

2) Think back to when you were 9-11-years old. What did you enjoy doing the most? What dreams did you have for your life?

3) Are you allowing space in your life for working on your dreams?

ATTITUDE

All my country has is spirit. We don't have petroleum dollars. We don't have mines or great wealth in the ground. We don't have the support of a worldwide public opinion that looks favorably on us. All Israel has is the spirit of its people. And if the people lose their spirit, even the United States of America cannot save us." — Golda Meir

An optimist thinks the glass is half-full. The pessimist thinks it's half-empty. The realist knows that before long he'll have to wash the glass.

Day 32

Benjamin Hoff has made an interesting analysis of Milne's classic *Winnie the Pooh* story for children. Compared to his friends, Pooh remains unfrazzled, down to earth, calm, and above all, patient. Owl constantly pontificates, showing off his wisdom, but never solves problems or makes things work. Rabbit is an impetuous activist, always calculating and clever, but always out of touch with reality. Eeyore, the donkey, frets and complains but never brings himself to action. Pooh, on the other hand, doesn't force things or try too hard, because he knows that if he does what he can, yet remains relaxed, sensible, and in touch with what's important, things will work out. Hoff concludes his analysis with the following advice: "Within each of us there is an Owl, a Rabbit, an Eeyore, and a Pooh. For too long, we have chosen the way of Owl and Rabbit. Now, like Eeyore, we complain about the results, but that accomplishes nothing. If we are smart, we will choose the way of Pooh."

Day 33

"The mayor of Zurich had arranged a dinner in my honor," writes silent film star Collen Moore in her autobiography. "We'd no sooner sat down than the mayor signaled the orchestra who started playing 'My Country 'Tis Of Thee.' We all stood up. When we sat down, I said to the mayor, 'That was the English national anthem.' I should have kept my mouth shut. The mayor sent for the orchestra leader, spoke a few words to him in German, and the orchestra struck up again with 'The Stars and Stripes Forever.' We all stood up and when the orchestra finished the mayor asked me why I was laughing. Like an idiot I said that wasn't our national anthem, that was a march. The mayor, red in the face, sent for the orchestra leader and spluttered in German at him. The leader asked me the name of our national anthem. I said, 'The Star Spangled Banner.' A few moments later the orchestra struck up again with 'Yes, We Have No Bananas.' The mayor stood up, and the guests stood at attention once again. When we sat down, I smiled at the mayor and said, 'That was lovely.'"

Sometimes you have to roll with the punches in order to keep everyone happy and yourself sane.

Day 34

One time an old drunk was paid to sit up all night in a funeral home with an open coffin, in case anyone came by late to pay their respects. But he was actually being set up by some practical jokers. In the quietness of the early morning hours, the 'corpse' in the coffin suddenly sat up and screamed. The drunk got up, staggered over to the casket, and pushed the body back down, saying, "You're supposed to be dead. Now lie down and act like it."

You would have to say the intoxicated gentleman at least "kept his cool." In order to be successful at a task, you can't allow yourself to become unhinged at any unexpected occurrences, no matter how bizarre or unlikely they are.

Day 35

Do you enjoy your work?

A survey carried out by *Nation's Business* magazine asked respondents to select the top ten business people America produced in its first 200 years.

Readers nominated people such as Alexander Graham Bell, Thomas A. Edison, and Henry Ford. The criteria for these choices included the fact that each nominee was responsible for providing jobs to thousands of workers and raised and spent billions of dollars. At the same time, each was engaged in highly competitive industries which are often cited in health magazines as a cause of early death.

Oddly enough, the average age of death for these ten nominees was eighty-seven, way above the national average. A probable cause of this disparity: these men enjoyed their work.

Perhaps it's not the type of work you do but whether or not you enjoy your work that counts.

Day 36

President Ronald Reagan was one of the great positive thinkers of all time. Shortly after Reagan's attempted assassination, his approval ratings in the polls went up to around 90 percent, virtually the highest on record. A year later, during the 1982 recession, his ratings plummeted to almost 30 percent.

Throughout this time, Richard Wirthlin, Reagan's pollster, would visit him every other week to discuss the ratings. When the polls looked good, Wirthlin would go into Reagan's office accompanied by a dozen or so assistants who wanted to share in the good news. But when the low recession rating came down, they shoved Wirthlin in to break the new to the President alone. "You tell him, Dick."

So Dick went in and Reagan said, "Well, how was it? How are they? What do the figures look like?"

"Well, they're pretty bad, Mr. President."

"Well, how bad are they?"

"Well, they're as low as they can get."

"So what do you mean?"

"Well, they're about 32 percent."

"Anything lower than that in the second year of the presidency?" Reagan asked. "I think that's the lowest." Wirthlin replied, kind of ruefully.

At that point, Reagan's face brightened up and he smiled, "Dick, Dick, don't worry. I'll just go out there and try to get shot again."

Great attitude!

Day 37

Jim Davis, the inventor, owner, and illustrator of Garfield the Cat, learned to draw because he had long bouts with asthma and his mother encouraged him to use art as a way to keep distracted from his short breaths.

Then there is Calvin Stanley, an 11-year-old who plays baseball, rides a bike, and does everything except see. Calvin was born blind, and he sees with his hands. He swims and attends movies, goes to regular classes with sighted students, moving with trust and confidence through his darkened world.

The most prolific mystery writer, Agatha Christie, had Miss Marple observe: "Some people . . . seem to think life owes them something. It's what's in yourself that makes you happy or unhappy."

Day 38

On March 5, 1944, when Chuck Yeager was twenty-one years old, he bailed out of a burning P-51 over occupied France. Wounded and alone in enemy territory, he hooked up with some French resistance fighters who assisted him in reaching the foothills of the Pyrenees.

Risking death by freezing in the icebound mountains, Yeager and a navigator from a downed B-24 hiked up into the Pyrennees. Unfortunately, a German patrol spotted them and opened fire, and the navigator was wounded. Single-handedly, Yeager dragged his unconscious companion up over the mountain and back down the other side. Then he walked twenty miles south to the nearest town.

He turned himself in to the local police who threw him in jail, but Yeager sawed through the window bars and escaped to the nearest pension. That's where an American consul found him two days later.

Weeks later, back in England, he was told he was going to be sent home, which was Army Air Corps policy for pilots who had been shot down in enemy territory. Chuck refused to go. He had come to fly airplanes—and that was what he intended to do.

"Without realizing it," he later recalled, "I was about to take charge of my life. If I had submitted to being sent home, I doubt whether the Army Air Corps would have been interested in retaining my services when the war ended. I would probably have been mustered out and my flying career abruptly ended."

Yeager got an interview with General Eisenhower, convinced the general to let him stay, and a few days later he was flying again.

Forty-four years later, author Dennis Conner asked Chuck what advice he would give to someone who wanted to be successful in a career.

"I'd tell you to pick something you enjoy doing. Forget the money angle, within reason. If you enjoy what you're doing, you'll adjust your lifestyle to meet your income. And if you enjoy it well enough, you'll be outstanding because you'll always like doing it."

For Reflection

Eugene Ormandy dislocated his shoulder one time while conducting the Philadelphia orchestra. Writer Maurice Boyd speculates that Ormandy may have been conducting Brahms. In the margin of one of his symphonies Brahms wrote, "As loud as possible!" Only a few bars later, however, he wrote in, "Louder still!" Boyd concludes, "I know some people who have reached middle-age and have never had an enthusiasm great enough to dislodge a necktie, let alone their shoulder."

Enthusiasm is definitely a positive aspect in our world. Do you have it?

1) How might your enthusiasm spur your team on to new and better ideas?

2) List some ways you could calm yourself in a crises. Practice those techniques ahead of time.

3) What are some actions you could take to bring more humor into your life and into your workplace?

4) Attitude is a choice. Will you choose to be happy today?

CHANGE

From the time of Christ until 1760, world knowledge doubled once. From 1760 to 1880 it doubled again. In 1914 it had doubled the third time. Now the raw mass of human knowledge doubles twice a year.
— Ralph L. Lewis

Progress is impossible without change; and those who cannot change their minds cannot change anything.
— George Bernard Shaw

Day 39

In 1867 the following news item appeared in a leading Chicago newspaper: "Joshua Coppersmith has been arrested in New York for attempting to extort funds from ignorant and superstitious people by exhibiting a device which he claimed will convey the human voice any distance over metallic wires, so that it will be heard by listeners at the other end. Well-informed people know this is impossible and of no practical value. The authorities who apprehended this criminal are to be congratulated."

Change is always thought to be impossible—until somebody does it.

Many of the Ivy League schools used to live up to their name by having ivy growing up the walls of many of their buildings. But today the Ivy League colleges have little or no ivy. Why not? They found that the ivy was destroying the mortar in their buildings. The pride of tradition is too expensive if it jeopardizes the future.

Day 40

In 1934 there was a National Football League championship game played between the New York Giants and the heavily-favored Chicago Bears. The weather was bitterly cold, and the playing field was covered with ice. The Bears were leading at half-time with a score of 10-3.

During the half-time, however, the Giants switched from cleats to sneakers, which they had borrowed from the Manhattan College basketball team. Suddenly, the Giants had the edge. They scored four touchdowns in the second half with their new equipment and beat the Bears 30-13.

Don't be afraid of trying the unconventional. Changing conditions require that new procedures be implemented to get the job done.

Day 41

Philip Holzman and George Klein conducted an experiment in perspective some time ago. They showed subjects drawings of two- and five-inch squares. Then they gradually showed them larger squares, without telling them that they were doing so. The two-inch square was replaced with a three-inch square, and the five-inch square was replaced by a seven-inch square, then a ten-inch square, and then larger squares.

When asked about the size of the squares, some participants simply wouldn't change their original estimates on the size of the squares, even though the size of the squares was steadily increasing. If they had originally told themselves that they were seeing a two-inch square, then that's what they kept seeing, even as the square grew much larger. Especially rigid subjects were estimating squares to be only four inches on sides that were, in fact, thirteen inches!

Be aware of this tendency not only in other people, but in yourself as well. Don't be afraid to re-evaluate a situation, even if you don't feel that it has changed that much. Be honest with yourself, and you may be surprised at how much things do change.

Day 42

If Thomas Edison invented electric light today, says Newt Gingrich, Dan Rather would report it on CBS News as "the candle making industry was threatened." You would get a downer. You would get a story explaining that electricity kills. There would be interviews with five candle makers. At least three politicians would pass a bill banning electricity.

Newt's probably right. Change threatens. Any change.

Radio Pastor Chuck Swindoll tells about a church back in the Midwest where he grew up. Somebody introduced the flannel graph in an adult Sunday School class, one of the trendy visual aids commonly used in the business world during that era. The poor guy was verbally crucified! He was called before the board and severely lectured. "How <u>dare</u> you contaminate our church with this worldly method!"

"Can you believe it?" asks Chuck. "All he did was introduce a flannel graph and use it as a teaching aid. You'd think he had released a truck full of cobras!"

Day 43

The rapid rate of change is a challenge to every professional in every field. We are trying to cope with an information explosion. I t came home to me several years ago when I was reading about the Voyager II spacecraft that was making its way deeper into deep space, sending back bulletins and pictures from Saturn, Uranus and Neptune. The people feeding flight instructions to Voyager II from home—"home" being the Jet Propulsion Laboratory in Pasadena, California—had to "spoon feed" the craft in tiny increments because the six computers on board had only about 32K of memory altogether, one one-thousandth of the capacity of your average desk-top word processor. Why was a ground breaking spacecraft equipped with only 32K of memory? Because it left this planet in 1977, when the desk-top and the lap-top were only dreams of the future; when the hand-held calculator and the silicon chip were very new news. Voyager II has been traveling since before the personal computer explosion, before the VCR, and CD player, before the telephone answering machine. In today's world of rapid technological change, that is many generations ago.

Day 44

Many years ago, a White House physician, Dr. Baker, told this story in a public meeting: "The happiest man I ever knew lived in St.

Louis. One day I went over to his home to ask him what the secret of his happiness was. This is the story he told me:

"When I was a young man I was heels over head in love with the sweetest girl that ever lived. I still am, and she still is. I have been married to her for thirty years, but she had one fault then, and she has it yet—she is always late.

"One day she begged me to take her to a concert to hear a certain singer. I promised her I would take her on one condition—that she would be ready a half-hour ahead of time. If she was not ready on time, we agreed I would tear up the tickets.

"When I got to her home about twenty minutes before time, her mother met me at the door and sadly shook her head. 'Nellie will never be ready in time. She just came in.' I walked the floor, and I watched the clock as the minutes dragged by, and I got more and more furious. Finally, when the half hour was up, I flung myself in a chair by the table and picked up a book. On the fly leaf of it were four little lines that changed my whole life. They read:

"For every evil under the sun,
there is a remedy or there is none.
If there is one, seek till you find it;
if there be none, never mind it."

"I decided there was no remedy for her tardiness and so I would simply accept it. I also decided at that moment that this would be my philosophy for life. Nothing ever took more misery out of my life than the determination that I wouldn't worry over the things I couldn't change.'"

For Reflection

Back during the days of the space race, Wernher Von Braun gave a lecture on the subject of putting a man on the moon. When his lecture was finished, he asked for questions.

A woman's hand immediately shot up: "Why," she asked, "can't you forget about getting people on the moon and stay home and watch television like the good Lord intended for you to do?"

Change is what carries us into the future. If you can't change, you will be stuck in the past.

1) Are you worrying over something you can't change? What can you do to "let go"?

2) How might a change in perspective or outlook improve your team's productivity?

3) What are the changes you'd like to make in your lifestyle? List the benefits of changing and the steps you'd need to take in order to change. Find people who will support you.

4) How might you be an encourager to a friend or colleague who is trying to make a change?

COMMUNICATION

You must be frank with the world. Frankness is the child of honesty and courage. Just say what you mean to do on every occasion, and take it for granted you mean to do right. — Robert E. Lee

Day 45

During the confrontation between Malaysia and Indonesia in 1964, a British officer asked a group of Gurkhas fighters from Nepal if they would be willing to jump from transport planes into combat against the Indonesians if the need arose. The Gurkhas were given the option to turn down the request because they had never been trained as paratroopers.

The Gurkhas usually agreed to nearly any assignment, but for some reason on this occasion they said no. The next day, though, one of their NCOs sought out the British officer who had made the request. The NCO said that they had discussed the matter further and would be willing to jump under certain conditions.

"What are they?" asked the British officer. The Gurkhas told him they would jump if the land was marshy, or reasonably soft with no rocky outcrops. They also wanted the plane to fly as slowly as possible and only one hundred feet or less off the ground. The British officer pointed out that the planes always flew as slowly as possible when dropping troops, but a jump from one hundred feet was impossible because the parachutes would not have time to open from that height.

"Oh," said the Gurkhas, "that's all right, then. We'll jump anywhere with parachutes. You didn't mention parachutes before!"

Always be as clear and complete as possible in correspondences. It's better to risk being a little redundant, than to risk a misunderstanding.

Day 46

When J. Edgar Hoover was the Director of the Federal Bureau of Investigation, a new manager in the Supplies Division implemented a number of changes. One of these changes was to narrow the margins on the memo pads in order to cut expenses by preventing the waste of paper.

When the new, narrower pads finally reached the desk of Mr. Hoover, he did not exactly like them. He wrote a simple message back to the supply manager: "Watch the borders!"

Somehow the message got diverted into the wrong hands, and for a while hardly anybody could get into the United States from either Mexico or Canada. Eventually Hoover sent out another memo saying that he had meant the borders on the new memo pads and not the territorial borders of the nation.

Be careful of how you word yourself, especially if your message could fall into the wrong hands.

Day 47

Young Matthew, age 4, was eating an apple in the back seat of the car. "Daddy," he asked, "why is my apple turning brown?" His father explained, "Because after you ate the skin off, the meat of the apple came in contact with the air which caused it to oxidize, thus changing its molecular structure and turning it into a different color."

There was a long silence, and then Matthew asked softly, "Daddy, are you talking to me?"

Know your audience. Be sure to conduct yourself appropriately so that those you are addressing will understand what you are saying.

Day 48

If you expect others to respond to what you say, you have to communicate at a level that they can understand. That is where United Airlines' luggage handlers failed sometime back.

A $50,000 champion Belgian sheepdog named Korsair had been on performing tours through Europe when he escaped from his cage at Chicago's O'Hare International Airport and refused to respond to employee commands to "sit," "stay," and "heel." The dog wasn't being disobedient as he ran off from the people who were yelling at him; he simply didn't understand. It seems that Korsair only knows French, but in that language he responds to commands immediately!

Day 49

Let them find their own solution: Gene Roberts is the former executive editor of *The Philadelphia Enquirer*. During the 18 years Roberts was with the paper, it garnered an astonishing 17 Pulitzer prizes.

Obviously, Roberts didn't do all the writing or shoot all the photographs himself. He succeeded by allowing others to take ownership of their jobs.

Robert's colleagues remember his long trance-like silences during meetings with them. This silence had the effect of forcing others to talk. "He once told me," said one of his former colleagues, Bill Kovach, "that one of the most important lessons I would ever learn about managing people . . . was that most people will solve their own problems and give you a solution if you only listen to them, if you keep them talking long enough."

Day 50

When a would-be politician asked Justice Oliver Wendell Holmes for advice on how to get elected to office, Justice Holmes wrote him:

"To be able to listen to others in a sympathetic and understanding manner is perhaps the most effective mechanism in the world for getting along with people and tying up their friendship for good. Too few people practice the 'white magic' of being good listeners."

Harpo Marx never received much in the way of a formal education, yet he was welcome in some of society's most sophisticated circles. Someone once asked him how he had managed to survive among the wits and the intellectuals of the Thanatopsis poker club and the Algonquin round Table.

"Very simple," said Harpo. "They had to have someone to listen."

The art of listening can be a very powerful aid in relating to other people.

Day 51

Margaret Lane in her book *Are You Really Listening?* shares an embarrassing moment that resulted from not listening actively: "Years ago, fresh out of college and being interviewed for a job on a small-town newspaper, I learned the hard way. My interview had been going well, and the editor, in an expansive mood, began telling me about his winter ski trip. Eager to make a big impression with a tale of my own about backpacking in the same mountains, I tuned him out and started planning my story. 'Well,' he asked suddenly, 'What do you think of that?' Not having heard a word, I babbled foolishly, 'Sounds like a marvelous holiday—great fun!' For a moment he stared at me. 'Fun?' he asked in an icy tone. 'How could it be fun? I've just told you I spent most of it hospitalized with a broken leg.'"

Keep in mind that other people wish to be heard just as much as you wish to speak.

Day 52

Inspirational speaker Naomi Rhode tells about a woman in Michigan who created a business out of listening. Newly divorced, she decided to advertise her offer to provide a sympathetic ear to the lonely and troubled.

The ad read:
When you need someone to talk to—
24 hours a day—
Call Kathy, Trained Listener, $10.

In the first three months alone she received sixty calls from people who needed someone to listen to them. Kathy doesn't offer advice, but restricts herself to sympathetic listening.

For Reflection

Sir Thomas More, in describing the mechanics of government in his fictional *Utopia*, writes the following: "There's also a rule in the Council that no resolution can be debated on the day that it's first proposed. All discussion is postponed until the next well-attended meeting. Otherwise someone's liable to say the first thing that comes into his head, and then start thinking up arguments to justify what he has just said instead of trying to decide what's best for the community. That type of person is quite prepared to sacrifice the public to his own prestige, just because, absurd as it may sound, he's ashamed to admit that his first idea may have been wrong—when his first idea should have been to think before he spoke."

1) Is there a recurring problem at your office that could be corrected by simply clarifying communications?

2) Repetition is crucial in conveying an important message. Are you giving people around you the opportunity to receive your message often?

3) What advantages would you gain by disciplining yourself to listen to others before speaking?

4) Who in your life needs for you to listen?

CONFIDENCE

"Always walk in a place like you belong — and most people will believe you do!"
—Ed McMahon

Basketball player Glen Rice on becoming an NBA All-Star for the first time: "I'd always had in my mind I was an All-Star. It just wasn't publicly announced until now."

Day 53

Television entertainer Ed McMahon says his father impressed him at an early age with a favorite saying: "Always walk in a place like you belong—and most people will believe you do!"

When Ed was a young boy, he had trouble relating to other children. "I went to 15 different schools before I finished high school," he explains. "You see, my father was a fund raiser, and we were constantly traveling. Consequently, I would be in a school where no one knew me—and that was a tough situation. You know how cruel people can be to strangers."

One of the problems he had was that he would develop a regional accent while he was living in one part of the country, and then his family would move to another state where he "talked funny." "You know, one year I'd be in New York with a Massachusetts accent, and then the next year, I'd be in Massachusetts with a New York accent," he said. "So I was called various things by various kids—'Hey, New Jersey!' 'Look out, Philadelphia!' whatever."

During this time, McMahon hung on to his father's advice for dear life. No matter how unfamiliar or uncomfortable a situation, he says, "I always tried to look like I was supposed to be there."

And it worked. "I moved from a naturally shy, wallflower type to being very aggressive. I really got on top of things."

If you appear confident, you will become confident.

Day 54

Some people seem to be born with confidence. True story. Jonathan, at 3, requested a grilled cheese sandwich at a restaurant. The waitress explained that grilled cheese was not on the menu.

Jonathan, determined to have his way, queried, "Do you have cheese and bread?"

The waitress nodded, "We do . . ."

"Then," Jon blurted, "do you have a pan?"

Jon got his sandwich.

When the sandwich arrived, the waitress took beverage orders. Jonathan ordered a milkshake, but this time the waitress was one step ahead. "Jonathan, we have milk and ice cream, but I'm sorry we don't have any syrup."

To which Jon asked, "Do you have a car?"

Jonathan will own the world some day. Most of us couldn't be that direct in making our desires known—even as adults. And yet a simple key to getting what you want is to ask.

Day 55

One day, all of the electricity went out at the Barnum and Bailey circus while the show was in progress. The animal trainer had just stepped into the tiger cage to begin his act when they were plunged into total darkness for several minutes. Some members of the audience and most of the circus crew feared for the trainer's life because they knew that big cats are able to see in the dark, placing the trainer at a distinct disadvantage.

But when the lights came on back he was still alive. He was later interviewed by both TV and newspaper reporters who asked him, "How did you feel in that cage with all those big cats in the dark, when they could see you but you couldn't see them?"

The trainer's answer was this: "But they didn't know I couldn't see them! So I just cracked my whip and shouted commands."

Day 56

One of Custer's scouts warned him they were in for a fight. He estimated there were enough Sioux to keep them busy for a good 2 or 3 days. General Custer replied rather smugly, "I guess we'll get through with them in one day." He even declined help from the 7th Calvary or even Gatling guns.

Custer was right about one thing: one day was all it took.

Confidence is good, but overconfidence can be deadly. Know your limitations.

AND THE REST OF THE STORY...

Shortly after the Sioux had defeated General Custer and fled to Canada, the North-West Mounted Police were charged with the task of controlling the Indians. But there were all of five Mounties stationed in the same area as the vast Sioux tribe. Consequently, the Mounties thought they had better seize the initiative.

The five Mounties and two guides rode directly into the Sioux camp and headed for Sitting Bull's tent. They laid down a list of rules for Sioux behavior if the tribe expected to be allowed to stay in Canada. Then, spotting an Indian sitting on a stolen horse, they arrested the Indian on the spot and rode quietly out.

There is a certain advantage for the person who can act boldly in an uncertain situation. The very boldness of the Mounties' actions conveyed to the Indians that here was an authority to be obeyed.

Day 57

William Purkey tells a delightful little allegory concerning the value of feeling good about ourselves:

A mouse ran into the office of the Educational Testing Service and accidentally triggered a delicate point in the apparatus just as the College Entrance Examination Board's data on one Henry Carson was being scored.

Henry was an average high-school student who was unsure of himself and his abilities. Had it not been for the mouse, Henry's score would have been average or less, but the mouse changed all that, for the scores that emerged from the computer were amazing—800s in both the verbal and quantitative areas.

When the scores reached Henry's school, the word of his giftedness spread like wildfire. Teachers began to re-evaluate their gross underestimation of this fine lad, counselors trembled at the thought of neglecting such talent, and even college admissions officers began to recruit Henry for their schools.

New worlds opened for Henry, and as they opened he started to grow as a person and as a student. Once he became aware of his potentialities and began to be treated differently by the significant people in his life, a form of self-fulfilling prophecy took place. Henry began to put his mind in the way of great things. . . Henry became one of the best men of his generation.

Day 58

Bullfighters have a confidence in themselves that borders on arrogance. One day a reporter asked the great Spanish bullfighter Manolete to name the five or six great bullfighters of the time. Manolete froze the reporter with a look and then answered:

First there is Manolete.
And then there is no one.
And then there is no one.
And then there is no one.
And then there is no one.
And then there is no one.

Bullfighting is a brutal sport that demands that kind of self-confidence. The truth of the matter is that every task we face requires self-confidence. Believe in yourself. It's the only way to face all the bull that's out there.

For Reflection

There was a study performed at the University of North Carolina recently that dealt with the importance of making a good impression. A group of psychologists there set up a false corporation office, advertised job openings, and began conducting interviews with students at the school as if they were a major employer. They further arranged matters so that some of the students who applied for jobs there could dress up, but others could not.

They found that the dressed up students, as a rule, asked for $4,000 more in salary and felt much more confident with the interview than those who were not allowed to dress up.

When we look our best, we feel better about ourselves. When we seek to impress others, we often impress ourselves as well.

1) What are some things you could do to make yourself feel more confident?

2) Think of someone you know who appears to you to be very confident. What does he or she do to give that appearance?

3) What is the connection between integrity and confidence?

4) How does fear get in the way of confidence?

CONFORMITY

Tacitus once described Tiberius, the unpopular Roman emperor, as follows: "He feared the best, was ashamed of the worst, and chose the innocuous middle."

Day 59

Jean Henri Fabre, the French naturalist, once encountered some unusual caterpillars while walking in the woods. They were marching in a long unbroken line front to back, front to back. What fun it would be, Fabre thought, to make a complete ring with these creatures and let them march in a circle.

So Fabre captured enough caterpillars to encircle the rim of a flowerpot. He linked them nose to posterior and started them walking in the closed circle. For days they turned like a perpetual merry-go-round. Although food was near at hand and accessible, the caterpillars starved to death on an endless march to nowhere.

We, too, can get so caught up in following other people around that we forget the essentials and collapse. Don't be afraid to look outside of the group of people you are in if you feel you lack something.

Day 60

Roger von Oech in *A Whack On The Side Of The Head* tells two true stories that are classics: A man walks into a doctor's waiting room and, much to his surprise, discovers that everyone is sitting in their underwear, waiting on the doctor. After a few moments of confusion, the man slowly removes his clothes, hangs them on a coat rack nearby and quietly takes a seat to wait his turn.

Second true story: A man gets on an elevator. Strangely enough, everyone is facing the back wall. There is no door at the back, just a wall, and everyone is facing it. So the man rides up to his floor facing the back wall, too.

Two stories from the television series *Candid Camera*.

Conformity is never necessarily the right thing. If breaking with tradition will improve things, then break with tradition.

Day 61

Two young daughters of a Queen came to her with eyes full of bright new fashions from the catalogs and magazine and storefront windows. "Mother!" they cried, "We want to dress like that! Everybody's doing it!" After hearing them go on like this for a time, the Queen asked them: "Whose daughters are you?"

"Your daughters, Mother! The daughters of the Queen!"

"Queen's daughters don't follow fashions and styles," she said, "They set them!"

Years ago Harry Emerson Fosdick made the observation that the world persecutes two kinds of people: those who live below the standard, and those who dare to live above it. As someone has noted, in 399 BC the jail at Athens held many criminals, but also Socrates. Two criminals were crucified on Calvary, but so was Christ. In Birmingham, Alabama in the 1960s the jail was full of thieves and criminals, but it also held Martin Luther King, Jr.

Standing out from the crowd for the right reasons may be risky or even dangerous. Do you have the courage to excel?

Day 62

One time during the Coolidge administration, an overnight guest in the White House wanted to make a good impression. He was having breakfast with President Coolidge, and noticed with some discomfort that the President, having been served his coffee, took the cup, poured the greater portion of the coffee into a deep saucer, and added a little bit of sugar and a little cream. The guest felt that since the President had done this, that it was what was expected, and so he should follow the example. So he also poured out much of his coffee into his saucer and added sugar and cream.

Then he watched as the President took his saucer and put it on the floor for the cat.

Don't be afraid to ask for directions if you don't know what to do in a situation. Ignorance is nothing to be ashamed of, but blind acceptance of a bad idea will hurt you in the long run.

Day 63

A number of years ago a rather unusual advertisement was played over the radio. The announcer gave several scenes in the life of a certain person.

The first scene portrayed a crying baby and a proud father. The father was saying, "Oh, it's a boy. It's a boy. We're going to name him Stanley, and one day he will become the president of the United States."

In the second scene, Stanley was getting married. The father of the bride was telling him, "I know you would like to go to medical school, son, but I think you should join me in the purse manufacturing business."

In the third scene, Stanley and his wife were on an expensive vacation. He had obviously become a successful manufacturer and made a lot of money.

In the final scene, the minister was preaching Stanley's funeral. He said, "Stanley was much beloved by all those who lived here at the Shady Nook Rest home. He was the best gin rummy player in Shady Nook, and a few people knew that he also had the lowest cholesterol count of anyone here."

Then the announcer came on and said, "Isn't it sad to live your whole life and never make a ripple and never rock a boat? Join the Peace Corps."

Day 64

It is perhaps a measure of our times that we are rarely without some form of light. And that is due, in part at least, to the efforts of Thomas Edison. It is said that after several thousand experiments, when he finally achieved that breakthrough which would affect all of human history, he heard the voice of his wife call out, "Tom, for goodness sake, would you turn off that light and come to bed!"

It is very difficult for some people to realize the significance of a new discovery. Those who do recognize it, like Edison, will profoundly affect the future.

For Reflection

Captain William Westy sometime back wrote an article titled "The Right to Be Different" in which he said: "Psychologists attempt to help persons adjust to society. Big business and big labor try to fit the individual into the organization pattern. Advertising extols the virtues of conformity... This same sort of logic should have convinced Columbus that the world was flat and the Wright brothers that man could never fly. Thank God that some men of all ages have dared to dispute the majority opinion when it was in error."

1) In what ways are you conforming now to ideas and expectations which are not true to your nature? Looking at these ideas and expectations objectively, is conformity really necessary?

2) What types of conforming behavior negatively impact the effectiveness of your team or company?

3) In working with or supervising others, do you communicate an insistence on conformity which hampers their creativity?

4) What can you do today to step out of a rut?

CREATIVITY

In the most primitive societies, the only source of energy is the human organism itself. The amount of power that an average adult can generate is less than 1/10 of 1 horsepower. Obviously, societies that rely on human power alone never get very far. And you as an individual won't get very far either if you rely on physical labor alone.
— B. Eugene Griessman

Day 65

I'm one of those people who would like to see tighter controls put on hand guns. I do not think it will do much to deter crime, though. People who want to get into mischief will find another way. The newspapers carried two incidents sometime back that illustrate this point.

Two robbers in Dallas have learned to consider all of their resources. The two, apparently lacking a knife or gun, decided to hold up a Domino's Pizza delivery man as the guy stood talking in a phone booth. According to the Domino's driver, the men pinned him in the phone booth, thrust a snapping turtle in his face, and commanded, "Don't move or you're gonna get bit." They then left with $50 of the frightened driver's money.

About that same time there was a story about a tractor-trailer driver following behind a car who was pulled over and attacked by two individuals with swords. The car's driver and other passenger apparently felt the truck driver had been following them too closely. Because of previous felonies, the car's driver was prohibited from carrying a gun. He had adjusted, however. He merely switched to carrying antique swords!

People will be creative! The challenge is to channel that creativity into profitable and constructive activities.

Day 66

Back in the late 19th and early 20th centuries, there was a great German chemist named Johann von Baeyer, who made many contributions to science and was awarded a Nobel Prize in 1905. One morning Baeyer came into his laboratory and found that his assistants had built an ingenious stirring device operated by water turbines. The professor was fascinated by the complex machine, and he called in his wife from their apartment next door. Frau Baeyer watched the apparatus in silent admiration for a while, and then exclaimed, "What a lovely idea for making mayonnaise!"

There's a basic distinction to be made here: the good professor's students were the inventors, but his wife was the innovator. As Peter Drucker says, "Above all, invention is not innovation. It is a term of economics rather than technology. The measure of innovation is the impact on the environment."

Day 67

A tenth grade boy had a crush on a girl in the eleventh grade, but he assumed that because he was younger, she wouldn't be interested in dating him. He daydreamed about her all the time but couldn't get up the courage to ask her out.

Suddenly one day, out of the blue, his dreams came true. The eleventh grade girl walked up to him, right in the middle of the cafeteria, and invited him to the junior-senior prom. He was absolutely bowled over! He accepted her invitation gleefully. He rented a tux, ordered a corsage for her—and then his dream fell apart!

It hit him with a sickening thud. He realized that he had no car and, even worse, no driver's license. All his older friends with cars already had made their plans, so there was no chance of double dating. He was in an embarrassing situation. But as they say, necessity is the mother of invention, and the young man came up with an ingenious plan.

He remembered that his grandfather owned a big, shiny, black car. With that in mind, he went to a nearby pawn shop and bought a chauffeur's cap. Then he went over to his grandfather's house.

Somehow, the young man persuaded his grandfather to put on a black suit, a black tie, and the driver's cap, and serve as his limousine driver for the night—not telling anyone that the driver was his grandfather! Well, it worked perfectly. He was the hit of the prom. His date loved it. And Grandfather played his part to the hilt—driving well, opening the "limousine" doors for them with a flourish, and throughout the night, calling his grandson "Mr. Johnson"!

Just think what a little creativity can accomplish!

Day 68

It's hard to believe that one of the most popular pants today, the blue jean, began as unsold tent canvas.

During the 1850 California gold rush, Levi Strauss tried to peddle the canvas to prospectors. Unsuccessful, he realized that the material could be used to make sturdy pants for the miners. The pants went over big, and Levis (later made from indigo-dyed denim) soon were being worn by the general public.

Creativity is not some dark, mysterious process. It is stepping back and gazing at what already is and asking if there is a new approach you might take to reach your goals.

Day 69

The Flick Reedy Company of Bensenville, Illinois, needed a large supply of water for emergency fire use. The most obvious solution was to purchase water towers, but they are costly to build and keep up, and besides that, they are ugly. In shifting mental gears and brainstorming creatively, the company hit upon the idea of an indoor swimming pool. It could be big enough to hold the required amount of water, yet the cost would be half that of a water tower.

Thus the company created a pool for employee and community use, enhancing its public image in the community while saving money. The company was so pleased with this solution that it created a backup supply of water in artificial lakes which it stocked with fish, creating new opportunities for fishing and canoeing.

Day 70

Many of our most important inventions were produced by people who were looking for an easier way to do something.

Thomas Edison was fired from an early job as a telegraph operator when it was discovered that he had created a device to let him take short naps on the job.

Henry Ford, while still a boy, designed a device that allowed him to shut the gate without having to get out of the wagon.

Years later, after he had become a world-famous manufacturer, Ford was still creating devices that made work easier. He implemented a feeder line to the factory so that workers wouldn't have to waste their energy walking to get parts. After the feeder line became a standard part of the car-building process, Ford realized that workers' stooping over the assembly line increased fatigue and led to sloppy work and accidents. So, he insisted that the entire line be raised by 8 inches. This simple adjustment, which made work less tiring, led to a major increase in productivity.

Sometimes creative effort can result in an idea or invention that allows you to spend more time on your real priorities.

Day 71

TV Guide had an article recently about Estelle Getty of TV's *Golden Girls*. When she was an unknown in Hollywood, she auditioned four times for the part of Sophia, the 80ish lady in *The Golden Girls*, but she wasn't able to nail down the part.

Getty, a New York stage actress, was very, very interested in the part, but after each audition's failure, she was left wondering what the producers' reservations about her might be.

Assuming that the decision-makers were concerned about the disparity between Getty's true age (in the neighborhood of 60) and

Sophia's scripted age, Getty, with her managers' encouragement, hired a Hollywood makeup artist to age her before she went into her fifth reading for the part. She also went shopping and bought a thrift-shop polyester dress a couple of sizes too big for her, a funny little hat, lace-up shoes and a flat little handbag that she could carry on her wrist. Getty shuffled into NBC that way, stayed in character throughout the audition, and when it was over she shuffled out again, still in character.

She was hired that day.

Sometimes it helps to show a little creative enthusiasm. It will make you feel better about what you are doing, and may impress someone about your earnestness.

Day 72

Irving Berlin spent his childhood as a waiter in Chinatown. He never learned to play the piano, except by ear and only in the key of F-sharp. Many 12 year-olds read music better than the man who wrote the only American piece which John Alden Carpenter has included in the world's greatest music.

Alexander Woollcott knew Berlin well. He denied the rumor that Irving could play with only one finger. But he loved to tell about Chico Marx who, upon hearing that Berlin had cut his thumb, observed in withering accents, "Well, that won't interfere with his piano playing."

Woollcott's highest tribute to Berlin was this: "He can neither read music nor transcribe it—he can only give birth to it."

Irving Berlin did not fret over the gifts he did not have. Rather he made maximum use of the wonderful creative genius he did have—and the world is a happier place because of it.

For Reflection

Consider the videotape recorder. Invented in the United States by Ampex, the initial models weighed more than one hundred pounds and cost $250,000. The Japanese then took this idea in the A phase and successfully worked out the systems and practices needed to drive it out of A and into the B phase of development where they could economically apply this new paradigm to the problems of entertainment and education.

1) Do you know of a good idea which has been "waiting in the wings"? How could you or your team creatively build on that idea?

2) Have you been beating your head against a problem which seems to have no solution? Deliberately shove that problem out of your mind for at least a day. Then, after your 24 hours are up, commit yourself to at least a half-hour of brainstorming possible answers to your problem. Allow yourself to be outrageous, and see if you don't come up with a solution.

3) Are you developing your innate creativity? Try reading outside of your field, playing, daydreaming, walking and thinking, conversing with creative people, listening to music, and/or journaling.

CUSTOMER SERVICE

Bruce Nash and Allan Zullo tell about a warranty Cable Electric Products has on its Snapit 6 + 2 = 8 multi-outlet system. Just complete and mail the registration form and retain the warranty. So what's the hitch? The warranty is on the back of the registration form.

Day 73

Don Webner of the Michigan Department of Transportation, Lansing, Michigan suggests we learn to break what he calls "the RUPOLES."

Rupoles are the rules and policies that protect company personnel from meeting the needs of their customers. RUPOLES are excuses for not providing quality service. And they're written for the convenience of people who are supposed to be providing customer service.

Here are some excuses that help RUPOLES survive:
* "We have very strict rules about that."
* "I just work here."
* "I'm sorry; it's against our policy."
* "We've always done it that way."
* "We deliver only on Tuesdays."
* "If I do that for you, everyone will expect it."
* "I'd like to help you, but you don't have the proper form."

Quality service demands that we get out of the comfort zone created by RUPOLES. Customers are interested in having their needs met. They want service in a timely fashion. Try changing or bending a few RUPOLES.

Day 74

The next time you are in Atlanta, stop in at one of the QT markets (a convenience store). I did on a Sunday morning. I needed a ball-point pen to take some notes. I stopped in at this little convenient type market. I was in a hurry and asked as I breezed past the cash register, "Do you have any ball-point pens?" The young man answered, "Yes, we do," and directed me to them. I brought a pen back up to the register and the young man said, "The next time you need to pick up a pen, all of our markets are laid out the same way. You'll find the pens in exactly the same spot. Now would you like a cup of our freshly brewed coffee to take along with you?" That sounded good, so I said yes. "And how about a Sunday morning paper?" he asked. I was afraid I was going to run out of money before I got out of that store, but I told my wife that the next time we were in Atlanta, I would be stopping at QT. Don't you appreciate it when a sales person is attentive and pleasant and well-trained?

Day 75

We live in a crazy world. Did you ever notice that?

Did you read about that Burger King employee in Ypsilanti, Michigan a couple years back, who was confronted by a hold-up man? It was 7:20 in the morning when a man walked into the Burger King carrying a gun. The young man behind the register asked, "May I help you?" The hold-up man said, "Give me all the money in your register." The young man behind the counter answered, "I'm sorry, I'm not allowed to open the register without a food order." The hold-up man said, "All right. Give me some onion rings." And the young man behind the counter answered, "I'm sorry. Onion rings are not on our breakfast menu." And the hold up man became so frustrated, he walked out. I believe that young Burger King employee has waited on me at several major department stores.

Day 76

Bedside manner: When he was adjunct professor at UCLA Medical School, Norman Cousins took a random survey of 1500 high-income people who were not ill. In asking about the doctor-patient relationship, he discovered that 85 percent had either changed doctors in the last five years or were considering it. Of the five reasons cited by the respondents, the least important was the doctor's competence. The four more commonly mentioned reasons related to the physicians' relational style and included not taking enough time, not allowing patients to express themselves, being preoccupied with phone calls, and having poor personal habits. Medical competence was taken for granted. It was "bedside manner" that made the difference.

Day 77

Treat every customer with dignity. The results might surprise you.
Some years ago a 10 year-old boy entered a restaurant and sat at the counter. The waitress went over and put a glass of water in front of him. "How much is an ice cream sundae?" he asked. "Fifty cents," replied the waitress.
The little fellow pulled his hand out of his pocket and studied a number of coins clutched in it. "How much is a dish of plain ice cream?" he asked.
There were many people waiting at the counter, and the waitress was getting impatient. "Thirty-five cents," she said brusquely. Again he counted the coins. "I'll have the plain ice cream," he said. The waitress took his money, brought the ice cream, put it in front of him, and walked away. When she came back a few minutes later, the boy was gone. She stared at the empty dish and then swallowed hard at what she saw. There, placed neatly beside the empty dish were two nickels and five pennies—her tip.

Day 78

John Maxwell tells of a time when he was traveling in the South and stopped at a service station for some fuel. It was a rainy day, yet the station workers were diligently trying to take care of the customers. Impressed by his first-class treatment, John fully understood the reason when he read the following sign on the front door of the station:

WHY CUSTOMERS QUIT
1% die
3% move away
5% other friendships
9% competitive reasons (price)
14% product dissatisfaction
BUT . . .
68% quit because of an attitude of indifference toward them by some employee!

In other words, 68 percent quit because the workers did not have a customer mindset working for them.

Day 79

The *Atlanta Journal-Constitution* did an interesting study sometime back. They interviewed a wide range of persons who had bought new homes within the past five years. The first question they asked was, have you had any problems with your new home—problems that you had to call the contractor back to repair? As you might imagine some of them had nightmare situations to report. Some of them had the contractor back several times over those five years for one thing or another.

Then they asked the question, Would you have the same builder build your next home? What they found was that the feelings of the home owners had nothing to do with how many problems they had experienced with their house. The only thing that mattered was whether the contractor listened to them and came back and repaired the problem. Even those who felt they had lived through nightmares said they would use the same builder again if the builder listened to them and responded in a timely manner. People will forgive us a multitude of sins in any profession if they really believe we care.

Day 80

There once was a man who owned a small drugstore. For some reason he hated his work, and he spent his mornings looking for something better to do, and his afternoons at the ball park.

Finally he decided it was foolish to live like this so he decided to quit moping and begin to build up his business by giving the best service possible.

In keeping with his new outlook, when a customer who lived near called in an order on the telephone, he would repeat each item being ordered and his assistant would hurriedly fill out the order sheet. With the order filled, the owner would keep the customer on the line while the delivery boy dashed out the front door. When the delivery boy reached the customer's house, the customer would still be on the line with the drugstore owner. She would excuse herself for a minute to answer the door. Coming back to the phone, the customer would express great surprise and appreciation at the quickness with which the order was delivered.

News got around about the drugstore that filled orders so promptly, and soon Charles R. Walgreen, founder of the nationwide chain of pharmacies that are his namesake, had more business than he could handle.

Perhaps great customer service requires only a change in attitude.

Day 81

There was a story in *USA Today* about a woman who received a sizable check from the Veteran's Administration. The check was not made out to her, she did not know the person that the check was made out to, nor had she ever been in the military.

She put it back outside for the postman to pick up on his next round. Five days later she got it back in a different envelope. She telephoned the VA office in her district and was directed to send the check there. She did, and one week later she received it back, in the same envelope. Next she mailed it to the Treasury Department office in Kansas City, where the check was originally issued, along with a certified letter advising them that it did not belong to her and that she did not know the person to whom it had been issued. The check was returned to her in a different envelope.

Next she took it to the local postmaster. After explaining the situation to him, he advised her to give it to him for returning it to the Veteran's Administration. Two weeks later she received the check again. She was then instructed to mail it to Waco. It returned yet again. After the seventh delivery she called the Dallas VA branch and was told they didn't know what else they could do.

Finally she called the secret service office and told one of their agents that she intended to destroy the check. He informed her that to destroy the check would be against the law—it was government property. She told him she'd cash it, but he answered that she could not keep it either—it wasn't hers! She is currently awaiting further instructions.

Getting the run around is a common experience. Let your company be the exception.

Day 82

Writer Michael Crichton once revised a screenplay in his hotel room by physically cutting apart the script and taping the pieces back together. To get the long pieces of tape he needed, he ran pieces of tape down the front of the desk drawers so that they stuck lightly to the knobs. When he was ready for a piece of tape, all he had to do was cut between the knobs. He continued to revise the script in this manner for several weeks while he was at this hotel.

Now, this hotel has a tradition of catering to its guests' whims. When Crichton returned to the same hotel a year later, he found that a very comfortable room had been prepared for him, but with a peculiar feature: pieces of tape ran down the front of all the desk drawers.

Be prepared to make that extra effort for clients. That added extra is what sets apart the okay from the outstanding.

For Reflection

Several years ago, American Airlines was sued by one of their former employees, Robert W. Cox, who had been fired for not smiling enough. In his suit Cox contended that he had met all of the requirements for the job except for the smile. But the judge ruled in favor of the airline, saying that their policy of requiring a "friendly facial expression" was essential in the competitive airline industry.

Looking positive is just as important as feeling positive. You'll find that people are much more willing to do business with you if you wear a smile.

1) Do you, your colleagues, and your employees treat customers with respect, kindness, and enthusiasm?

2) What would happen if you, your colleagues and your employees thought "win/win" in every interaction with a customer?

3) Sometimes it takes that "extra touch" or special sensitivity to a customer's needs to move a company from adequate customer service to excellent customer service. What would that "extra touch" be for your company?

DECISION

Tycoon T. Boone Pickens, speaking at George Washington University, gave this advice to the young people there: "Be willing to make decisions. That's the most important quality in a good leader. Don't fall victim to what I call the 'ready aim-aim-aim-aim syndrome.' You must be willing to fire."

Day 83

The ability to make concise and accurate decisions is one of the great secrets of successful living.

There was a college football team whose starting quarterback was injured, and the number two quarterback was too ill to play. This left only a freshman quarterback who also did their punting, but who had absolutely no game experience as a quarterback in college. But the coach was forced to throw him into the fray.

It was first down, but the ball was resting on their own three yard line. The coach's main concern was to get them away from the goal line so that they would have room to punt out of danger.

The coach told the rookie quarterback, "Son, I want you to hand-off to Jones, our big fullback, for the next two plays, let him run into the middle of the line and get us a few yards. Then I want you to punt."

The young quarterback did as he was instructed. On the first play he handed off to Jones, and Jones found a hole in the defense and managed to run fifty yards. The young quarterback called the same play again, and once more, miracle of miracles, the hole was there. This time Jones ran forty five yards. The fans were going wild. The ball was on the opponent's two yard line—six short feet from the goal. Confidently the team lined up, and the young quarterback received the snap, stepped back and punted the football into the stands.

As the team came off the field, the coach grabbed the young quarterback angrily and shouted, "What in the world were you thinking about when you called that last play?!" The quarterback stared back, "I was thinking what a dumb coach we have."

Always have enough confidence in yourself to change the game plan if the situation calls for it.

Day 84

Joseph Henry, the man who founded the Smithsonian Institute in Washington, D.C., tells a story of his boyhood days. His grandmother once offered to pay a cobbler to make him a new pair of shoes. The man measured his feet and told him there were only two styles: a rounded toe or a square toe. Little Joseph couldn't decide: new shoes were too exciting. The cobbler told him that he could take a couple of days to choose, since there were other steps in the preparation that could be done first. Day after day Joseph went to the shop, sometimes three or four times a day, but he couldn't make up his mind. The round-toed shoes were more practical, but the square toes looked more fashionable.

Finally, one day he came to the shop and the cobbler handed him a parcel wrapped in brown paper. It was his new pair of shoes! When he got home, he tore through the wrapping and found a matched set of leather shoes, one with a rounded toe, and the other with a square toe.

If you don't make a decision, someone else will do it for you. And you may have to live with the consequences.

Day 85

Once upon a time Brer Rabbit was invited to dinner on the same evening at the same hour at both Brer Terrapin's and Brer Possum's. When he came to the crossroads that led one way to Brer Terrapin's and the other to Brer Possum's, he stood hungrily in indecision . . . "Do I eat with Brer Terrapin or do I eat with Brer Possum?"

First he ran down the road toward Brer Possum's. Then, changing his mind, he reversed himself and started towards Brer Terrapin's. Then he changed his mind again and started towards Brer Possum's. Thinking of the two meals awaiting him, he ran back and forth, unable to make a decision until finally he missed dinner at both places.

Indecision can lead to no decision, which is often worse than a bad decision.

| Day 86 |

In 1974 the government of Nigeria decided to bring their country into line with the developed Western nations in one bold move. The planners calculated that building the new roads, airfields, and military buildings they wanted would require some 20 million tons of cement. This was duly ordered and shipped by freighters from all over the world, to be unloaded onto the docks at Lagos, Nigeria.

Unfortunately, the Nigerian planners had not considered the fact that the docks at Lagos were only capable of handling two thousand tons a day. Working every day, it would have taken them twenty-seven years to unload the ships that were waiting out at sea to get into Lagos at one point. They had tied up a third of the world's supply of cement and were unable to use it. Much of it set solid in the holds of the freighters.

| For Reflection |

When Luciano Pavarotti graduated from college, he was unsure of whether he should become a teacher or a professional singer. His father told him, "Luciano, if you try to sit on two chairs, you will fall between them. You must choose one chair."

Pavarotti chose singing. It took seven more years of study and frustration before he made his first professional appearance, and it took another seven years before he reached the Metropolitan Opera. But he had chosen his chair and had become successful with it.

1) Do you feel stuck because of indecision? Try this: a) state the decision or dilemma; b) write out pros, cons, and possible consequences of each option; c) seek out all relevant information; d) choose the best option and "just do it." Don't waste time over-thinking the situation.

2) Has a bad personal or company decision kept you from being as effective as you could be? What could you do to reverse or modify that decision?

3) Decision-making always carries with it an element of risk. Take the risk, and rely confidently on your creativity to carry you through if the decision fails. Most decisions allow a Plan B.

DETERMINATION

"I have not yet begun to fight."
— John Paul Jones

Day 87

During the 1976 Olympics in Montreal, Canada, Shun Fujimoto from the Japanese gymnastics team, broke his knee during the floor competition. Speculation ran high that he would be forced to withdraw from the rest of the competition. But the next day Fujimoto, a true competitor, returned to compete in his best event—the rings. His routine went very well, but his dismount was the critical point.

When the moment came, the crowd held its breath as Fujimoto performed a twisting, triple somersault. There was not a sound to be heard as he hit the mat for a jolting impact on his injured knee. But he held his ground, and remained standing. The applause that followed was deafening. Later, when the reporters asked him about the landing, he said, "The pain shot through me like a knife. It brought tears to my eyes. But now I have a gold medal and the pain is gone."

Day 88

Mt. Everest is the tallest mountain in the world. It rises over 29,000 feet above sea level, and can be seen from 100 miles away. The top of the mountain is so high that it reaches into the jet stream, where winds often exceed 200 miles per hour.

The first attempt to climb this immense mountain was made in 1921 by a man named George H. Leigh-Mallory. The attempt failed, but he tried again in 1922. This time seven members of the expedition were lost in an avalanche.

Mallory was determined, however. In 1924 he led his final expedition to conquer the huge mountain. It looked as if they were going to make it, but as the climbers neared the top, both Mallory and another climber disappeared into the mist, and were never seen again.

At a banquet given in the memory of the brave climbers, one of Mallory's friends gave a speech that epitomizes the spirit of all enterprising people, everywhere. He turned from the podium towards a huge picture of Mt. Everest hung on the wall, and addressed the mountain: "I speak to you, Mt. Everest, in the name of all brave men, those living and those yet unborn. Mt. Everest, you defeated us once. You defeated us twice. You defeated us even three times. But we shall some day defeat you, Mt. Everest, because you can't get any bigger—and we can!"

Eight more attempts were made on the mountain after that, and each of them failed. But finally, on March 29, 1953, after eleven total attempts, Edmund Hillary finally beat the challenge and stood with his guide on the summit of the mountain.

The key to reaching the summit of the mountains in your path is persistence. Failure is not the end, it is the end of only one step in reaching your goal.

Day 89

Women have always had a powerful influence on society. Unfortunately, few women have had the opportunity to do so publicly. Sheila Murray Bethel, in her book *Making A Difference*, tells about one of these women:

Susan B. Anthony was born into a well-to-do Quaker family that produced strong-minded women. In the Victorian era, when ideal womanhood was supposed to resemble a flower both in appearance and intelligence, Anthony was a militant.

Anthony spent her life campaigning for women's rights and Negro suffrage, as well as temperance. She was a radical abolitionist before the Civil War. Her campaign to include women in the Fourteenth Amendment was unsuccessful, but before her death in 1920 at the age of eighty-six, she saw the Nineteenth Amendment successfully ratified.

One person's determination can change the world.

Day 90

A story is told about former University of Tennessee and NFL halfback, George Cafego, during the early days of pro football. Playing for the old Brooklyn Dodgers football team against the New York Giants one day, Cafego brought the ball up field practically by himself. Just before the half ended, he broke away over left tackle.

First one man hit him, then another. But Cafego kept going. Finally, about five Giants ganged up on him, and still he plowed goalward. At last he started down—just as the timer's gun exploded.

"My gosh?" a spectator shouted. "They had to shoot him to stop him!"

Day 91

Carole Doi was born during WWII in one of America's internment camps for Japanese Americans. She grew up in America and married a man of Japanese descent. They were thrilled when they had a little girl.

At birth, however, the child's feet were severely twisted so that her toes faced inward. Carole was determined to help her baby grow up to have a normal life, so she decided that the child's feet would not ever be an issue in her life. They bought her orthopedic shoes, and encouraged her to build up her feet and legs. They even supported her when, at a young age, she wanted to try out ice skating.

The hard work and encouragement paid off. In 1992, these proud parents watched as their daughter, Kristi Yamaguchi—the little girl born with the twisted feet—won the Olympic gold medal for ice skating.

Day 92

A bespectacled little girl, many pounds overweight, sat in a Sunday school class listening to a speech by an Olympic gold medalist. She kept jumping up and down saying, "I'm going to be a great tennis champion." None of her classmates in their wildest imaginations could visualized that happening. But she could. And it did. Yes, that little girl carried a determined spirit and a fixed idea in her mind. Today she ranks among the greatest of all women tennis champions. Her name? Billie Jean King.

An eight-year-old boy used to say, "I am going to be the greatest baseball catcher that every lived." His mother told him, "That's impossible."

When he graduated from high school, the Superintendent stopped him and said, "Tell the audience your future plans." "I am going to be the greatest baseball catcher that ever lived." The audience snickered.

Today they applaud Johnny Bench who, in the minds of many, is probably the greatest baseball catcher who ever lived.

For Reflection

A woman came running up to Arthur Rubinstein once after he'd finished another brilliant concert. "Oh, Mr. Rubinstein!" she said, "I'd give anything to be able to play the piano like you do!" And he replied, "No you wouldn't, because you didn't!"

1) Achieving your dreams requires hard work. Are you giving your most important aspiration all the time and energy it deserves?

2) Are you living your life reactively, waiting for someone else to make the decisions, looking for some exterior sign, hoping for the "perfect time"? Isn't it time for YOU to direct your life?

3) How can you keep unimportant distractions from ruining your sense of determination?

ENCOURAGEMENT

A driver made his way nervously along one of the most treacherous Rocky Mountain roads. He was approaching an extremely narrow pass, and there was no guard rail—nothing to keep him from plunging thousands of feet down the deadly side of the mountain. Then he spied a small sign. It said, "O yes, you can. Millions have."

| Day 93 |

A couple moved into a small town in Massachusetts. Both of them liked to read, and made extensive use of the library, but they were constantly frustrated by the lack of assistance they received in finding the books they needed. One day the wife grumbled to a neighbor about the poor service at the library, hoping that her friend would repeat the complaint. And the next time she entered the library, the librarian was indeed all smiles and extremely helpful! She visited her neighbor again and reported the miraculous change.

"I suppose you told her how poor we thought the service was?"

"No," confessed her friend; "I hope you don't mind, but I told her that you were amazed at the way she had built up this small town library, and that you thought she showed good taste in the new books she ordered."

Complaints often have the reverse effect of what we intend to accomplish by them, because people are insulted by them. Try a little praise concerning what has been accomplished. This may drive the person to try even harder.

| Day 94 |

In 1944, during World War II, Admiral Halsey received an intercepted Japanese communication that revealed the destination of an enemy submarine. The admiral planned to send three destroyers to try to intercept the sub.

One of his aides begged the Admiral to reconsider one of the three, a boat called The England. The aide recited the dismal record of this particular destroyer and her crew to the admiral: As soon as she was commissioned, her crew had rammed her into a buoy in San Francisco harbor. On her check-out cruise she destroyed a dock. Her crew was a joke and she held the record for the worst firing ever seen by the aide on a training exercise report. Also, her crew were brawlers, and 6 of them were currently in the brig for breaking up two bars in Honolulu.

Admiral Halsey laughed, ordered the 6 men released from the brig, and sent The England out. Twenty-four hours later The England had chased down and sunk her first sub. Over the next 11 days The England sank 5 more Japanese submarines, wiping out all but two of the enemy underwater armada. Every sub that The England contacted, she sank. Often her sister ships would locate an enemy submarine and fire unsuccessfully for awhile before The England was given a chance. She usually dispatched the enemy on the first try. Even the Japanese assumed that no one ship could inflict so much damage. They shifted their air and naval forces to that sector, believing that their subs were being sunk by the main U.S. naval group carrying the invasion forces.

Often the only thing standing between someone and success is an opportunity and an objective vote of confidence by someone.

Day 95

Many years ago, at the University of Wisconsin, there was an undergraduate literary club which consisted of male students who had demonstrated an outstanding talent in writing. At every meeting, one of the students would read aloud a story or essay he had written, and then submit it to the others for criticism. Of course, the criticism was always brutal: the students showed no mercy in dissecting the material line by line. The sessions were so cruel that the members dubbed themselves "The Stranglers."

Later a similar club was formed called "The Wranglers" which consisted of female students with outstanding writing abilities. Like their male counterparts they would read their writings at meetings and would critique one another. But the Wranglers' criticism was thoughtful, positive and kind. One of their primary concerns was to encourage one another.

Twenty years after the two clubs were formed, a university researcher looked at the careers of the members of both groups. Not one of the bright young men in "The Stranglers" had achieved a literary reputation of any kind. "The Wranglers," though, had produced half a dozen prominent, successful writers.

The formats of both groups were similar. Both groups had very talented students. But "The Stranglers" employed negative criticism while "The Wranglers" used positive. Criticism can be very beneficial when properly used, or damaging when not used well. Learn to tell the difference between the two, and use the positive whenever possible.

Pablo Picasso once said rather immodestly, "When I was a child, my mother said to me, 'If you become a soldier you'll be a general. If you become a monk you'll end up as the Pope.' Instead I became a painter and wound up as Picasso."

Day 96

There's a story from Dwight Eisenhower's academy days that helps shed some light on a part of his character.

It is an accepted practice at West Point, where Eisenhower attended, for upper class men to haze the freshmen, or "plebes." Eisenhower was a second year student, and participated in the hazing activities with his fellow students.

One day one of the plebes bumped into him, an unpardonable offense, and Eisenhower responded by yelling and screaming at the young cadet. Calling on the most demeaning insult he could summon, Eisenhower told the plebe that he looked like a barber. At this, the man lost his stiff composure, drew himself up, looked Eisenhower in the eye, and said, "I am a barber."

Eisenhower, made ashamed of his remark by the man's pride, returned to his room and told his roommate what had happened. "I've just done something that was stupid and unforgivable," he said, "I just managed to make a man ashamed of the work he did to earn a living." Then he vowed that he would never belittle another person again.

Even when he became the leader of the combined Allied war machine, and even as President of the United States, Dwight Eisenhower never broke that promise. He had decided early to encourage, rather than discourage, and it showed in his leadership ability.

Encouragement can help people develop to their full potential. The mark of a good leader is the ability to encourage people to do their best.

> **For Reflection**

Few coaches ever demanded more from their players than did Green Bay Packers coach Vince Lombardi. Yet when Lombardi was seriously ill in a Washington, D.C. hospital, one of his former players, Willie Davis, flew from Los Angeles to Washington just to spend a few minutes with his coach. "I had to go," said Davis. "That man made me feel I was important."

People will go to the ends of the earth for someone who makes them feel important. There is something liberating about knowing that our lives really do matter, that somebody notices us and cares.

1) How could you use encouragement as a technique in motivating people?

2) Are there people in your life who discourage instead of encourage you? How will you handle them? Can you communicate to them your need for encouragement? Is it time to break off a discouraging relationship?

3) Can you think of an acquaintance of yours who needs a little encouragement? What are you waiting for?

EXCELLENCE

The late baseball owner Bill Veeck used to say about players' salaries, "It's not the high price of stardom that bothers me. It's the high price of mediocrity."

Don't be afraid to give up the good to go for the great. —Kenny Rogers

Day 97

There is a story about an Italian duke who was wandering through his flower garden when he came upon a young workman building a box for his flowers. He noticed that the workman was finishing the box with intricate carvings that required painstaking detail. "Why are you wasting your time on this flower box?" The duke asked the workman. "No one will ever notice the intricate details. What is your name?" The young workman answered, "My name is Michelangelo."

One of the factors contributing to Michelangelo's greatness was that he was willing to do his best even for a humble flower pot. Are you willing to put your best effort into those "unimportant" tasks?

When asked whether there are some words she lives by, Nancy Hanks, chairwoman of the National Endowment for the Arts, said, "My parents always told me that people will never know how long it takes you to do something. They will only know how well it is done."

Day 98

Driving between Amarillo and Witchita Falls, Texas you pass through a series of small towns. One of those small towns is a place called Clarendon—population 2067. If you want to spend the night in Clarendon, you'll have to stay in a quaint little establishment named the "It'll Do" motel. That name caught my attention. It'll Do. I didn't stay that night in Clarendon even though I was weary and was still a good distance from my destination.

The It'll Do is probably a fine establishment but something about the name didn't inspire my confidence. And yet that name perfectly describes how many of our institutions function—both public and private. It'll do. Unfortunately, "it'll do" won't do anymore.

Day 99

The second Norman king, William II, came to the English throne in 1085. He brought into his retinue a master silversmith by the name of Walter of Esterlin (or Easterling). Walter always signed his metalwork with four stars. He was a perfectionist in his work and used only the purest silver that could be refined. In fact, the coins he fashioned soon became the standard of weight and purity for much of Europe. His influence is felt even today, as the pennyweight is still the basis for commercial weight and his anglicized name is found on all pure silverware today. That name is Sterling.

Day 100

Peter Drucker in *The Effective Executive* tells about a newly appointed hospital administrator conducting his first staff meeting. The staff had just settled a rather difficult matter to the satisfaction of the new boss when one of the staff asked, "Would this have satisfied Nurse Bryan?" The arguments erupted all over again and did not stop until a better solution was resolved upon.

Naturally the administrator was curious to know who this Nurse Bryan was. He found out that she had been a nurse at the hospital who had retired ten years before. Whenever a decision regarding patient care came up while she had been there, she had asked, "Are we doing the best we can for this person?" As a result, the patients on her floor generally felt better and recovered faster. By the time she retired, the whole hospital had adopted the "Nurse Bryan Rule," and even ten years later the rule was still in force.

Don't just work, work at doing your best.

Day 101

Arthur Rubenstein once astounded a young inquirer with a statement that he practiced piano eight hours a day, every day of his life. "But, sir!" exclaimed the young man, "You are so good. Why do you practice so much?"

"I wish to become superb," replied the master pianist.

Antonio Stradivari distinguished himself as the world's greatest violin maker. His instruments were unsurpassed. Modern violin makers have been unable to equal the instruments of the old Italian masters of the seventeenth and eighteenth centuries. Stradivari once remarked, "If my hand slacked, I should rob God."

Excellence doesn't just happen. It is the product of dedication and extraordinary hard work.

Day 102

A beloved old physician was retiring in a little French village. He had labored among the villagers for decades. It was a poor village, so the mayor proposed that a keg be set up in the village square and that everyone should bring a pitcher of wine from his own cellar to pour into the keg. Then they would present the keg to the doctor as an expression of their good will for all he had done for them.

On the appointed day, a steady stream of people brought pitchers of wine to pour into the keg. That evening a presentation was made to the good doctor, and he took the keg home with him. Not long afterwards, as he sat near his fireplace, he decided to have a glass of wine. He drew a glass from the keg and took a sip. He nearly choked from the taste. He drew another glass to be sure, but it had the same awful taste—water! Confused, he returned the keg to the townspeople. The mayor was understandably upset, and he called for a town meeting to see what had happened. Much to his disgust, and the town's embarrassment, it was discovered that every family had brought water to pour into the keg, thinking it would never be noticed since everyone else was bringing wine.

Are you contributing your best? Or are you merely supplying water, hoping that nobody will notice it among all the wine?

Day 103

At Federal Express, package sorters are tested once a quarter for accuracy, and anyone who falls below the standard of 100 percent is sent back for retraining. This perfectionism may seem expensive, but the reasoning is that if a Federal Express sorter makes only one mistake in 100 tries, that single mistake may be a 100-percent disaster to the customer. Since a typical Federal Express customer is someone who uses the service repeatedly, only one mis-sent or delayed package can cost the company an untold amount of future business.

Sony president Akio Morita was once asked, Why are the Japanese reluctant to build consumer products in the United States? His answer: They can't find American parts that meet their quality control standards.

Take the Sony camcorder, he explained. Sony has a production standard that tolerates only one out of a hundred of them to fail. That seems easy to meet—until you realize that the device is made up of two thousand component parts. With that many parts, each one must work flawlessly—less than one failure in a hundred thousand, or even a million—in order for the whole unit to meet the standard. The whole is far greater than the sum of the parts.

Day 104

Lou Holtz, the head football coach at Notre Dame, is a stickler for detail. Here's an example:

The team has a road game at Purdue. Their coach has instructed them to wear coats and ties to the stadium because they'll be closely observed as representatives of the University of Notre Dame. They're waiting to board the bus to go to the stadium for the game when coach Holtz shows up. He doesn't say a word—just goes down the line and looks them over. And over. Finally he goes up to one of the players, smiles, reaches up and straightens the player's tie, and then nods to the driver of the bus. Not until then is the door to the bus opened and the team permitted to load up.

He hasn't said anything, but the message is clear: If you're going to be a winner, look like a winner. Little things mean everything.

Day 105

A visitor had come to see Michelangelo and was examining a statue that he was sculpting. The visitor said, "I can't see that you have made any progress since I was here last time."

Michelangelo answered, "Oh, yes, I have made much progress. Look carefully and you will see that I have retouched this part, and that I have polished that part. See, I have worked on this part of the statue, and have softened the lines here."

"Yes," said the visitor, "but those are all trifles."

"That may be," replied Michelangelo, "but trifles make perfection and perfection is no trifle."

Without small things, there can be no big things. Everything is made up of something smaller. And if the parts are done well, the finished whole will also be done well.

> **Day 106**

James Francis Burns, Secretary of State under Franklin Roosevelt, once said, "I discovered at an early age that most of the difference between average people and great people can be explained in three words: AND THEN SOME.

"The top people did what was expected of them and then some. They were considerate and thoughtful of others and then some. They met their obligations and responsibilities fairly and squarely and then some. They were good friends to their friends and then some. They could be counted on in an emergency and then some."

Those are good words to remember. Do what everybody else does . . . and then some.

> **Day 107**

Lee Buck tells about a young actor in a play many years ago. The play was called *Up and Up*, but it was nearly down and out, and about to fold. It had received dismal reviews, and the audiences were dwindling. In such a situation it would be natural for any young actor to do less than his best. After all, what difference would it make? The play was a loser.

One particular young actor, however, believed that it did make a difference. Someone once told him, "Whatever task lies to your hand, do it with all your might." He believed that, and so he gave his best even in this dismal play. The play eventually did fold, and he went on to play in some other productions.

Over a year after *Up and Up* closed, he received a call from Howard Hughes, who, at that time, was a major film producer. Hughes had been in the audience of one of the performances of *Up and Up*. He had not been impressed by the play, but he had been impressed by a young actor named Pat O'Brien who was giving all he had in the role he had been given. Hughes remembered that performance and cast Pat O'Brien in the movie *The Front Page*, the first of an impressive collection of films in which he would star. Give your very best regardless of your circumstances. That is a great secret of successful living.

For Reflection

A Rolls Royce owner experienced a mechanical failure in his car while traveling on vacation. When he called the company's headquarters in England and explained the problem, they flew a mechanic out to him to repair it. After waiting a number of weeks and not receiving a bill for the repair job, the man wrote to the company and asked for one. He received a telex in reply which read: "We have no record of a Rolls Royce with a mechanical failure." That's a commitment to quality!

1) In what way is your company "just getting by"? Are employees given adequate time to do excellent work?

2) How might your insistence on excellence influence your colleagues or employees?

3) How would a personal commitment to excellence improve your attitude toward your work?

FAILURE

The man who is incapable of making a mistake is incapable of anything.
>—Abraham Lincoln

I can pardon everybody's mistakes but my own. —Marcus Cato, Roman Statesman

If at first you don't succeed, destroy all the evidence that you've tried.

Day 108

It is encouraging to know that Henry Ford forgot to put a reverse gear in the first car he invented. Also, he didn't build a door wide enough to get the car out of the building he built it in. If you go to Greenfield Village, you can still see where he cut a hole in the wall to get the car out. But he did get it out and the world has never been the same.

Things don't always have to be perfect to be good. Would the world have been much different today if Ford had remembered the reverse gear, or the door? Probably not.

Einstein, reputed to be the smartest person who ever lived, said, "I think and think for months and years. Ninety-nine times the conclusion is false. The hundredth time I am right."

Day 109

Most everyone knows about the "Home Run King" Babe Ruth. He had 714 home runs in his career—a record that held until Hank Aaron broke it in 1976. But does anyone remember the ball player with the most strike-outs? The man who holds the dubious honor of having the most strike-outs during his career is Babe Ruth. He struck out a total of 1330 times. Only in swinging often and hard was he able to hit so many home runs—only by striking out so many times was he able to achieve greatness.

Everybody strikes out occasionally. Elias Howe invented the sewing machine, but it nearly rusted away before American women could be persuaded to use it. With their sewing finished so quickly what would they ever do with their spare time? Howe had vision and had made his vision come true, but he could not sell! So his biographer paints a tragic picture—the man who had done more than any other in his generation to lighten the labor of women is forced to attend—in a borrowed suit of clothes!—the funeral of the woman he loved.

Day 110

Robert Frost, one of the greatest poets that America has produced, labored for twenty years without fame or success. He was 39 years old before he sold a single volume of poetry. Today his poems have been published in some twenty-two languages and he won the Pulitzer Prize for poetry four times.

When Enrico Caruso, the great Italian tenor, took his first voice lesson, the instructor pronounced him hopeless. He said his voice sounded like wind whistling through a window.

Walt Disney was once fired by a newspaper editor for lack of imagination. Disney once recalled his early days of failure: "When I was nearly twenty-one years old I went broke for the first time. I slept on cushions from an old sofa and ate cold beans out of a can."

Gregor Mendel, the Austrian botanist whose experiments with peas originated the modern science of genetics, never even succeeded in passing the examination to become a high school science teacher. He failed biology.

Woody Allen flunked a motion picture production course at the City College of New York. Leon Uris, writer of one of the most popular novels of this century, *Exodus*, failed English three times in high school.

Everyone who makes a major contribution to life knows what it is to have failures. Indeed, early failures can be a major contributor to later successes.

Day 111

Maybe you know somebody who flunked their driving test the first time around. Maybe you know someone who flunked it twice. But 273 times? That's how many times England's Betty Tudor bombed her driving test. Says Betty, "I'm a disaster when I'm driving."

After one test, her examiner was admitted to a mental hospital. During another, her examiner lost his cool. Why? 'Cause Betty started driving the wrong way around a traffic circle. Betty told the guy to chill out: "If it hadn't been for the cars coming in the opposite direction honking their horns, he wouldn't have noticed anything wrong."

After 19 years of trying to get her license, Betty finally gave up—and started riding a mo-ped instead.

Failure is no disgrace. Still, one of the secrets of success is knowing when to cut your losses.

Day 112

There was once a young man who failed miserably in both business and politics, the two things that he was determined to succeed at.

He began by starting a small business which soon failed, so he ran for the legislature and was defeated. He then started another business, which also failed. Three years later he had a nervous breakdown. A year after his breakdown he was defeated for two more public offices, and again when he ran for Congress, and then the Senate, and then the position of the Vice President of the United States. And then he was defeated one more time for a seat in the Senate.

Most people with any sense would have given up by this time, but this man ran for office once more, and Abe Lincoln was finally elected President of the United States in 1860.

Day 113

In his first season with the Yankees, Mickey Mantle had a terrible batting slump. He couldn't seem to hit anything. In a double-header against Boston, Mantle struck out three times in the opener and twice more in the second game. His coach, Casey Stengel, finally had to pull him from the lineup.

A few weeks later, while playing in Kansas City, Mickey got a call from his father. Mantle told his father he was planning to quit pro ball.

Five hours later, after a late-night drive all the way from Spavinaw, OK, Elvin Clark Mantle stalked into his son's hotel room and let him have it.

"So you've had your slump," Mickey's dad said. "You're not the first and you sure won't be the last. Everybody has them, even DiMaggio. Take my word. It'll come together. You'll see."

Mickey Mantle promised his dad he would give it another try.

During the next forty games, he hit eleven home runs and fifty RBIs, for a .361 average.

Day 114

Although Vincent Van Gogh painted hundreds of pictures in his lifetime, he actually sold only one. Van Gogh called himself "a poor bungler who can't sell a picture."

Ninety-nine years after he killed himself, one of his paintings, "Portrait of Dr. Gachet," was sold to a Japanese collector for $82.5 million.

How sad it is that Van Gogh didn't live to see his success. How much sadder it would have been for the world if Van Gogh had given up. Failure is not a condition; it is merely an event.

Day 115

Creativity expert Edward De Bono in his book, *New Think*, tells about the tribulations of the father of the wireless radio, Guglielmo Marconi. As he increased the power and efficiency of his equipment,

Marconi found that he could send wireless waves over longer and longer distances. Finally he became bold enough to consider transmitting a signal across the Atlantic Ocean itself. It seemed only a matter of having a powerful enough transmitter and a sensitive enough receiver.

The experts who knew better balked at the idea. They assured him that since wireless waves, like light, traveled in straight lines, they would not follow the curvature of the earth, but would stream off into space. Logically the experts were quite right. But Marconi tried, persisted, and succeeded in sending a signal across the Atlantic.

Neither Marconi nor the experts of the time knew about the electrically charged layer in the upper atmosphere, which bounced back the wireless waves that would have otherwise streamed off into space as the experts predicted. It was only this layer which made transatlantic wireless communication possible.

By being wrong Marconi arrived at a conclusion he could never have reached had he followed rigid logic. More often than not, being wrong like Marconi will end in failure. But the few times that being wrong ends in success makes the effort worth it.

Day 116

Stephen Glenn tells a story about a famous research scientist who had made several very important medical breakthroughs. He was being interviewed by a newspaper reporter who asked him why he thought he was able to achieve so much more than the average person.

He responded that, in his opinion, it all came from an experience in his life which occurred when he was about two years old. He had been trying to remove a bottle of milk from the refrigerator when he lost his grip on the slippery bottle and dropped it, spilling its contents all over the kitchen floor and creating a sea of milk!

When his mother came into the kitchen, instead of yelling at him, giving him a lecture or punishing him, she said, "Robert, what a great and wonderful mess you have made! I have rarely seen such a huge puddle of milk. Well, the damage has already been done. Would you like to get down and play in the milk for a few minutes before we clean it up?"

What an opportunity for a two-year-old! Of course he wanted to play in the milk, and play he did. After a few minutes, his mother said, "You know, Robert, whenever you make a mess like this, eventually you have to clean it up and restore everything to its proper order. So, how would you like to do that? We could use a sponge, a towel or a mop. Which do you prefer?" He chose the sponge and together they cleaned up the spilled milk.

His mother then said, "You know, what we have here is a failed experiment in how to effectively carry a big milk bottle with two tiny hands. Let's go out in the back yard and fill the bottle with water and see if you can discover a way to carry it without dropping it." The little boy learned that if he grasped the bottle at the top near the lip with both hands, he could carry it without dropping it. What a wonderful lesson!

This renowned scientist then remarked that it was at that moment that he knew he didn't need to be afraid to make mistakes. Instead, he learned that mistakes were just opportunities for learning something new.

Day 117

Bernie Marcus was a poor Russian cabinetmaker's son from Newark, New Jersey. Arthur Blank was raised in a lower-middle-class neighborhood in Queens, New York, where he ran with a juvenile gang. His father died when Arthur was 15. "I grew up with the notion that life is going to be filled with some storms," Blank says.

In 1978, Arthur Blank and Bernie Marcus were working at a hardware retainer in Los Angeles when a new owner canned them. The next day an investor friend suggested they go into business for themselves. "Once I stopped stewing in my misery," says Marcus, "I saw that the idea wasn't crazy."

Marcus and Blank began opening the kind of stores they had dreaded competing against: hangar-size, no-frills outlets with high-grade service and a huge selection. Today their Home Depot tops the fast-growing home-improvement industry.

Day 118

"I never understood the impact I had on people," says Anne Busquet of American Express. Four years ago, Busquet was the general manager of its Optima Card unit. When it was discovered that five of her 2000 employees had deliberately hidden $24 million in losses, she was held accountable. An intense perfectionist whom others saw as intimidating and confrontational, Busquet may have made her subordinates so fearful of reporting bad news that they simply lied about it.

She lost her Optima job but was offered a chance to try to salvage one of American Express's smaller businesses. Her self-esteem shaken, she almost turned down the offer. But then she decided to view the Optima failure as a call to action.

"I realized I needed to be much more understanding," she says. She disciplined herself to become more patient and a better listener. She learned to solicit bad news: "I question why profit numbers are good as well as why they're not. If I had done this before, I might have uncovered the Optima problem sooner."

Busquet is now an executive vice president. "Anne is an example of someone whose career stalled but who had the courage to take on a difficult challenge," says former boss Thomas Ryder. "Too many people look for the safe place and as a result stay stuck."

Day 119

Jim Burke actually encourages mistakes at Johnson & Johnson, saying, "I decided that what we needed more than anything else was a climate that would encourage people to take risks."

Burke went on to tell of his own experience with a mistake: "I once developed a new product that failed badly, and General Johnson called me in, and I was sure he was going to fire me . . . Johnson said to me, 'I understand you lost over a million dollars.'

"I can't remember the exact amount. It seemed like a lot then. And I said, 'Yes sir. That's correct.'

"So he stood up and held out his hand. He said, 'I just want to congratulate you. All business is making decisions, and if you don't make decisions, you won't have any failures. The hardest job I have is getting people to make decisions. If you make that same decision wrong again, I'll fire you. But I hope you'll make a lot of others, and that you'll understand there are going to be more failures than successes.'"

Day 120

Edison could not conceive of any experiment as a flop. As Israel puts it, "He saw every failure as a success, because it channeled his thinking in a more fruitful direction."

Israel thinks that Edison may have learned this attitude from his enterprising father, who was not afraid to take risks and never became undone when a business venture crumbled. Sam Edison would simply brush himself off and embark on a new moneymaking scheme, usually managing to shield the family from financial hardship.

Israel says, "This sent a very positive message to his son—that it's okay to fail—and may explain why he rarely got discouraged if an experiment didn't work out."

In addition to teaching him what wouldn't work, Israel says, failed experiments taught him the much more valuable lesson of what would work—albeit in a different context.

Day 121

In his autobiography, *The Tumult and the Shouting*, the great sports columnist Grantland Rice gives this advice about past mistakes:

"Because golf exposes the flaws of the human swing—a basically simple maneuver—it causes more self-torture than any game short of Russian roulette. The quicker the average golfer can forget the shot he had dubbed or knocked off-line—and concentrate on the next shot—the sooner he begins to improve and enjoy golf. Like life, golf can be humbling. However, little good comes from brooding about mistakes we've made. The next shot, in golf or life, is the big one."

Day 122

Roy J. Plunkett was a 27-year-old research chemist for Du Pont in 1938 when he discovered a substance that was useless as a refrigerant, but it had other unusual properties—above all, nothing stuck to it. Du Pont marketed it as Teflon, which soon coated three-quarters of the pots and pans sold in the United States.

Had a setback? Look for some way you can use what you've learned from it to accomplish something even more lasting and significant.

Day 123

When Rossini's opera, the *Barber of Seville*, was first performed, it was hooted off of the stage. The audience was loud and passionate in its displeasure.

Afterwards the cast was nearly hysterical. There is a lot of pain involved with being in a theatrical production that has just bombed. The cast was commiserating with one another when they noticed that Rossini was not among them.

Fearing that he might have done something desperate, they rushed to his house. He was asleep. "Maestro, are you all right?" they asked.

"I was until I was awakened," he responded.

"But what about the opera?" they asked in obvious despair.

Quietly Rossini answered, "So it is not good enough. I will have to compose something better, that is all. But please, let us discuss that in the morning. I would like to go to sleep now."

Don't let failures overwhelm you. They will happen to everyone sooner or later, and they do not end the world. Simply go back and do something else.

Day 124

As a teenager, the late comedienne Minnie Pearl played the piano very well. Unfortunately, she had a great fear of piano recitals. She was afraid that once she was in the public eye, she would not be able to play.

Once at a recital, she balked and refused to perform. When she realized what was happening, her mother walked quietly up to her and whispered firmly in her ear, "Don't say you can't play the piano. Go up to that piano and show them you can't play."

The fastest way to defeat is to not make the attempt. Make the attempt. If you fail, you will not be any worse off than if you had given up. But you may succeed.

For Reflection

Do you know how to fail? If you do, you will also know the secret of succeeding, for the two are forever locked together.

"On a thousand gridirons each fall coaches prepare their charges to take the field of battle in the grand sport of football. Do you know the first lesson those candidates for the team will be taught? Not how to make a touchdown, that is easy. The first thing they must learn is how to fall down, and for days the coach will be teaching his team how to be tackled, how to fall limp so as not to be hurt, how to expect to fall and then rise again and press onward toward the goal."— William E. Phifer, the Christian Observer

1) With what kind of attitude do you approach failure? Do you make it more of an obstacle to future success than it should be?

2) Are you allowing a past failure to influence you self-esteem? How can you mentally "re-frame" that experience so that you deal with it in a more positive way and move on with your life?

3) In dealing with other peoples' failures, do you view them as disasters or potential learning experiences? How might you help those you supervise to effectively use their failures as stepping stones toward success?

FOCUS

The National Football League once did a study on scoring in the NFL and discovered that more points are scored in the last two minutes of the first half and the final two minutes of the second half than in any other TWENTY minutes of the football game!

Day 125

An Englishman named Roger Banister was the first man in history to officially run a mile in less than four minutes. A lot of people have done it since, but he was the first. The very next month after Roger Banister ran his four-minute mile, an Australian by the name of John Landy topped his record by 1.4 seconds.

Soon after, the two athletes met in British Columbia to compete against each other. As they moved into the last lap, the other contestants were trailing far behind. Landy was ahead, and it looked as though he would win. As he neared the finish line, though, he began to wonder how close Banister was to him. His apprehension finally got the better of him, and he looked over his shoulder. When he did that, his step faltered and Banister surged by him to win the race.

Don't look back to see where your competition is. Keep your eyes on the future and you won't falter.

Day 126

During the darkest days of the Civil War, one of Abraham Lincoln's heavy burdens was sustaining the hopes of the Union. Once when a delegation called at the White House with a catalog of crises facing America, Lincoln told this story:

"Years ago, a young friend and I were out one night when a shower of meteors fell from the clear November sky. The young man was frightened, but I told him to look up in the sky past the shooting stars to the fixed stars beyond, shining serene in the firmament. And I said, 'Let us not mind the meteors, but let us keep our eyes on the stars.'"

Day 127

It is amazing what you can do if you are focused. A couple of years ago a group of doctors went to lunch together. One of them spent the whole hour talking about some new treatment that he had heard of for a condition known as sepsis—a spreading of poison throughout the body from a bacterial infection. The conversation was interesting professionally, but it was neither particularly relevant nor diverting for lunchtime.

A short time later, though, a patient of one of the other doctors who had been in that lunch group began to fail rapidly. The problem was diagnosed as Gram-negative sepsis. Fortunately the doctor remembered the lunchtime conversation and telephoned his friend. Together they sent an emergency request to the FDA, who allowed the patient to conditionally try the new treatment. She eventually recovered.

Now what if that doctor had his mind on something else during lunch that day, like the stock market or his golf game? When people are focused, when they are committed to a particular ideal or calling, when that calling dominates every aspect of their life, then those people find ways to make all of life contribute to their endeavor.

Day 128

William H. Hinson tells us why animal trainers carry a stool when they go into a cage with large cats. They have a whip, of course, and a pistol, but invariably they will also carry a stool. Hinson says that it is the most important tool of the trainer. The trainer holds the stool by the back and thrusts the legs toward the face of the animal. Those who know maintain that the cat tries to focus on all four legs at once. In the attempt to focus on all four, a kind of paralysis overwhelms the animal. It becomes tame, weak and disabled because of its fragmented attention.

Jungle cats are not the only creatures affected by this problem. We also tend to become unable to perform our duties when our attention is divided among too many things.

"This one thing I do," said the apostle Paul. Dwight L. Moody said most people would have to alter that and confess: "These 50 things I dabble in."

Day 129

One day a pilot was flying his light plane low over Devil's Creek in Alaska. To his surprise, he saw a black bear walking aimlessly in circles with a large can stuck over its head.

It appeared as if the bear had been rummaging through some garbage for food and had pushed its head into the can but could not pull it out again.

The pilot had a rescue party flown in to tranquilize the bear and remove the can. By the five smooth and worn circular paths in the thick blanket of leaves, the rescue party estimated that the bear had probably walked close to 500 miles in circles before being freed.

A man went into Walmart on an errand for his seventh grade son. "Do you have any compasses?" he asked a clerk. "We have, she answered, "compasses for making circles, but not for going places."

Many people have confused the two. They go on their merry way just making circles—often larger and larger—but still circles nevertheless. A leader needs to be "going places not just going in circles."

Day 130

One of the men who helped to hunt down Nazi war criminals after World War II speaks in his autobiography about the dangers he faced. He admitted that he sometimes felt like giving up. Sometimes he was discouraged.

But he carried around with him a photograph of his mother and father who had been killed in one of the Nazi death camps. Often he would take out that picture of his parents and just look at it and be inspired by that picture to go on with his task.

Day 131

One day a man was driving through the Black Hills near Mount Rushmore when he ran into a snowstorm and lost all sense of direction. Luckily, when he peered out his side window, he saw a snowplow. Relieved, he kept as close to the vehicle as he could while it removed snow from the pavement. At times the heavy snowfall made it difficult to follow the machine.

After a while, the plow stopped and the operator got out and walked over to the car. "Mister, where are you headed?" the driver asked.

"I'm on my way to Montana," the man responded.

"Well, you'll never get there following me. I'm plowing out this parking lot!"

Day 132

Successful living and successful business begin with a plan. There is an ancient fable that brings that truth home.

Behold a king took forth his three sons to judge their fitness to govern the kingdom, and they stopped by a field, where a vulture sat in the branches of a dead tree. And the king said to the oldest son, "Shoot—but first tell me what you see."

And the son replied: "I see the earth and the grass and sky..."

And the king said, "Stop! Enough!" and he said to the next son, "Shoot—but first tell me what you see."

And the son replied, "I see the ground and a dead tree with a vulture sitting in the branches...."

And the king said, "Stop! Enough!" and he said to his youngest son, "Shoot—but first tell me what you see."

And the young man replied, his gaze never wavering, "I see the place where the wings join the body." Those were the words the king wanted to hear. "Shoot, then," he replied. And the shaft went straight—and the vulture fell.

Day 133

B. Eugene Greissman asked Gunther Gebel-Williams, the celebrated circus performer, what advice he had given his son, who's following his father's career as an animal trainer.

"I told him to be there," Gebel-Williams replied.

Greissman was not sure exactly what Gebel-Williams meant. Perhaps it was a father telling his son to always show up for work—the way he had for over 10,000 straight performances. But Gebel-Williams had something else in mind.

"When he's in the ring with lions, tigers, and leopards, he can't be somewhere else. He must never let his mind wander," the best-known animal trainer in the world explained. "He must be in the ring mentally."

It's pretty obvious how dangerous it is to let your mind wander in a circus ring when you're surrounded by dangerous animals. But letting your mind wander can be disastrous to virtually any career.

Day 134

There is a story about a man who went ice fishing. He cut a hole in the ice, placed his chair, and readied his line and hook when a man came up to him and said, "There are no fish here."

So he got up, looked for a better spot, moved his chair, cut a new hole in the ice, and put his hook in. After a moment, the other man came up to him again and said, "There are no fish here, either."

The fisherman, annoyed, looked at the man and said, "Who in the dickens are you anyway?"

The other man replied, "I'm the manager of this ice rink!"

Make sure you know where you are and who you're talking to before you commit all your resources to a particular endeavor.

Day 135

Thomas Edison had a reliable method for weeding through applicants when he was hiring engineers. Each applicant would receive a light bulb and would be asked, "How much water will a light bulb hold?"

The applicants fell into one of two groups. The first group would measure all the angles of the bulb. Then, by a series of calculations, the applicant would figure out the volume of the bulb. These maneuvers could take up to twenty minutes.

The second group would pour water into the bulb, then pour the water from the bulb into a measuring cup. This took about a minute.

Edison always hired from the second group.

Calculations and procedures often come in handy for resolving difficult situations. But an over-reliance on any system can lead to shortsightedness and an inability to think for oneself.

Day 136

At one point in *Alice in Wonderland* by Lewis Carroll, Alice comes to a fork in the road. The Cheshire Cat appears in a nearby tree, and she asks him which path she should take.

"Where do you want to go?" he asks.

"I don't know," says Alice.

"Then it really doesn't matter, does it?"

You have to know where you're going before you can decide how to get there. The future belongs to the focused.

For Reflection

"I never look at feeding the masses as my responsibility," Mother Teresa has said. "I look at the individual. I can love only one person at a time. I can feed only one person at a time. Just one, one, one . . . So you begin . . . I begin. I picked up one person. Maybe if I didn't pick up that one person I wouldn't have picked up 42,000. Same thing for you . . . just begin, . . . one, one, one."

1) Are you trying to gobble up a problem whole? What about taking Mother Teresa's advice and breaking it up into manageable parts?

2) What circumstances in your life keep you from focusing? Unexpected distractions? Worry? Busy-ness? Constantly trying to please people? What are some practical things you can do to simplify your life?

3) Have you written down and set a plan for achieving your life goals, or are you still moving in a circle toward nothing?

4) Are you spending the bulk of your time on your priorities?

GOALS

You've got to think about big things while you're doing small things, so that all the small things go in the right direction.
— futurist Alvin Toffler

Do not turn back when you are just at the goal. — Publius Syrius

Day 137

There is a famous study involving graduates of Yale University from the class of 1953. The students involved in this study were asked if they had a clear, specific set of goals for their future, and if they were written down with a plan for achieving them. Only three percent of those interviewed said that they did.

Twenty years later the researchers went back and interviewed the surviving members of that class. They discovered that the 3 percent with specific written goals had achieved more in financial terms than the entire other 97 percent put together. They also seemed to be happier and more "together" in every way.

Do you know where you are headed? Do you know how you are going to get there? Do you have it written down?

Day 138

Sometime back TV host Merv Griffin was interviewing some body builders and asked one of his muscle-bound guests what he used all his muscles for.

The body builder answered by striking one of the standard body-building flex poses. "No, you don't understand me," said Merv. "What do you use all those muscles for?"

The guy said, "I'll show you." And he flexed again, striking a different pose.

"No. No. You still don't understand my question," Merv said insistently. "Read my lips. What do you use them for?" And the guy posed again.

Do you know what you are supposed to do with your talents? Or do you just use them to make yourself look good, without contributing much of anything?

Day 139

Coach John Madden gives a good example of how perception affects performance when he tells about Ray Wersching, kicker for the San Francisco 49ers'. It seems that Wersching doesn't even look at the goal posts when he lines up for a field goal. In fact, he NEVER looks at the goal posts. The quarterback has to tell him if a kick is successful. "But how do you aim," Madden once asked him, "if you don't look at the goal posts?"

"I just look at the hash marks," said Wersching, "They tell me all I have to know." Madden goes on to note that Wersching is right. The hash marks, the chalked lines on the field that are about 23 yards inside each sideline, are 18 ½ feet apart, the same width as the goal posts.

"The farther away you are, the narrower the goal posts look," Ray Wersching explains, "But the hash marks always look wide."
If you think about it for a moment, you will see the intelligence in that. Why concentrate on the narrow goal posts instead of the wide hash marks? Concentrate on your short term goals, and your long term goals will take care of themselves.

Day 140

Carlton Fletcher tells about his Uncle Walter who lived in Waldorf, Germany, during the Second World War. Uncle Walter was a descendant of Huguenots who had run away from France during the persecution of the Protestants in the 1600s. During the war he wanted to build himself a house, but all the necessary materials were reserved for the army. Commoners couldn't build houses for themselves. But to a member of Germany's middle-class, a house is very important: building a house and getting out of an apartment is a priority. And nothing–not even a world war–would deter Uncle Walter, even if it meant building a house and hiding it under a junk pile.

Here is how he did it. He bought a lot and loaned it out for people to throw junk on it. And then he would go there at night and build, layer by layer of brick, and cover it up with junk. When the end of the war came, there was a big pile of junk, but there was a nearly completed house under it. All it needed was a roof. In 1946, when the war was over, he raised the roof like a madman, and he was jubilant. He said, "I beat the Nazis, I beat them. I got my house."

Nothing overcomes adversity like a powerful desire to accomplish a goal.

Day 141

Ben Feldman will be remembered as a legend in the insurance business, an industry in which only about 5 percent of the agents exceed annual sales of $1 million. Ben Feldman sold more than eighty times that amount in one year. His lifetime sales exceeded $1 billion.

"What is the difference between you and the agents selling a million dollars in one year?" I once asked him. "Are you eighty times better than they are?"

"Not at all," he replied. "The average person just doesn't think big enough."

His advice to others reflects that. Speaking before thousands, this superstar from East Liverpool, Ohio, was known for statements like these:

"Don't be afraid to dream big dreams."

"Let go of lower things and reach for higher."

Day 142

The story of goal setter John Goddard was published in *Life* magazine in 1972. When John was fifteen years old, he overheard his grandmother and aunt saying, "If only I had done this when I was young.

. ." At that moment he resolved not to be a part of the army of "if only's," and sat down and decided what he wanted to do with his life. He wrote down 127 goals. He listed seventeen mountains he wanted to climb and ten rivers he wanted to explore. He wanted to have a career in medicine, visit every country in the world, learn to fly an airplane, retrace the travels of Marco Polo, and ride a horse in the Pasadena Rose parade. Other goals were to read the Bible from cover to cover, read the works of Shakespeare, Plato, Aristotle, Dickens, and a dozen other classic authors. He wanted to become an Eagle Scout, go on a church mission, dive in a submarine, play the flute and violin, marry and have children, and read the entire Encyclopedia Britannica.

In 1972, when John Goddard was forty-seven years old, he had accomplished 103 of his 127 goals. As a result, he became a highly paid lecturer and toured the world telling of his adventures.

We can accomplish much in our lives, but we will accomplish the most if we have our goals written out. If our goals are vague and ambiguous, our attempts to fulfill them will also be vague and ambiguous.

Day 143

It's an average day at work, and you come home dead tired. After collapsing in your favorite chair, your spouse reminds you that tonight is your league bowling night. So after about an hour's rest, you go to the lanes.

Once there, you bowl for hours and throw that 16-pound ball about a hundred times, and you feel great. But think of this: if you have the manager remove the pins from the lane, how long do you think your energy and interest would last? After about four or five throws, you would be pooped and ready to go home and into bed.

Set yourself a goal. If you have a goal to reach, you will be given enough drive to achieve it.

Day 144

To be effective, goals must be realizable.

Doug Sherman and William Hendricks tell this story in their book, *How To Succeed Where It Really Counts*: "When I was a boy my family had a little poodle, just a tiny thing. When I came home from school, that dog would greet me and beg for dog biscuits—the sort of disgusting "treats" that only a dog could love. I'd take a biscuit and hold it in my hand about waist high, and the dog would jump up and grab it out of my hand. Then I'd hold another one up about level with my eyes, and he'd jump up and get it. It was amazing how high he could get. Then I'd hold one way up above my head—and he'd bite my foot!"

Day 145

Mark Victor Hansen is a professional speaker and motivator with a talent for getting the best out of people. In a book written and compiled by Mark Victor Hansen and Jack Canfield, Mark tells of one of his many strategies for getting people to follow their dreams. He created the Mark Victor Hansen Children's Free Enterprise Fund, which loans money to children for some worthy project or invention. Every child is expected to pay back the loan, and so far every child has.

One day after speaking about this fund at his church, Mark was approached by a six-year-old boy named Tommy Tighe. Tommy wanted to borrow money for a very special project—a bumper sticker that would promote peace in the world. Tommy had already made up the bumper sticker. It read: PEACE, PLEASE! DO IT FOR US KIDS, and it was signed, TOMMY. A printer had told Tommy that he needed to raise $454 in order to print out 1,000 bumper stickers, and so Tommy had come to Mark Victor Hansen for help.

Mark wrote out the check for $454, and gave Tommy a set of his motivational tapes. He told Tommy to listen to each one twenty-one times, until he knew and believed in his message. On the tapes, Tommy learned that he was supposed to start selling at the top. So Tommy asked his parents to drive him to former President Ronald Reagan's house. Tommy walked right up to the door and talked to the gatekeeper, who bought a sticker. A few minutes later, Tommy was talking to Ronald Reagan, who also bought a bumper sticker. Next, Tommy sent a bumper sticker, and the bill for the bumper sticker, to Mikhail Gorbachev. Gorbachev sent Tommy a signed picture that said, "Go for peace, Tommy." He also included money for the bumper sticker. Soon, other people heard Tommy's story. He was interviewed by his county newspaper. Joan Rivers called and asked him to be on her show. Tommy wowed Joan and her audience, and they were eager to buy bumper stickers from him.

So far, Tommy has sold more than 2,500 bumper stickers, and repaid his loan to the Fund. He has a goal to send a free bumper sticker and a letter to every president or leader in the world. So, what are your goals?

Day 146

There is something to be said for breaking down a large project into small, manageable pieces. *The Guinness Book of World Records* records the true story of a man who ate a bicycle. That's right—he ate an entire bicycle, tires and all! Of course, he didn't eat it all at once. Over a period of 15 days, from March 17 to April 2, 1977, Michel Lotito of Grenoble, France, melted the parts into small swallowable units and consumed every piece. The reason some people never accomplish "big things" in life is that they never reduce them to small units that can be handled.

Day 147

Former all-Pro wide receiver Paul Warfield said this about catching passes: "I would block out everything else that was occurring. It was just the football, and I had an obsession with catching it."

In 1992, American Kevin Young came to the Olympic Games in Barcelona, Spain, with two goals in mind: he wanted to win the gold medal in the 400-meter hurdles, and he hoped to break the world record in that event. To remind himself of those goals, Young wrote the time he wished to run, "46.89" on the wall of his room in the Olympic village. Every morning as he prepared for his workout, Young had his eyes and his heart fixed firmly on his goal. On Thursday, August 6, Young won his event—and the gold medal—in the world record time of 46.78 seconds!

Day 148

When Curtis Carlson founded the Gold Bond Stamp Company in Minneapolis at age 24, he also set a goal of earning $100 a week—a princely sum in the Depression. He wrote down that objective and carried it in his pocket for years until the paper was frayed. Today, Carlson Companies, Inc. ranks among the nation's largest privately held corporations, with annual revenues topping $9 billion.

While Lee Iacocca was still in college, he boasted to his classmates that he would become a vice president of the Ford Motor Company before his thirty-fifth birthday. Seventeen years later, just thirteen months after his self-declared deadline, he achieved his goal.

When the great architect Frank Lloyd Wright was asked at the age of 90 to single out his finest work, he answered, "My next one."

> **For Reflection**

Commentators seem to regard one as something of a phenomenon because one set out in politics with conviction... I say, if you're embarking on a great voyage across the ocean, you have to have some stars to steer by. And the stars have to be constant. It's no good steering by a shooting star. — Margaret Thatcher

1) Have you made your goals more concrete by writing them down? Have you posted them in a place where you'll refer to them often?

2) In one sentence, write down your mission in life. How do your goals help you fulfill your mission?

3) Are you feeling "burnt out" in any area of your life? Setting attainable goals for yourself in that area may help motivate you to change your attitude.

4) What is the relationship between your personal career goals and your company's goals? Do they match up pretty well? How could you improve two-way communication with your boss or colleagues concerning goals?

INTEGRITY

A cartoon in "New Yorker" magazine: Two clean-shaven middle-aged men are sitting together in a jail cell. One inmate turns to the other and says: "And all along, I thought our level of corruption fell well within community standards."

Day 149

A company in Phoenix, Arizona during the 1970s was shut off from the Mexican market because they refused to give payoffs to Mexican government officials. But the company's ethical behavior in refusing the payoffs impressed some Mexican business people, and a group of influential Mexicans lobbied their government to allow the company to import two dealerships. Today they are doing a booming business because people know that they can be trusted.

A study of the most successful leaders in corporate America found three universal characteristics: a high level of energy, a definite plan for personal success, and a high level of personal integrity. Indeed, integrity is one of the hottest words in business today. Companies want leaders and workers who can be trusted.

Day 150

In Henrik Ibsen's play *An Enemy of the People*, Dr. Stockman is the medical supervisor of the mineral baths in a resort town. When he discovers that the baths are polluted and potentially dangerous, he reports it to the town's authorities, who fear financial disaster if the report is not suppressed. The doctor's brother, the mayor, tells him to retract his findings, but the doctor refuses to do so. The mayor says he will fire him if he doesn't retract. When the doctor discusses the issue with his wife, she urges him to think of his family and retract the findings lest they lose their income. At that point their two young sons come into the room and the doctor becomes convinced that he must risk all to be a person of integrity. "I want to be able to look my boys in the face when they grow up into free men," he says, and he leaves to do what he must, in spite of the rejection of his fellow citizens.

Day 151

Recently, officials in the Sierra Club, an important force in the environmental movement, admitted that they didn't use recycled paper in their lushly illustrated nature calendars. The reason they gave was that photographs don't reproduce well on recycled stock.

Two Denver-area club branches, calling that stance hypocritical, stopped selling the annual fund-raising calendars, and one state chapter official warned that a "real revolt" was possible among members.

"As a group, we can't walk one way and talk another way," said Michael Reis, a spokesman for another branch. "How can we take a hard stand in promoting recycling when our own group doesn't use recycled paper?" Other branches have been equally vocal. One sin that the American public will not forgive is that of hypocrisy.

Day 152

A family from South Carolina went to New York City for their vacation. They told all their friends that they were going to attend the Broadway play, *My Fair Lady*. Unfortunately, the play was sold out by the time they tried to get their tickets, and they couldn't get in. Naturally, they were disappointed, but they were also embarrassed to have to go back home and tell their friends they missed the highlight of their trip. In fact, they were so embarrassed that they decided to lead their friends to believe that they had seen the musical. They picked up some discarded tickets from the show, purchased a program, and bought the musical tapes. Back in their motel room, they learned all the songs and reviewed the program. Once home again, they sang and whistled the tunes to all of *My Fair Lady's* hits, hoping that no one would suspect that they never saw it.

Many people go to great lengths to hide their lack of experience or competence. It is better to admit to a lack of knowledge and thereby learn what you need to know, than to look like a fool after all the posturing is over and it is time for results to be revealed.

Day 153

Lou Holtz has established his reputation as an outstanding and principled football coach. Before a major game at USC in the late 1980s, two of his Notre Dame players were late for the team dinner—for the fourth time. They apparently had been touring and shopping, and hadn't bothered to get back on time. One was a valued member of the starting offensive team, and the other was a similarly key starter for the defense. Yet Holtz felt that in the long run his team would perform more effectively if he disciplined the two players—even at the possible expense of the next day's performance. So the players were sent back to South Bend before the game and the news wires hummed with the story. (Oh, by the way, Notre Dame, playing well as a team, won the game!)

In one of the more perceptive editions of the comic strip "Frank and Ernest," a client is sitting across the desk from a lawyer, and the client is saying, "The question of right and wrong is very clear. I want you to cloud it up for me."

Day 154

A young man decided to impersonate Derwin Richards. The real Derwin Richards is a boxer with the title of Texas junior middleweight champion. The fake Derwin Richards decided that a false identity could get him a bout with Roy Jones, Jr. Roy Jones, Jr. just happened to be a boxer in the 1988 Olympics.

The plan went off without a hitch . . . until 2 minutes and 2 seconds into the first round of the fight. That's how long it took Jones to leave his opponent lying out cold on the canvas.

For Reflection

"I'm certainly not the type of person who can ask the Cubs organization and the Cubs fans to pay my salary when I am not happy with my mental approach and performance. Therefore, I am here to announce my retirement immediately."— Ryne Sandberg.

COMMENTING:
"It takes a lot of pride and dignity to kiss off that kind of wad."
—Tribune columnist Mike Royko, on Ryne Sandberg's walking away from $7 million a year because he didn't think he was earning it.

1) How has your dishonesty hurt you in the past? How have other peoples' dishonesty hurt you?

2) How successfully are you managing the following components of integrity: punctuality? Honesty? Following through? Compassion? Reciprocating kindnesses? Going beyond what's expected? Fighting injustice?

3) How might an emphasis on integrity change the way your company does business? What would be the long-term benefits of this new emphasis?

KINDNESS

A man named Stephen Grellet was born in France, a Quaker, and died in New Jersey in 1855. That's about all we know about him, except for a few lines he penned that have made him immortal:

"I shall pass through this world but once. Any good I can do, or any kindness that I can show any human being, let me do it now and not defer it. For I shall not pass this way again."

Day 155

Though the Cincinnati Reds won 1990 World Series in a four-game sweep over the Oakland A's, they blew it in terms of public relations.

Eric Davis, the Reds' left fielder, was seriously injured while diving for a ball in the fourth game in Oakland. He was rushed in severe pain to the hospital, where doctors discovered he had a lacerated kidney. Although he was in critical condition for several days, the doctors told him he could go back to Cincinnati, provided he hired a private plane. The cost for the plane would be $15,000.

Unfortunately, his team had already returned home, so Davis tried to call Reds owner Marge Schott to ask whether the team would pay for the plane. She never called him back, and Davis was forced to hire the plane himself.

His feelings were so hurt by the way he'd been treated that he took out a newspaper ad. The situation had been badly mishandled, and it made the whole Reds organization look bad. In 1991 Davis left the Reds to play for the Los Angeles Dodgers.

Day 156

A sociologist was returning to Paris after a year of research in Africa. He had discovered that in most places in Africa the people are very, very gracious, and hospitable. They will treat you like one of the family, taking you into their hut, sharing what they have with you, and treating you like royalty. This is what the sociologist had become used to in Africa.

Then he returned to Paris, and he took a bus from the Charles DeGaulle Airport into the city. He noticed how the passengers on the French bus sat silently, no one saying a word to anyone else. No one even shared a glance with another person unless it was a critical or disapproving one.

As that sociologist sat on the city bus and reflected on his experience in Africa, the thought came to him that it is we who are undeveloped. We have much we can learn from the people in the Third World about the things that really matter.

Day 157

Soon after the dentist moved into his new house, he found that the neighborhood teenagers had a habit of littering his yard and riding their bicycles over his lawn.

One night the leader of the neighborhood's teenagers developed a bad toothache, and the boy's mother sent him to the dentist to be examined. The dentist found that the boy needed expensive repair work, and offered to take care of it, but the boy refused. He said his family could not afford it. The dentist persuaded the lad to let him do the repairs anyway.

Of course, he didn't send the boy a bill, and he soon forgot all about it. That summer he left town for an extended vacation. When he returned, he found that his lawn had been well cared for while he was gone—by the teenager whose tooth he had repaired. When asked why he had done this, the boy just smiled and said, "A tooth for a tooth."

Who knows the rewards you may reap when you go that extra distance for someone.

Day 158

Do you know who is credited with the invention of the white line down the center of the highway? Dr. June A. Carroll of Indio, California, and she painted the line herself back in 1912 along a one-mile stretch of treacherous highway to help uncertain travelers find their way. Shortly afterward the California Highway Commission adopted the idea—and you know what happened from there. Dr. Carroll earned a measure of immortality as a result of her thoughtfulness.

During the bombing of London, it was found that people suffering from nervous disorders experienced unexpected recoveries while ministering to the terrible needs of air raid victims. The reason many of us have no energy, no vitality, no joy, is that we are living only for ourselves.

Day 159

Alexander Bryan and Cortland Heyniger owned and operated a modest company that manufactured small, flat-decked sailboats during the late forties and early fifties. When Aileen Bryan, Alexander's wife, became pregnant, she complained that the flat decks of the boats were extremely uncomfortable for her to sit on. As a result, the two men designed a boat with a well for her feet, which they called a Sunfish.

So far, thousands of Sunfish have been sold, making it the most popular class of sailboat ever designed. Yet the sole idea behind the now-successful boat was to make a pregnant woman more comfortable. Many of our finest enterprises have been built by those who put the well-being of others first.

Day 160

George Eastman, inventor and founder of the Eastman-Kodak Company, often said that he never set out to become rich. Nor was it specifically his intent to promote photography.

Eastman had lost his father while he was still young, and he was forced to watch his mother struggle to provide the bare essentials for George and his two sisters. Memories of his mother mopping floors and washing clothes for other people haunted George like a bad dream throughout his life. Consequently, he vowed to make enough money so that his mother would never have to work again.

Actually, he made millions, and he revolutionized photography—but his real goal was to make a comfortable living for his mother. And that is the power that compassion for another can have.

Day 161

A young soldier had been utterly humiliated by his senior officer. The officer had gone far beyond the bounds of acceptable behavior in disciplining the young soldier. Both knew it, and so the officer said nothing as the younger man growled, "I'll make you regret this if it is the last thing I ever do."

A few days later their company came under heavy fire. At one point, the officer was cut off from his troops and wounded. But through the haze of pain, he saw someone coming up to him: the young soldier. Both of their lives were at risk, but the young soldier managed to drag the officer to safety.

On the edge of consciousness the officer gasped, "Son, I owe you my life." The young man laughed and said, "I told you that I would make you regret humiliating me if it was the last thing I ever did."

Day 162

Arthur F. Sueltz told about a man he knew who had just bought a house in the suburbs. On the day he moved in, his new neighbor came over to visit in an obviously belligerent state.

"Did you buy this house?" asked the neighbor.

"Yes I did," was the reply.

"Well, I want to tell you something: you bought a lawsuit. You see that fence of yours? It's at least seven feet over on my side of the line, and if it takes every dollar I've got, I intend to sue you and get that fence moved."

The new homeowner said, "Well, neighbor, I'm sorry to hear this. I bought this house in good faith, but I believe you're telling the truth, and I'll tell you what I'm going to do. First thing tomorrow morning, I'll have that fence moved back those seven feet."

The neighbor looked shocked: "What did you say?"

"I said I'll have that fence moved back seven feet."

"No, you're not," the other man shot back, "You leave it right where it is, and anything you need is yours for the asking."

We don't know what had occurred between that angry man and his previous neighbor. But all he seemed to be wanting was a little respect. That is all most people want, and when you give it to them, you usually get it back.

Day 163

Before the start of Game 1 of the 1981 World Series, Dodger manager Tommy Lasorda was busy managing—managing the turnstile at the press gate, that is. Lasorda spent ten minutes making sure the wives and girlfriends of his players were admitted into Yankee Stadium, despite their lack of tickets or credentials.

"You'd do the same thing for your wife, wouldn't you?" asked Lasorda. "Being a manager involves taking care of your players. I don't see any harm in this. I'm just making sure that everybody is happy."

For Reflection

American Health magazine reported the findings of a study by the University of Michigan's Research Center. This study says that, more than any other activity, doing regular volunteer work dramatically increases life expectancy. It's more important than jogging, aerobics or even a low-cholesterol diet. The results are clear, and the prescription is simple: help somebody else and you will live longer.

1) How would an attitude of compassion affect your next conversation with a difficult person?

2) What benefits would you receive by volunteering a couple of hours a week serving others?

3) Think of a time in your life when someone's unselfish act of kindness has made all the difference for you. To whom will YOU give that gift?

4) Performing a "random act of kindness" can be a real mood-booster. Why don't you try it today?

KNOWLEDGE

The test of intelligence is the ability to hold two contrasting ideas in the mind at the same time and still retain the ability to function.

— F. Scott Fitzgerald

Day 164

Dr. Robert Gilruth, the first director of the space center at Houston, observed that one reason people themselves must go into space is that a human being is still "the best instrument for measuring the unknown." He added that "if scientists were to design an instrument to measure all the things in the unknown of space that they wanted to know about, it would look surprisingly like... a man."

Along the same lines, another Space Age sage, Dr. Wernher von Braun, once observed: "Man is still the best computer that we can put aboard a spacecraft—and the only one that can be mass-produced with unskilled labor."

Day 165

Benjamin Franklin once received a gift of a whisk broom from India. He happened to notice that a few seeds were still fastened to the wisps of the broom, and he planted them. When the first crop came up, he distributed the seeds among his friends and neighbors. Their crops flourished. In this way Franklin was responsible for introducing broom corn into the American colonies, from which the American broom manufacturing industry was born.

Great harvests sometimes come from a few tiny seeds. But you have to find the seeds first, and know what to do with them.

Sir Isaac Newton was once asked how he discovered the Law of Gravity. "By thinking about it," he answered.

Day 166

In a 1985 assessment of math achievement in twenty industrialized and Third World nations, American students ranked no higher than tenth. Japan was number one.

American students spend 180 days a year in school. Japanese students spend 240, including the half days they put in on Saturday. Overall, by the time a Japanese student graduates from high school, he or she has been to school one to three years longer than an American student. As a result, the average Japanese high school graduate has the same basic knowledge of the average American college graduate.

The Japanese are so fanatical about education that when a child is sick his mother will often show up at school in his place and take notes for him.

Is it any wonder that the Japanese are out-maneuvering the United States in the world market?

Day 167

In the spring of 1608, the settlers at Jamestown, Virginia discovered gold. At least they thought they did. They almost totally abandoned their efforts at planting crops, preparing buildings, and readying themselves for winter. They had found gold, and they devoted themselves entirely to digging out and washing the precious metal.

The colonists probably would not even have survived the summer and fall if the Indians had not fed them. However, they were finally able to send a ship back to England with a heavy load of the metal for which they had labored all spring. Unfortunately their gold turned out to be iron pyrite, or "fools' gold." They had given their time, their talent, and all their energies to "fool's gold."

Before you start digging for gold, have someone who knows look over your samples. The expense of an expert is negligible compared to the cost of mining a worthless material.

Day 168

A Native American artist was asked to draw a picture illustrating the Indian perspective on Little Big Horn. He agreed. It took awhile, but finally the picture was finished.

In the center was a large picture of General Custer. In the bottom right corner was a cow with a halo. In the left bottom corner was a southern plantation complete with cotton fields as far as the eye could see. Filling the cotton fields were Indians. When he was asked what the picture meant, the artist explained, "General Custer said: "Holy Cow! Where did all those cotton-pickin' Indians come from?"

Ignorance is not bliss; it can bring death. In July of 1876, the body of General George Armstrong Custer was found naked, reclining against the carcass of a horse, and surrounded by the remains of his unfortunate command. He and his men had not known that they were going out against an Indian force that was the largest ever assembled on the Plains. Had he not been ignorant of this fact and acted accordingly, he and his regiment would have survived.

Today's successful companies put their emphasis on well-trained, informed employees. In competitive times like these, the training budget is not the place to make cuts.

Day 169

There is a story about a missionary in Kenya who was given a car to help him in his rounds, traveling from village to village. After he had the car for only a few months, it refused to start. He looked under the hood, but not knowing anything about engines, he couldn't see anything wrong, and assumed that the battery was worn out.

He found, however, that he could get the car started by getting some boys from a local school to push it 50 feet or so; or he could park it near the top of a hill and roll it off, engaging the clutch. He started his car this way for two years.

Then came the day when he needed to take his family back to the United States. His replacement arrived before he left, and he showed him around. He introduced the replacement to his old car, and described various ways to push or roll it to get it started. The new missionary looked under the hood for a moment, then said, "Dr., I think that the battery cable has come loose from the starter." The new missionary reconnected the loose cable, got in the driver's seat, turned the key, pressed the starter, and the engine roared to life.

Don't make assumptions through ignorance. The result may be a great deal of trouble for yourself.

Day 170

When Henry Ford started his car company in 1903, he took on a business partner, James Couzens. Couzens was strong where Ford was weakest—in administration, finance, sales, etc. Couzens contributed as much to the success of the early Ford motor company as did Ford himself. Many of the best known policies and practices of the Ford Motor company for which Henry Ford is often given credit were actually Couzens' ideas.

Couzens became so effective in administrating the company that Ford grew increasingly jealous of him, and forced him out in 1917 over an argument about the future of the Model T. Couzens maintained that the car was obsolete and that they should move on to other things. Ford disagreed, got rid of Couzens, and kept making Model T's until he had nearly run his car company out of business.

If there is someone more knowledgeable than you on a subject, listen to them. Don't let your own biases make a bad decision for you.

> Day 171

Adrian Rogers tells a great story about a wealthy gold miner who had a son whom he named to take over the family business. He sent the young man back East to study in the finest engineering school and to learn all he could about managing the mines.

The young man studied hard and proudly took his degree. After his graduation he spoke to his father about his inheritance. "Dad," he said, "I'm ready to go to work. Give me your best mine, and I'll show you how to run it."

The father replied, "No, Son, first you need to change into your work clothes and go down into the mine. There you will gain experience. You may start at the bottom and work your way up." But the son was adamant. "Look, Dad, I've been to school, and I got my diploma. With all due respect, I know more about mining than you will ever know. And if you will just give me your best mine, I will prove it to you."

And so the father, against his better judgment, gave his son the most productive mine. And for a while it did do well. But one day the father received a letter, stating, "Dad, you know that the mine I am working is backed up to the lake. Well, the water is seeping in. We've shored it up, but the shoring doesn't want to hold. What do you think we ought to do?" The father did not answer.

In a few more weeks the son wrote again, "Look Dad, this is serious. We are not able to stop the water. What do you think we ought to do?" The father still did not answer.

Finally the son sent a frantic wire: IF YOU DO NOT GIVE ME AN ANSWER SOON, WE ARE GOING TO LOSE THE ENTIRE MINE. WHAT SHOULD I DO?

The father wired back: TAKE YOUR DIPLOMA AND SHOVE IT INTO THE LEAK.

Education is a good teacher, but so is experience. You need to have both in order to do your best.

Day 172

As a young man Benjamin Franklin was somewhat arrogant in his opinions, and he wanted to do most of the talking in conversations with his friends. He was so quick to tell people where they were wrong that they began crossing to the other side of the street to avoid speaking to him.

A Quaker friend kindly pointed out this unpardonable fault to him, and convinced Ben by mentioning several instances in which he had rudely dismissed the opinions of others. Franklin was so stricken by this revelation that over half a century later, when he was seventy-nine years old, he wrote these words in his famous autobiography:

"Considering that in conversation knowledge was obtained rather by the use of the ears than of the tongue, I gave Silence second place among the virtues I determined to cultivate."

Remember this. Knowledge is gained by listening, not by speaking.

Day 173

A group of Apaches once attacked a Cavalry unit and successfully captured the paymaster's safe. They had never seen a safe before, but they knew it had gold inside. And by then gold was as precious to the Indians as it was to the white man.

The Indians tried and tried to open the safe, but were unsuccessful. They beat it with their tomahawks. They dragged it all over the ground with their horses. They threw it in a fire. Their medicine man tried his magic. They even tried blasting it with gunpowder. Finally, they tried dropping it from a cliff, hoping it would burst open like a pumpkin, but nothing worked. In spite of all their best efforts, the safe was still locked tight, so they gave up and left it behind.

Later the army found the stolen and abandoned safe. The paymaster came over, turned the combination, and had the safe open within a minute. What had been impossible for the Indians was simple for the paymaster.

The mystery was impenetrable until the right person, who knew the right combination, came along. That is what the art of leadership is all about.

John Maxwell compares it to the professional logger. When he sees a log jam, the professional logger climbs a tall tree and locates a key log, has that log blown up and lets the stream do the rest. An amateur would start at the edge of the jam and move all the logs, eventually moving the key log. Obviously, both methods will get the logs moving, but the professional does his work more quickly and effectively.

For Reflection

In 1942 the U.S. sent the first consignment of Mustang fighter planes to England for the RAF. Very little actual training was given to pilots in those days: the extent of their pre-flight instructions for the new plane was a pat on the back and a few words of encouragement. However, the new Mustangs were so much hotter and faster than previous ones that 3 out of the 5 pilots assigned to the plane were killed trying to make the transition.

Proper training is essential for good productivity. The time spent on learning a new job or technique will be more than made up for in the amount of work accomplished through knowledge.

1) Do your employees and assistants have the proper skills to carry out their jobs successfully? How could you train them to work more efficiently and independently?

2) How might you benefit by having a knowledgeable and highly skilled team?

3) What could you do to enhance your own knowledge of your business or field?

LEADERSHIP

A historian was commenting on Winston Churchill's importance to the people of England and, indeed, to all the Western world during the Second World War. He said, "There was a time in the dark days of the London 'blitz' when the only thing that stood between England and oblivion was one stubborn old man."

Day 174

When was the only time in Stanley cup history that a coach stepped in to play? This unique event occurred on April 17, 1928, in the second game of title play for the coveted Stanley Cup. The game took place between the New York Rangers and the Montreal Maroons at the Montreal Forum. Ranger goalie Lorne Chabot was struck in the eye by the puck from the stick of Nelson Stewart and was carried from the ice. The coach for the Rangers, forty-five-year-old Lester Patrick, who had previously played as a professional goalie, took over the goaltending duties, as there was only one goalie on the Rangers' roster. The Maroons soon found that Patrick was no easy target and that the Rangers were fiercely protecting their prized goalie. The game was 0-0 into the third period, when the Rangers scored. Montreal soon tied, sending the game into overtime. Seven minutes into overtime, Ranger Frank Boucher sent the puck into the Montreal net. The final score was Rangers 2, Montreal 1. New York went on to take the Stanley Cup.

Now, that's "hands-on" management. If you are a manager, be prepared to roll up your sleeves from time to time and work alongside the troops. You will benefit and so will they.

Day 175

Forecasting International did a study in 1983 of what types of firms were failing and found that "the largest number of firms going out of business were the authoritarian, the second were participative—everybody's called together and everybody discusses what they want to do; the workers and the managers, everybody—then they do it, then they go out of business . . . But the most important one that works is called consultive . . . bringing people in, getting their views, making sure we modify things to get people involved . . . but you, the boss, make up your own mind. That's consultative management, that's the best."

Harry Truman once put it this way: "How far would Moses have gone if he had taken a poll in Egypt? What would Jesus Christ have preached if he had taken a poll in the land of Israel? What would have happened to the Reformation if Martin Luther had taken a poll? It isn't polls or public opinion of the moment that counts. It is right and wrong and leadership."

Day 176

A few years ago, a major corporation announced that it would be moving its corporate offices to the other side of the country. During an interview with the media, the board's chairman was asked if he expected most of the employees to make the move. He said that he felt that most of the important employees would transfer, but secretaries and others would not. When the secretaries read in the paper the next day that they were not among the "important" employees, they decided to prove their importance by not answering any phones for one day. They did all of their other duties, but answered no phones. The chaos which resulted from this demonstration of importance forced the board chairman to make a public apology.

A noted novelist was talking with a friend about two of their greatest countrymen. Of one they said, "His greatness is that he makes everyone around him seem smaller." But then they decided that the other was even greater because he made everyone around him feel larger.

Day 177

In July, 1099 the city of Valencia, Spain was under siege by the Moors, who were trying to reclaim it from Rodrigo Diaz, better known as El Cid, who had taken it from them five years earlier. There were nearly forty Moorish kings surrounding the city with their combined armies, holding it in a vice-like grip. Diaz was sick with a fever and near death, but he knew that he had to come up with a plan for breaking the Moors' hold and lead his troops, or he would lose his beloved city again. Working with his advisors from his bed, he plotted strategies all night so they could wage battle the next morning.

Just as the sun was rising the next day, the city opened its gates, and a flood of soldiers came forth, led by Diaz, mounted on his white stallion, with his sword gleaming in the sun. The Valencian army followed their charging leader straight into the ranks of the startled Moors. The fight raged for some time, but eventually the Moors fled, with over half of their kings and 10,000 of their troops dead. The victorious Valencians then made a disturbing discovery: El Cid was dead. He had died early that morning. But before he died, he had ordered his advisors to strap his body onto his horse, and a sword in his hand. In this way he had inspired his troops and led them to victory.

It is often merely the presence of a respected leader that can inspire people to achieve great things.

Day 178

There once was an awful uproar in a particular neighborhood in Scotland. One father was so upset that his boys had been involved in the incident that he ran out of his house with a gun in order to get the ones who led his boys astray.

In one cartoon published which portrayed this particular incident, the man followed a path that he suspected would lead him to the guilty party. He followed it through the woods and through the valleys and over the mountains and finally to a door. He knocked on it, ready to shoot whoever answered. But it was his own wife who opened the door. He was standing in front of his own house.

Look to yourself first as a possible source of error when something goes wrong. Charity isn't the only thing that begins at home.

Day 179

In New York's garment district, there was an older gentleman who had worked for the same garment factory for 30 years. In all that time, he had never missed a single day of work, nor had he ever been late—not once. All of his co-workers admired his dedication and reliability.

But one day, at 9 a.m, he didn't show up as he always had. Nine-fifteen, Nine-thirty. He still wasn't there. Everyone started wondering and talking. "What do you think happened to Stanley? Where can he be?" Nine-forty-five and still no Stanley.

Finally, at 9:55 Stanley staggered in, bruised, tattered, and shaken. His concerned co-workers immediately gathered around to comfort him. "What happened to you?" they asked.

Stanley sat down to catch his breath. "I fell down four flights of stairs. Almost got killed." The boss, who had just walked in, said sternly, "And this took you an hour?"

Day 180

Alexander the Great once approached a great walled city with only a handful of soldiers and demanded that the inhabitants surrender to him. But the people inside the city just laughed at him and his pathetic army.

So Alexander had his men line up in single file and begin to march towards a nearby cliff. Alexander guided his soldiers directly to its edge, and one by one they stepped over it and fell to their deaths on the rocks below, as the people in the city watched in horror. At a certain point Alexander halted the march and ordered the rest of the men back to his side. They responded without any sign of fear, relief, or panic.

The shaken residents of the city surrendered at once, realizing that defeat was inevitable from the hands of a leader who commanded such loyalty.

It is doubtful that many people today could command the kind of loyalty that Alexander did, but loyalty is still no less important to a leader now than it was then.

Day 181

A charismatic man, Sam Walton usually wore moderately priced suits, casual shoes, and an ever-present Wal-Mart baseball cap while tooling around town in his worn red and white pickup. At the time of his death in April 1992, "Mr. Sam" had amassed a personal family fortune of twenty-two billion dollars and nearly forty-four billion dollars in annual sales.

How could a man of such massive wealth live and work so unpretentiously? Sam's simple stay-in-touch-with-your-people style is one of the secrets of his success.

In 1983, Walton challenged his officers to produce a pre-tax profit of 8 percent for the coming year. If they succeeded, he promised to celebrate by dancing the hula on Wall Street. Much to the delight of Chairman Walton, Wal-Mart employees awarded their beloved founder his projected profit margin—and then some! And much to the delight of his employees, Mr. Sam kept his promise. Accompanied by a band of Hawaiian dancers and musicians, he slipped into a grass skirt and jiggled away!

Day 182

One unknown author provided the following insight into the misunderstood role of the executive:

An executive has practically nothing to do except decide what is to be done; to tell someone to do it; to listen to reasons why it should not be done or should be done by someone else, or done in a different way; to follow up to see if the work has been properly done at last, only to discover that it has not; to ask why; to listen to excuses from the person who should have done it; to follow up to see if the work has been properly done at last, only to discover that it was done incorrectly; to point out how it should have been done; to conclude that as long as the work has been done to let it stay as it is; to wonder if it isn't time to get rid of a person who cannot do a thing right, but also to reflect that he probably has a wife and 10 children and that, anyway, someone else would be just as bad if not worse; to consider how much simpler and better the work would have been if one had done it himself in the first place; to reflect sadly that one could have done it right in 20 minutes and that, as things turned out, one has had to spend two days to find out why it has taken three weeks for someone else to do the work the wrong way.

The solution: Do it right the first time!

Day 183

Bishop Arthur Moore was a bishop in Georgia for twenty years. He wore the mantle of authority with dignity and grace. The story is told that on one occasion he entered the elevator in a building in Chicago. "Good morning Governor." Bishop Moore replied, "I am not a governor." The operator said, "Well, good morning Senator." Again the bishop replied, "I am not a Senator. I am a bishop of the United Methodist Church." The elevator operator paused a moment and said, "Well bishop, I knew whatever racket you were in, you were the head of it."

It helps if a leader looks the part. If you have aspirations for leadership, begin looking like a leader now.

Day 184

Great Leaders are encouragers. Fran Tarkenton, the scrappy little quarterback of the Minnesota Vikings tells about throwing a key block in a game the Vikings won again the St. Louis Cardinals. He says that during the Monday films he kept waiting for the coach to point out his contribution to that critical play. The coach praised the linemen and the runners and the water boy and the pom-pom girls, it seemed, but he never mentioned Tarkenton and that key block. Tarkenton went to him after the team meeting and said, "Coach, why didn't you say anything about my block?"

"Fran," he said, "you always give a hundred and fifty percent. You're out there gung-ho all the time. So I just didn't feel that I needed to praise you for it."

"If you ever want me to do it again, you needed to," Fran said.

Day 185

E.M. Kelly once said, "Remember the difference between a boss and a leader: a boss says, 'Go!'—a leader says, 'Let's go!'"

President Eisenhower used to say that he could demonstrate leadership style with a piece of string. He'd lay the string on a table and say, "Pull it and it'll follow you wherever you wish. Push it and it will go nowhere at all. It's that way when it comes to leading people."

It's taken many organizations a long time to discover that Ike was right. Leadership styles are changing, but it will not happen over night. In today's world of self-directed work teams, though, the man or woman who can lead by building consensus will be much in demand.

Day 186

After the British captured Gibraltar in the 18th century, the Spanish retaliated by laying siege to "the Rock." The Queen of Spain was so sure that her armies would defeat the British in a matter of hours that she ordered a chair to be placed on a hillside against Gibraltar, where she vowed to sit until she saw the Spanish flag waving again from the top of the Rock. But the siege wore on for several days.

Mindful of her vow and her status as queen, she refused to budge from the chair. Her court was embarrassed, but she was adamant: she had made a promise, and she was going to see it through! Finally, even the British felt sorry for her. The British commander ordered a truce, and asked the Spanish general for a flag. He waved it over Gibraltar just long enough for the Queen to go back to her palace with dignity.

Day 187

Late in the summer of 1943, a young naval officer was driving a jeep near the Marine Air Base in Tontouto. World War II was raging throughout the Pacific and there was active fighting just a few miles north in the Solomon Islands.

At the sound of sirens, the driver pulled over and watched as two jeeps full of military police cleared the way for a motorcade. Expecting to see some high-ranking general, the young officer was genuinely surprised when the Army weapons carrier sped by. The passenger was a civilian, wearing a big floppy hat to protect herself from the blistering sun.

Eleanor Roosevelt had come into a dangerous war zone to encourage the troops. "Her visit made a great impression on all of us," the naval officer wrote years later. His name was Richard Nixon.

Leading by influence begins with being visible. It begins with going to where your people are—letting them know you care.

Day 188

A small Cessna 206 was just lifting off the wet jungle airstrip, flying out of Ecuador. The pilot had the throttle pushed all the way forward to the firewall. He had done this many times before and was confident they would clear the huge trees towering at the end of the little airstrip.

Next to him in the cockpit was a passenger, an American who had been visiting the Indians. This passenger had never taken off from a jungle airstrip. Looking out the front window, all he could see were on-rushing trees. Fearing that they were going to crash into the trees, he grabbed the pilot's wheel and pulled back. Now, a plane needs to build up a certain amount of airspeed before the nose can be pointed skyward, or it will stall.

And the plane stalled. It pitched up, lost critical airspeed, and began to fall toward the jungle below. The pilot wrenched the controls back and tried desperately to get the nose down, but it was too late. The airplane reached stalling speed, the engine pulled the nose over sharply, and the craft fell to earth. Luckily no one was killed, but they all suffered injuries because of a passenger's lack of trust in his pilot.

There is time for trust and there may be a time to question your superiors. But the time for questions is not in a crisis. If you can't trust the driver, don't get in the plane.

Day 189

Going into the Olympics in 1968, Mark Spitz was considered the best swimmer in the United States. George Haynes, the coach of the U.S. team, predicted that Spitz would win as many as six gold medals.

In Mexico City, however, Spitz only won a total of four medals—two gold medals, both in relay events, a silver in the 100-meter butterfly and a bronze medal for third place in the 100-meter freestyle. It was widely considered a disappointing performance, and Mark Spitz was more disappointed than anyone. That experience made him closely examine the way he was managing his athletic career. It forced him to analyze his personal strengths and weaknesses.

Four years later, at the Munich Olympics, he returned to become the most successful athlete in Olympic history by winning seven gold medals in swimming. Why the change? In those four intervening years, Mark had surrounded himself with people who could coach him, manage his career, and handle the publicity and public relations. That way, Mark Spitz could concentrate on his single greatest strength—competitive swimming.

> **For Reflection**

I have seen competent leaders who stood in front of a platoon and all they saw was a platoon. But great leaders stand in front of a platoon and see it as 44 individuals, each of whom has aspirations, each of whom wants to live, each of whom wants to do good. — General Norman Schwarzkopf

1) How are you being sensitive to the individual needs and characteristics of those you supervise?

2) If you made "empowering other people to be the best they can be" your No. 1 priority, how might that change the way you go about your work?

3) Great leaders are role models. In what ways could you model your expectations for those you supervise?

4) Think of a person you know who exhibits leadership ability, and list his or her characteristics. Let that list be a guide for you.

LIFESTYLE

Yesterday is but a dream; tomorrow is only a vision. But today well-lived makes every yesterday a dream of happiness, and every tomorrow a vision of hope.
— **Ancient Sanskrit Proverb**

> **Day 190**

A man who was experiencing difficulty coping with anxiety and fear went to visit his physician. The doctor handed the patient an envelope and told him to take a day off work and visit the beach. When he got to the beach, he was to open the envelope and follow the instructions inside.

So the man did as his doctor suggested: he found a quiet spot at the beach and opened the envelope. Hand-written on a small piece of paper inside were the words "listen carefully." Later the patient spoke of how peaceful and reviving it was to hear, for the first time in years, the lapping of the waves, the song of the bird, and the sighing of the wind.

Everyone needs to take a break now and then from the rush of modern society. Regular breaks will keep you mentally fit and better able to focus.

> **Day 191**

In their book, *Staying OK*, Amy Bjork Harris and Dr. Thomas Harris list ten obstacles to making the best use of our time. The first obstacle is simply things. The second is not saying no. The third is unmade decisions. The fourth is not interrupting (you can be so polite that you never get anything done). The fifth is television. Then come lack of planning and clutter. The eighth obstacle is ignoring maintenance, the ninth is idle waiting, and the final one is agonizing about the future.

The secret, of course, to time management is to realize there is no such thing. We can't manage time. It moves right along regardless of our efforts to slow it down. The only thing we can manage is ourselves. Set priorities. Then refuse to let anyone keep you from your appointments with those vital objectives you have designated.

Day 192

Dr. Anthony Campolo tells about a study in which fifty people over the age of ninety-five were asked one question: "If you could live your life over again, what would you do differently?" It was an open-ended question, and many diverse answers were given. However, there were three answers which kept appearing and which dominated the results of the study. They were:
1. I would reflect more.
2. I would risk more.
3. I would do more things that would live on after I am dead.

Are you doing these things now? Will you regret not having done them when you reach ninety-five?

One psychologist described our daily living like this: "The average person's back is breaking under an oppressive weight of tedium, drudgery, and boredom induced by constant attention to the trivial and inconsequential."

Day 193

A story once appeared in the newspapers about a man in Evansville, Indiana who had his life saved in a most unusual way: a truck smashed into his house.

At 2:35 a.m. a driver lost control of his truck on wet pavement, struck the curb, and sailed onto the porch of Lee Roy Book's home. Later, a utility crew came by to restore electricity to Book's home and to check for gas leaks. They discovered that Book's chimney and pipes were plugged with two feet of soot and leaves. This was causing odorless, poisonous carbon monoxide fumes, generated from burning natural gas, to back up into the house.

For the previous two years Book, who lives alone, had been ill with classic flu-like symptoms: including chills, nausea, shakes and headaches. But these are also the symptoms of carbon monoxide poisoning. He had blacked out on several occasions and couldn't remember doing such things as visiting a friend. "I'd come to when I got in the fresh air," said Book, "but every day it was getting worse and worse. It was awful." Chances are that if the car had not smashed into his house, by now Lee Roy Book would be dead.

The kicker to the story, however, is that Book once worked as a building contractor. He is very much aware of the dangers of improperly vented furnaces. He always warned his customers to check their flues every two or three years to make sure they weren't clogged. "But somehow or another," he said, "it never did dawn on me to check my [own] chimney."

Don't become so involved with the welfare of others that you neglect your own.

Day 194

One day in his later years, the composer Brahms reached a point in his life when his work almost came to a halt. He had started many things—serenades, part-songs and so on—but nothing seemed to work out properly. Then he thought, "I am too old. I have worked long and diligently and have achieved enough. Here I have before me a carefree old age and can enjoy it in peace. I resolve to compose no more." This determination cleared his mind and relaxed his faculties so much that he was able to begin composing again without any difficulty.

Everyone needs a vacation every now and then. Even the thought of not having anything to do is enough to rejuvenate some.

Day 195

John Sculley, CEO at Apple Computers, writes of the corporate culture in which he once worked at Pepsi Cola. There the discipline of the body was held in high esteem. Note the passion for discipline he describes:

"The culture demanded that each of us be in top condition, physically fit as well as mentally alert. At lunch time, the glass-walled corporate fitness center was packed with the rising stars of the corporation. Like me, they were the kind of people who would rather be in the Marines than in the Army. Even our exercise regimens became part of the competition." Placards on bulletin boards charted each executive's progress against his colleagues.

Competition may not be bad if it motivates you to keep yourself in shape.

Day 196

Some of the most recent demonstrations in the Soviet Union have not been over politics. Nor have the issues been shortages of food, clothing, and shelter, or human rights. Instead, the street demonstrations have been over cigarettes.

In this country of 285 million people, it is estimated that one out of every four people smokes. Hence, the current inability to buy cigarettes in the U.S.S.R. has left 70 million smokers angry.

As the black market price of a pack of American Marlboros has reached $32 in Moscow, the government has acted to ensure that the valuable cigarettes are equitably distributed. Ration coupons have been issued and cigarette shipments are carefully monitored to see that they reach their destination. Further, a special car is on hand to deliver cartons of cigarettes to any spot where shortages threaten to erupt into violence.

The response of smokers in the U.S.S.R. demonstrates an interesting aspect of human nature. Most of us confuse the urgency of our desire with the importance of that desire. There are, however, lots of things that we momentarily crave which should not be allowed to rule us.

Day 197

A study of air traffic controllers, conducted at O'Hare Airport just prior to the controller's strike several years ago, confirmed the high stress level of that demanding job. But the study found that the stress was not caused only by the controllers having to make decisions that affect the lives of others, it was also caused by the fact that, although they are called controllers, they often feel that they are not in control of anything because of fluctuating weather, pilot error, and equipment failure.

It has also been found that nurses have more stress than physicians because they have less control while still having the responsibility. Having a measure of control can help prevent stress and improve productivity.

For Reflection

Ulysses S. Grant had a famous weakness for drink. A biographer of Grant wrote that "fondness of drink seemed to stay with him, although it is notable that he never indulged it when the chips were down. His benders always took place in dull periods, when nothing much was going on."

Keep yourself busy. More importantly, keep yourself interested in what you are doing. Constantly challenge yourself with new ideas and projects.

1) List some of the things that made you enthusiastic about your career when you were first starting out. How can you arrange your present schedule to allow you to work on those things?

2) In what ways can you simplify your life to achieve greater balance among work, play, rest, relationships, exercise, spirituality, and personal interests?

3) Do your day-to-day activities contribute to your main priorities in life, or do you get bogged down in the inconsequential? What do you need to do to get better focused?

4) Have you tried more than a few times to stop a destructive habit? List the positive benefits you would gain by stopping this habit, then give yourself permission to seek outside help. You deserve to be whole!

MOTIVATION

I can teach a man to sail, but I never teach him why. — Timothy E. Thatcher in *The American Scholar*

Perry Como once asked Pearl Bailey if she ever sang just for the pleasure of singing. Pearl replied, "Well, if you look at the musical scale, you'll find that it begins and ends with "Dough."

Day 198

After completing his term as thirtieth President of the United States, he issued his famous "I do not choose to run" statement. Reporters bombarded him with questions seeking more details concerning this decision. One persistent journalist refused to leave this line of questioning. "Exactly why don't you want to be President again?" he grilled.

Calvin Coolidge, undoubtedly frustrated with the probes, looked the reporter straight in the eye and responded, "Because there's no room for advancement."

Day 199

A group of Jews were trying to escape the Nazis. They were walking over a mountain and they carried with them the sick and the old and the children. A lot of old people fell by the wayside and said, "I'm a burden; go on without me." They were told, "The mothers need respite, so instead of just sitting there and dying, would you take the babies and walk as far as you can?" Once the old people got the babies close to their bosom and started walking, they all went over the mountain successfully. They had a reason to live.

Day 200

Neil Eskelin tells a story he heard about the former President of Sears, Roebuck and Co., Robert Elkton Wood. Wood believed so strongly in incentives that he tried the technique in his own family.

He really wanted to have a lot of grandchildren. So he told each of his four daughters, "I'll give you a mink coat at the birth of your third child."

Wood had fifteen grandchildren! Now that's productivity!

Day 201

Thomas A. Edison was once asked what triggered his quest for the electric light. He said, "I was paying a sheriff $5 a day to postpone a judgment on my small factory. Then came the gas man and because I could not pay his bill promptly, he cut off my gas. I was in the midst of certain very important experiments, and to have the gas people plunge me into darkness made me so mad that I at once began to read up on gas technique and economics, and resolved I would try to see if electricity couldn't be made to replace gas and give those gas people a run for their money."

Day 202

Long ago in the old country there was a rag-and-bones man by the name of Mendel Klutznik.

Mendel drove around in a wagon pulled by a doddering old horse. One day Mendel came crying: "My horse! My wonderful old horse!"

"What happened?"

"I had been training my horse to live off less and less hay. Each day I gave him a smaller ration. In three weeks time he would have been working with no food at all. The perfect horse! And then he died on me."

Day 203

The French writer, Victor Hugo, author of the book on which the Broadway hit *Les Miserables* is based, had a habit of asking his servant to steal his clothes every morning. This meant Hugo could not go outside, and so was forced to carry on with his writing.

Sometimes we must take drastic measures in order to make sure that we do what we are supposed to do. But often these measures may be worth the inconvenience.

Tom Landry, the coach of the Dallas Cowboys, once said something that may be true of nearly any motivator: "I have a job to do that is not very complicated, but it is difficult: to get a group of men to do what they don't want to do so they can achieve the one thing they have wanted all of their lives."

Day 204

Most people in the world are day people: they get their best work done in the late morning hours. But some people work best late at night, like Anton Rubinstein. Mornings were like poison to this famous Russian pianist: he found it very difficult even to get up early. But sometimes he had to get up early to meet the schedule of a concert tour, and it was Mrs. Rubinstein's task to help him do this. In the early years of their relationship, she had tried alarm clocks of all kinds, and she had tried pushing him out of bed, but nothing worked. He would either fall back to sleep, or be so sluggish that he'd miss his appointment anyway.

Finally, though, after years of experimenting, she managed to find a way to wake him up in the morning. He had spent his life refining his sensitivity to music, to the point that he could hear the smallest flaw in a piece. Mrs. Rubinstein found that the easiest way to get her husband up was to go to the piano and begin playing scales—but only seven of the eight notes. After she had played the faulty scale a few times, Anton would be out of bed and at the piano, wide awake, and itching to finish the scale properly.

We all have problems with motivation from time to time. The trick is to find a system that will get us moving again. Your system may be tied in with your personality, hobbies, or life goals. But try to find that thing which will re-motivate you, and keep it near at hand.

Day 205

Historians have written that, on the night before a great battle, all of Napoleon's commanders went to their commander's tent one by one. It was a strange procession: no one said a word as they came into Napoleon's presence. Each man simply looked into his commander's eyes, shook his hand, then turned and walked out of the tent ready to lay down his life.

There are many ways to encourage people. Just knowing that your leader will acknowledge you is a good one.

Day 206

Some years ago, in Miami Springs, Florida, a crowd of residents rushed to the water department to pay overdue bills. The surprised clerk said, "I never saw anything like it. They came dashing in as fast as they could with the money in their hands." Later, the reason for the hurry became apparent. A road grading machine had accidentally cut a main water line, shutting off the supply to a large area. Unaware of what had taken place, the residents assumed that their water had been turned off for failure to pay their bills.

Don't allow threats to be your prime motivation!

Day 207

Many years ago the *Times of London* had difficulties with their typesetters: too many mistakes were being made in their daily editions. The editors thought long and hard about how to correct this problem. Finally, they gathered all the workers together and announced that from that time forward the first copy of every edition would be sent free to Buckingham Palace for the king and queen to read.

People always seem to try harder when they know that someone important is going to be using their handiwork.

Day 208

Knute Rockne was a motivator. During the first half of one game, his Notre Dame Fighting Irish were playing rather poorly. At halftime the team walked dejectedly to the locker room where they braced themselves for the pep talk. They knew Rockne was going to tear into them. So they waited, and waited, but Rockne did not appear.

Finally, as the team was heading toward the door for the beginning of the second half, Rockne came walking in. He looked around as if surprised and embarrassed and started to walk back out again. Then he said simply, "Sorry, I was looking for the Notre Dame football team." They won the game.

Day 209

A manager, who had just returned from a motivation seminar, called an employee into his office and said, "Henceforth you are going to be allowed to plan and control your job. That will raise productivity considerably, I am sure."

"Will I be paid more?" asked the worker.

"No, no. Money is not a motivator and you will get no satisfaction from a salary raise."

"Well, if production does increase, will I be paid more?"

"Look," said the manager. "You obviously do not understand the motivation theory. Take this book home and read it; it explains what it is that really motivates you."

As the man was leaving, he stopped and said, "If I read this book, will I be paid more?"

Paying more money is not the only way to motivate people—it may not even be the best way to motivate people—but until people have at least their basic perceived needs met, it will certainly be important.

Day 210

When asked by a news reporter how she thought she would do in one of her early career swimming meets in the United States several years ago, 14-year-old Australian Shane Gould replied, "I have a feeling there will be a world record today." She went on to set two world records in the one-hundred-and two-hundred-meter freestyle events.

Later she was asked how she thought she would fare in the more grueling four-hundred-meter event. Shane replied with a smile, "I get stronger every race, and besides . . . my parents said they'd take me to Disneyland if I win, and we're leaving tomorrow!" She went to Disneyland with three world records. At 16 she held five world records and became one of the greatest swimmers of all time, winning three gold medals in the 1972 Olympics. She learned early about the power of self-expectancy.

Day 211

The Tower of Pisa said to Big Ben, "You got the time?" Big Ben replied, "Yes, but not the inclination."

Let's face it: more people have the time for success than they have the inclination. Sometimes we have to depend on negative alternatives to motivate:

Bea Thorpe told about her 74-year-old neighbor who was a telegraph operator. Bea asked her if it wasn't difficult learning all those dots and dashes. "It sure was," she replied. "But it was either that or pick cotton."

I don't know about you but picking cotton would certainly motivate me.

It's like a cartoon in *Hagar the Horrible* comic strip. Hagar looks at his football team and says, "Today we play in the big championship 'No Rules' football game, men . . .

I know you're all seasoned players and don't want to hear a lot of rah-rah sentimental baloney from your coach, so I'm going to put this pep talk in the form of a short inspirational slogan: "WIN OR DIE!"

Day 212

In his book *The Peak to Peek Principle*, Robert Schuller relays this story about Tommy Lasorda, manager of the Los Angeles Dodgers baseball team. Tom was a manager in the minor leagues in 1971, when his team lost seven straight games. About that time sports writers across the country had voted to select the greatest major league team in the history of baseball. By a majority vote the honor went to the 1927 Yankees.

Defeated and exhausted, Tom's losing team headed for the locker room. A few minutes later he walked in and found the players sitting around, dejected, with their heads down. "Hey, get your heads up!" Tom yelled. "I don't even want to see you fellows with your heads down again.

Just because you lost seven games doesn't mean you are not a great team. You're going to start winning! As you know, according to the recent poll, the greatest major league team ever was the 1927 Yankees. And they lost nine straight games!" Suddenly heads went up and expressions changed. It was the turning point for the team, and by the end of the season they were champions!

A few days later Mrs. Lasorda asked, "Tommy are you sure the Yankees lost nine games in a row?" Tom answered, "How would I know? I was only a year old, but it made the point." The team had to believe they could do it!

Day 213

After a tour of combat duty, Corporal Jones was reassigned to a stateside induction center, where he was given the task of advising new recruits about their government benefits, particularly GI insurance. Soon he had an almost perfect, 100 percent insurance-sales record. His officers were amazed. Rather than ask him how he did it, an officer stood in the back of the room one day in order to listen to Jones's sales pitch.

Jones explained the basics of GI insurance to the new recruits, and then said, "If you HAVE GI insurance, and go into battle and are killed, the government has to pay $35,000 to your beneficiaries. If you DON'T have GI insurance, and go into battle and are killed, the government has to pay only a maximum of $3,000.

"Now," he concluded, "which bunch do you think they are going to send into battle FIRST?"

Day 214

What is incentive? One famous psychological study demonstrated that a financial incentive program designed for all female employees would not work with some because of group identifications. The extra money was a terrific incentive for girls of Norwegian descent because in their families, they were permitted to spend their own money. But for girls of Italian descent, money was not the right incentive. These girls, by family tradition, were required to throw their money into family funds from which they drew allowances—no matter how heavy their contributions, no matter how hard they worked.

Day 215

"I had a club member give me two apricot trees seven years ago. I planted, waited, fertilized and cared for them very carefully. They never had an apricot. I got a large ax out this last winter and proceeded to cut them down. They were about 15 feet high and had huge trunks. I laid the ax beside one of the trees but never had time to cut them down.

"This spring they bloomed and produced thousands of apricots. I do not know if the ax had anything to do with it or not."
— Leonard John Roberson, Denton, TX

Day 216

He was born into a poor family in Arkansas. He dropped out of school before the eighth grade to help out in his uncle's sawmill, because his family needed the money. He made a little money on the side selling wood shavings as a filler for chicken coops. Later he spent some time in the Army. When he got out of the Army, he got married and became a truck driver.

He started out in life poor, statistically he should end his life poor. But as J.B. Hunt himself said, "Once you're hungry, you're different." He knew he never wanted to be hungry again. So J.B. Hunt worked hard at his job and learned all there is to know about the trucking business. Then he started a small trucking business of his own. This year J.B. Hunt's trucking business will make approximately $900 million dollars. Hunt's personal holdings in the company plus other investments makes his cut of the pie worth $375 million. J.B. Hunt took his hunger and created an empire.

Day 217

He was just an average scrawny, gangly fifteen-year-old. One night he was walking home alone when he was attacked and brutally beaten by a boy who was much bigger than he was. The beating had a profound effect on him: he decided that he would never be weak again.

One day while watching a lion at the zoo, he noticed that the lion had a way of flexing some muscles in opposition to other muscles. This activity obviously kept the lion in perfect physical condition, even though it had been in a cage for a long time. The boy took his new-found knowledge and created a system of exercise for humans that involved using opposing muscles against one another. Using this new system, the scrawny fifteen-year-old became a brawny man of muscle who never had to worry about bullies ever again. He was Charles Atlas.

Day 218

The Golden Gate Bridge was completed in 1937. It was the world's longest suspension bridge at the time, costing the United States government $77 million. While the first section of the bridge was being constructed very few safety devices were used, and twenty-three workers fell to their deaths in the waters far below.

The toll was significant enough that something had to be done before the second section was built. So an ingenious plan was devised. The largest safety net in the world (it alone cost $100,000) was made out of stout manila cordage and stretched out beneath the work crews. It proved to be an excellent investment, as it saved the lives of at least ten men who fell into it, all of them without injury. And the work on the bridge went 25 percent faster with the net in place.

Security and a show of concern by superiors are excellent motivators. People are always willing to work harder for someone that they know will help them with their problems.

Day 219

Several years ago, a California aerospace company hired a motivational consultant to examine and stimulate its work force. The consultant interviewed one of the senior vice presidents who told him about a particular section where production and performance were extremely high. Turnover and absenteeism in this department were the lowest in the company, and morale was very high. What seemed to puzzle the executive was that the work done there was mechanical, repetitive and stressful. This group of employees maintained the pipes in the plant. Their job was checking temperatures and pressures, and the delicacy of the equipment meant that the pipes had to work within strict tolerances or there would be expensive damage. So why was morale so high?

In order to help solve the mystery, the consultant visited the department and asked the foreman to take him on a tour. The consultant noticed that all the workers wore green surgical smocks, and he asked the foreman about it. The foreman explained that he got them from his son, a cardiovascular surgeon.

"Ah. So you wear them for comfort."

"No, no!" the foreman said, "It's because we are surgeons, just like my son. He takes care of the pipes of the body; we take care of the pipes of the plant! And the plant isn't going to have any breakdowns as long as we're working on its arteries." It was then that the consultant noticed the stencils on the workers' lockers, which said, "Dr." before each name.

One enterprising home builder has found a way to motivate his employees. For exceptional work he names streets after them in his housing developments.

Day 220

When an armed robber tried to hold up a Speedway market, the thief and an employee ended up in a major wrestling match.

Curtis Wyatt, an employee of the market, happened to come out of the back room just as the robber was holding up the clerk at the counter. Wyatt, realizing that the thief was holding only a BB gun, jumped him. The two struggled in the store, through the door, and out into the parking lot. When the robber broke free and jumped in his car, Wyatt jumped in after him. They fought for the next two blocks while the car proceeded down the street unmanned. Meanwhile, the struggling pair had managed to break the front seat backwards and were rolling on top of each other when the car went over an embankment. After the car rolled three times, it ended up with Wyatt on top of the robber. At that point the thief conceded.

Then a strange thing happened. The armed robber told Wyatt, "Thanks, I was hoping I would get caught." He further explained that he was strung out on drugs and was sick of the whole mess.

Motivation comes in all kinds of packages. Sometimes the pain of change is less than the pain of staying the same.

Day 221

In a National Football League championship game many years ago, Dallas was playing Green Bay at Wisconsin in what came to be dubbed, "The Ice Bowl." Green Bay was behind by five points, with just seconds to play. Green Bay had the ball on the Dallas one-foot line and it was fourth down. Everything hinged on the next, and final, play. In the huddle, Packers' quarterback Bart Starr turned to Jerry Kramer, the offensive guard, and said, "Jerry, if you can move Jethro Pugh twelve inches to the left, you will make $15,000." From that remark Jerry Kramer caught the vision of what he needed to do: simply move defensive lineman Jethro Pugh twelve inches and collect $15,000—the winner's share of the championship. Jerry responded, Jethro was moved, and Green Bay won.

Keep in mind the benefits that will be had when a goal is reached, and you will have a better chance to reach it.

Day 222

Ignace Paderewski had been advised by famous authorities on music in his day that he had no possible future as a pianist. The professors at the Warsaw Conservatory, where he went to study, pointed out that his fingers were not well-suited to performance, and they suggested that he concentrate on composing music instead.

"I want to be a great pianist," he told them. So Paderewski practiced arduously for hours every day. His swollen fingers were tortured with pain, and blood often seeped from them during concerts. But he became a pianist of world renown.

Paderewski persisted with his dream because his incentive motivation—creative fulfillment and recognition—was stronger than the motivation to quit.

For Reflection

Joseph Juran says that a person doing a dull job on an assembly line will do what is required, but no more. The same worker in, say, a softball game will use much more energy. "It's more taxing, and he may get exhausted," Juran says. "But he does it because now he's with people that he himself has chosen to work with, he's not having to take orders from a boss he had no voice in choosing, and there's an element of volunteerism and freedom that is not present in the working place, but that doesn't have to stay that way . . . One of the main things about getting workers enthusiastic is to give them interesting work that will stimulate them."

1) What aspects of your work still excite you and motivate you to do you best? Would it be possible for you to delegate the less exciting tasks to someone else so that you could be free to work on what interests you?

2) List some creative techniques you could use to motivate yourself. (Remember Rubinstein's wake up call and Hugo's lack of clothing!)

3) Although businesses tend to rely heavily on external rewards such as salary, benefits and promotions, often it is the non-material, relational incentives that truly motivate employees over the long term. Think of the people whom you supervise. What kinds of encouragement or incentive could you offer them that would be particularly meaningful to them?

OPTIMISM

The men whom I have seen succeed best in life have always been cheerful and hopeful men who went about their business with a smile on their faces, and took the changes and the chances of this mortal life like men, facing rough and smooth alike as it came.
— Charles Kettering

Day 223

He was a clergyman in his fifties who had written a manuscript for a book. He had sent this book to a host of publishers without success. Now he was so discouraged with these rejections that he gave up and threw the manuscript into a wastepaper basket. His wife tried to salvage it, but he wouldn't let her. He told her sternly, "We've wasted enough time on it. I forbid you to take it from the wastebasket."

The next day she decided that the manuscript should be seen by at least one more publisher. When she arrived at that publisher's office she pulled out a wastepaper basket and set it on his desk. (That way she didn't have to go against her husband's wishes!) Inside the basket was the manuscript: Norman Vincent Peale's *The Power Of Positive Thinking*, which at last report has sold more than 30 million copies.

We all get discouraged. But we do not have to be defeated.

Day 224

In a *Frank and Ernest* cartoon, you see Frank rousing slowly from his sleep, then looking out at the sun coming up. And he says, "Well, the sun is rising in the east... so far, so good."

The story is told of a general who found his forces completely surrounded by enemy troops. He assessed the situation for his soldiers in this way: "Men, for the first time in the history of this military campaign, we are in position to attack the enemy in all directions."

Sometimes being optimistic is the best weapon to use in what might otherwise appear to be a hopeless situation.

It's like a cartoon that shows two Eskimos fishing on the frozen ocean. One of them is fishing from a manhole-sized opening that he had cut in the ice. The other is fishing from a considerably larger hole—in the outline of a large whale. Some of us are thinkers and some of us are big thinkers.

Day 225

Studies of winners show that before they ever head for the track or the ball field or the gridiron, many of them will envision themselves performing effortlessly and flawlessly. The decathlon participant will see himself clearing the hurdles; the wide receiver will hear the crowd cheering as he catches the winning pass, the swimmer will feel herself touching the wall just before her competitor. They all experience the thrill of winning in their minds long before it happens before crowds of spectators.

A positive attitude can be a great source of strength for achievement. Success becomes easier in practice when you've seen it in your mind, because you know that it's possible.

Martin Seligman, a professor of psychology at the University of Pennsylvania, surveyed representatives of a major life-insurance company. He found that those who expected to succeed sold 37% more insurance than those who did not. People will generally fulfill their own expectations of how they perceive themselves, whether failures or successes.

Day 226

Many kinds of birds fly over our nation's deserts, but there are two specific ones that we need to consider here: the hummingbird and the vulture.

The vulture sees nothing but rotting meat because that is what it looks for. Vultures thrive on a diet of dead and decaying things.

The hummingbird flies over the same desert and past the same dead carcasses and is instead attracted to the tiny blossoms of the cactus flower. It will buzz around until it finds the colorful blooms hidden from view by the rocks.

Each bird finds what it is looking for. We all do.

Day 227

There are two prisoners shackled to the wall of a deep dark dungeon. Spread-eagled, they are securely lashed by manacles and chains and actually hanging suspended, side by side, a few feet above the damp floor of the dungeon. There is only one small window high above their heads, maybe thirty or forty feet up. They are immobile and alone, pinned inexorably to the wall.

One prisoner turns to the other and whispers, "Here's my plan!"

There is an autobiography titled *In Praise Of Imperfection: My Life and Work*. It is written by a woman named Rita Levi Montacini, an Italian scientist. By looking back over her life as a scientist, she is convinced that in research, neither intelligence nor efficiency are what really count. What counts, she says, is a tendency to underestimate difficulties. When you underestimate difficulties, she contends, you are more apt to tackle problems other, more reasonable, persons say can't be solved.

Day 228

In the fourth inning of that famous game in Chicago, Babe Ruth motioned toward a particular section of the outfield fence, swung his bat, and hit his second history-making home run directly over the part of the fence he had indicated. The crowd went wild, and his teammates literally carried Ruth over the bases. More than twenty minutes passed before the umpires could clear away the debris of celebration from the field and settle down the players and fans to continue the game.

After the game was over the sportswriters interviewed the Babe about the gesture of his bat toward the center field fence and his apparent intention to hit a home run. As they were concluding the interview, one reporter said, "Babe, I have just one more question to ask before we go. What would you have done if you had missed that third strike?" Babe

Ruth's jaw dropped with an expression of sincerity and he answered, "It never entered my mind to do anything but hit a home run."

Day 229

Nelson L. Price tells about Dr. Murdo Ewin McDonald, a Scottish soldier who became a prisoner of war during World War II. One morning, Dr. McDonald was awakened by a friend who had been listening secretly to the BBC and heard the news of the allied invasion of Normandy. The bearer of the good news whispered only three words to McDonald in Gaelic: They have come!

McDonald immediately threw all reserve and restraint aside, ran back to the barracks and began shouting, "They have come! They have come!" The response to his proclamation was instant and incredible. Weak men shouted as they jumped for joy, ragged men hugged each other and wept with glee. Some stood on tables and shouted, as others rolled on the floor in fits of elation. Their German captors, not knowing of the D-Day Invasion, thought them crazy. Even though the jubilant allies were still prisoners within the formerly intimidating walls, and nothing had apparently changed, inwardly, they knew that actually everything had changed. Freedom was yet to be had but they lived happily in the knowledge that a rescue was on the way.

Contemplating the successes to come will often carry you through any difficulties that you are having at the moment. Don't dwell on what might have been or what is, think about what will be.

Day 230

Charles Kuralt travels across the United States meeting interesting people. He told about an old farmer he met in Kansas. "We never caught his name," he wrote. The old man was a pilot. Charles and his crew were doing a story about an artist whose canvases were eighty-acre fields. Of course the best way to view this unusual art work was from a plane. At one point Kuralt and his photographer spotted an old J-2 Piper Cub parked in a barnyard, and they asked the owner if he would fly them. "Sure, I'll take you up," the farmer replied. "We need to take the door off so I can take pictures," the photographer told the farmer. "Fine!" was his reply. Flying at 2000 feet the photographer asked the old pilot, "How long ago did you get your ticket?" "Ticket?" the man asked. "You know, your pilot's license," the photographer explained. "I don't have any pilot's license," the old farmer told them. "I just found this thing wrecked out here and patched it up and taught myself how to fly it."

Never let anyone tell you that something is impossible until you've found it out for yourself.

Day 231

Bobby McFerrin had a smash-hit song several years ago called "Don't Worry, Be Happy!" He says his song "says something that's just common sense, common wisdom for humanity—that worry is counterproductive."

"Worry takes your energy away," says McFerrin. "You need to turn it into something very positive. And that is to put a smile on your face and say, well, try to take it a little more lightly." McFerrin, who once considered becoming an Episcopal priest, said that the song came out of his own need. "When I wrote the song," he says, "I was experiencing a period of stress and tension. There were some things going on in my life that I wasn't happy with, and this song was written for me just as much as anyone else."

As someone has said, "Worrying is like a rocking chair. It will give you something to do, but you won't get anywhere."

Day 232

Shalom Aleichem tells a story about an old man on a crowded bus. A young man standing next to him asked him politely, "What time is it?" But the old man refused to reply. After the young man moved away, the old man's friend asked, "Why were you so rude to the young man asking for the time?" The old man answered, "If I have given him the time of day, he would next want to know where I am going. Then we might talk about our interests. If we did that, he might invite himself to my house for dinner. If he did, he would meet my lovely daughter. If he met her, they would both fall in love, and I don't want my daughter marrying someone who can't afford a watch."

Too many people allow the problems that might occur interfere with their work. Look at what can go right instead of what can go wrong.

For Reflection

IS THE GLASS HALF-FULL OR HALF-EMPTY? Some 46 percent of men and 52 percent of women describe themselves as optimists while 8 percent of men and 11 percent of women see themselves as pessimists. (The rest say they're neither.) People 35 to 44 years are most likely to see the glass as half-full—56 percent—while only 11 percent of those over 45 see it that way.

1) In what ways does a negative attitude toward aspects of your work sap your energy? What could you do to make those aspects more fun and rewarding?

2) Do you refrain from planning certain activities because of all the problems which MIGHT occur? Next time, try focusing on all the REWARDS which might result.

3) Consider spending a few minutes each day reflecting on the positive things in your life, the things you usually take for granted.

4) How might your positive attitude help and inspire those around you?

PERSEVERANCE

The big shots are only the little shots who keep on shooting. — Christopher Morley

Day 233

By the end of World War II, prominent CBS newsman William Shirer had decided that he wanted to write professionally. His job as a newsman ended with the war, and during the next twelve years he was consumed with his writing. Unfortunately, his books rarely sold, and he often had difficulty feeding his family. Out of this period, however, came a manuscript that was 1200 pages long.

Everyone—his agent, his editor, his publisher, his friends— told him it would never sell because of its length. And when Shirer finally did get it published, it was priced at ten dollars, the most expensive book of its time.

No one really expected it to be of any interest to anyone except scholars. But *The Rise and Fall Of the Third Reich* by William Shirer made publishing history. Its first printing sold out completely on the first day. Critics praised the writing, and even foreign sales were strong. Even today it remains the all-time biggest seller in the history of the Book-of-the-Month Club.

Day 234

After surviving fifty-five hours adrift off the coast of South Carolina sometime back a man slipped off a life raft into the ocean. Saying, "I just can't take it any more," Robert Louis Watson moved to the stern of the raft, jumped off and drowned. An hour later, a Coast Guard rescue ship appeared.

The easiest way to snatch defeat from the jaws of victory is to give up.

Day 235

We are told that a German named Philip Reis was actually the first person to invent the telephone—fifteen years before Alexander Graham Bell. His instrument could transmit music and was very close to transmitting speech. But he could not interest investors in his new invention. The prevailing attitude was "the telegraph is good enough for us." So he became discouraged and gave up. Thus Reis missed the world-wide fame that went to Bell because he quit before the results were in.

The hardest part in promoting a new idea is getting people to accept it over the old way of doing things. But the public usually does come around, eventually.

A recent study of Nobel Prize winners indicates that they may not be any brighter intellectually than their colleagues. Something else explains their success. Among the traits that their colleagues used to describe them was this one: they were good finishers.

Day 236

An unconscious 12-year-old boy was wheeled in to the emergency room with a stab wound to his heart. The senior medical student on duty followed the proper procedure. He checked the boy's skin which was cold, shined a light into the boy's eyes which showed no reaction, and hooked him up to the cardiac monitor which showed a straight line.

The medical student looked at the nurse and said, "He's dead. Turn off the monitor." Just then a doctor came in, felt the wound on the dead boy, grabbed a needle and stuck it into the boy's chest. Immediately the boy's heart began to beat. A few hours and an operation later he was mumbling and moving his legs.

The medical student later commented, "I left the room and wandered down the hall, discouraged. I had just pronounced a boy dead who had been saved seconds later while I watched."

Sometimes the best axiom to follow is one of the oldest and simplest: Don't give up.

Day 237

Theatrical producer Arthur Hopkins used to receive dozens of manuscripts for plays. But before he would read any script, he always asked the author, "How is your second act?" He realized that many new playwrights had wonderful first acts, but allowed the drama to fade and the plot to drift in the later parts of the play.

There is always a second act, though, and it must be just as impressive as the first. Don't let yourself slack off in the middle of a project once the initial enthusiasm has died. People remember endings better than they remember beginnings.

When LeBaron Briggs was the academic dean at Harvard, a graduate student once came to his office to explain why he failed to complete his master's thesis on time. The student told him, "I haven't been feeling well."

Dean Briggs replied, "Young man, I think it's time you realize that most of the work done in this world is done by people who aren't feeling well."

Day 238

We're like the farmer who grows Chinese bamboo. After the bamboo is planted, only a tiny shoot is visible and the gardener must tend and nurture the bamboo for four years while the shoot remains the size of a thumb. For those first four years all the growth takes place underground, unseen, in the plant's root system. Finally, in the fifth year, the gardener's perseverance is rewarded as the bamboo grows 80 feet!

Hang in there. Keep striving.

Muhammad Ali once said he hated every minute of the training. But he said to himself, "Don't quit. Suffer now and live the rest of your life as a champion."

Dr. Robert H. Schuller says it best in his "The Possibility Thinker's Creed":

When faced with a mountain I will not quit! I will keep on striving until I climb over, find a pass through, tunnel underneath, or simply stay and turn the mountain into a gold mine with God's help!

Day 239

Mary-Claire King sees her life's work—in her words, "solving breast cancer"—as nothing short of a crusade. In 1990, King proved there is a mutated gene for early-onset breast cancer, which strikes before age 50 and kills thousands of women in America each year. About 600,000 women in the U.S. carry the gene, according to one report. King had been struggling to confirm her hypothesis—that familial breast cancer could be blamed on a single gene—for 17 years.

Giving up was never an option. "The reason I stayed with it was twofold," explains the 50-year-old genetic researcher at her bustling lab at the University of Washington in Seattle. "It's an enormously intriguing problem in a purely scientific way—and it mattered to me."

How did King feel in 1994, when a competing research team pinpointed the precise location of the gene, now known as BRCA1? She responds: "We said, 'Oh, my God, somebody else found the gene,' then we went in the next morning and did the next experiment. The next experiments are absolutely obvious. You have to go right on. The point was not to find the gene. The point is to keep women from dying of breast cancer."

Day 240

When Michelangelo painted the ceiling of the Sistine Chapel in Rome, he had to do it lying flat on his back. Unfortunately, Michelangelo had a bad back, and if he lay on it for a very long he suffered excruciating pain. Moreover, he had a peculiar nasal obstruction which cut off much of his air supply when he lay on his back.

In spite of this, he lay on his back all day, every day, for twenty months. He often even slept with his clothes on, so that he could go back to work without bothering to dress. In this way he painted one of the greatest masterpieces of all time.

The greatest accomplishments are achieved by those who are willing to overcome their difficulties through hard work and endurance.

Day 241

Karen Phelps, a distance runner, wrote recently, "On this particular day, I didn't feel like running at all. But I made myself, because running is a sport you have to practice every day. I wanted to win races, so I had a set plan for training:

1. Run daily, even if you don't feel like it.
2. Run daily, even if you sometimes have to skip fun and pleasure.
3. Run daily, even in bad weather—even if people think you're weird.
4. Run daily, even when it gives you aches and pains and you feel like quitting.
5. Run daily, even if you don't feel it's doing you any good.

"Sometimes you may not feel like practicing, or doing something else that needs your attention, but if you're in training you'll do it."

Day 242

The story is told of Emperor Tamerlane, whose army had been defeated and scattered in every direction. Tamerlane himself was in hiding in an old barn. While he was secluded there he observed an ant trying to carry off a kernel of corn. The kernel was considerably larger than the ant, and the ant needed to push it over a wall in order to get it out of the barn. Tamerlane watched that ant struggle with that kernel of corn for some time as it tried to push it up that wall. When the ant was nearly to the top, it fell, as did the kernel of corn. But the ant did not quit. It returned to the kernel and began pushing it back up the wall. It fell again. In fact, the ant fell off the wall sixty-nine times without giving up. Finally, on the 70th try, the ant successfully made it over the wall with its prize. Tamerlane, watching that ant, made a commitment. He said, "If an ant can do it, so can I," and he went out, reorganized his army and returned to defeat his enemy.

How wonderful it is when a person in trying circumstances simply will not give up until the victory is won.

Day 243

Some might label him a juvenile delinquent. He was dabbling in drugs and alcohol by the age of twelve. He got into all kinds of trouble and got kicked out of school. Then a coach at his new school challenged him to make something out of his life. And under the tutelage and tough love of his swimming coach, Nelson Diebel made the Olympic swimming team and went on to win the gold in the 100-meter breast stroke at the 1992 Olympics.

People make mistakes. Particularly young people. The key is not to give up. There may still be the blood of a champion coursing through your veins.

Day 244

The great Babe Dedrichson Zeharias was once asked how she could hit a golf ball like she did. She answered, "Simple, first you hit a thousand golf balls. You hit them until your hands bleed and you can't hit any more. The next day you start over again, and the next day, and the next, and maybe a year later you might be able to go eighteen holes. And after that you play every day until the time finally arrives that you know what you are doing when you hit the ball."

Persistence is the key to learning how to do anything. Nothing can be mastered quickly. If you think you have mastered something quickly, chances are you need to learn more.

In the words of the champion heavyweight boxer, Jim Corbett, the secret of success is often simply fighting one more round. Or as an aging Winston Churchill said in a speech to a group of young men: "Young men, never give up! Never give up! Never! Never! Never!"

Day 245

The final draft of Thomas Gray's masterpiece, "Elegy Written in a Country Churchyard" is kept in the British Museum in London. Lovers of English literature marvel how every word in the piece seems so carefully chosen. And they were. Gray wasn't satisfied with his first draft, so he rewrote it. Then he improved the poem a third time. He continued rewriting the poem for eight years. With all that persistent polishing, however, Gray never did consider his poem to be complete. The museum has each carefully penned copy in the work's display—all seventy-five drafts.

Very few projects are ever perfect on the first try. Always be willing to revise and re-revise in order to produce the best.

For Reflection

      If you would attain what you are not yet, you must always be displeased by what you are. For where you were pleased with yourself there you have remained. But once you have said, "It is enough," you are lost. Keep adding, keep walking, keep advancing; do not stop, do not turn back, do not turn from the straight road.

— St. Augustine

1) When in your life has your failure to "hang in there" kept you from enjoying an opportunity or a reward? When has perseverance paid off for you?

2) Are you plugging away at a problem without result? Try taking a rest, refresh yourself, then come back to the problem again.

3) Write down a phrase you can repeat to yourself when you need encouragement to keep going.

4) There may be someone you know who has given up—on himself, on work, on love, or on life. What will you do to offer hope to that person?

PERSPECTIVE

A woodpecker flew away from his home in the forest. Perched on the side of a tree, he decided to start his work on a certain spot. Just as he made contact with the tree a bolt of lightening split the tree from top to bottom knocking the woodpecker to the ground. He picked himself up and smoothed his feathers and exclaimed "A fellow doesn't realize what he can do until he gets away from home."

Day 246

An old Navajo Indian owned a piece of land in Arizona. One day, oil was discovered on his land, and suddenly, he became very wealthy. But he went on living just as he had before while his money piled up in the bank.

Every now and then, however, the old man would visit the bank and say to the banker, "Crops all dried up; sheep all dead; cattle all stolen." The banker knew exactly what to do. He would take the old man into the vault, seat him at a table, and place several bags of silver dollars in front of him for him to count. After a while the man would come out of the vault and say, "Crops fine; sheep all alive; cattle all back."

Why the change in attitude? He had simply reviewed his resources and reminded himself of everything he had to fall back on.

Day 247

There once was a king who had two servants. To the first he said, "I want you to travel for six months through my kingdom and bring back a sample of every weed you can find."

To the second servant he said, "I want you to travel through my kingdom for six months and bring back a sample of every flower you can find."

Six months later, both servants stood before the king. To the first, the king asked, "Have you carried out my command?" The servant replied, "I have, and I was amazed to find there were so many weeds in the kingdom. In fact, our kingdom contains nothing but weeds!"

The king then repeated the question to the second servant, who answered, "I have, and I was amazed how many beautiful flowers there are in the kingdom. In fact, our kingdom contains nothing but beautiful flowers!"

Both servants found what they were looking for, and their success caused them to stop seeing anything else. It is possible for anyone to be blinded by success.

Marcel Proust once put it this way: "The only real voyage of discovery consists not in seeking new landscapes but in having new eyes."

Day 248

Author Paul Tournier tells about taking a friend out to his farm. At one point his friend suggested that they take a little walk and collect some mushrooms for a mushroom omelette. "That will take some time!" Tournier thought to himself. But his friend picked up a basket and off they went. While they walked his friend was constantly bending down, picking, bending down, picking... In ten minutes the basket was full. Tournier kept searching, but couldn't see anything but grass. His friend was the son of a food inspector, and like his father knew all about mushrooms and how to find them. It was then that Tournier realized how true it is that one sees only what one is prepared to see. There were mushrooms all around, but he couldn't see them.

Day 249

A little boy said to his mother, "Hey, Mom, I'm eight feet tall." His mother said, "No you're not."

And the boy said, "Yes I am. I just measured myself, and I'm eight rulers high."

What did you measure yourself with?" the mother asked. So he showed her his measuring stick: a six-inch ruler.

Some of us are measuring ourselves with a six-inch ruler. Others are using an eighteen-inch ruler. Either way we get a distorted measurement.

"What position does your brother play on the football team?" a neighbor asked a little boy. "I'm not sure," the tot replied proudly, "but I think he's one of the drawbacks."

If we are going to avoid being one of the drawbacks, we will need to accurately assess our competencies and our inadequacies and adjust accordingly.

Day 250

An Eskimo man was rewarded for guiding North Pole expeditions with a trip to the Big Apple. He was amazed at what he saw. When he returned to his native village, he told stories of structures that rose into the very face of the sky (skyscrapers); of houses that moved along a trail, with people living in them as they moved (streetcars); of mammoth bridges, artificial lights, and all the other dazzling sights to be seen in the Big Apple.

His friends looked at him coldly and walked away. They began to call him Sagdluk, meaning "The Liar," and he carried this name to his grave. Long before his death his original name was entirely forgotten.

Sometime later another man from the same village named Mitek also visited New York, where he also saw many incredible things for the first time. But later, upon his return, he remembered the tragedy of Sagdluk, and decided that it would not be wise to tell the truth.

So he told his people how he paddled a kayak on the banks of a great river, the Hudson, and how, each morning, he hunted ducks, geese and seals. Mitek, in the eyes of his countrymen, was a truly honest man. His neighbors treated him with rare respect.

It is a sad state of affairs when liars are treated with respect, and truthful people are persecuted. But people don't want to hear that different ways of doing things also work. Keep your mind open, and one day you will be able to take advantage of a new situation while everyone else scoffs.

Day 251

Life really is a matter of developing the right perspective. The right perspective—which is another way of saying the right attitude—will help us deal with rejection, criticism and a host of bad breaks.

Once there was a disciple of a Greek philosopher who was commanded by his Master for three years to give money to everyone who insulted him. When this period of trial was over, the Master said to him: Now you can go to Athens and learn wisdom. When the disciple was entering Athens he met a certain wise man who sat at the gate insulting everybody who came and went. He also insulted the disciple who immediately burst out laughing. Why do you laugh when I insult you? said the wise man. Because, said the disciple, for three years I have been paying for this kind of thing and now you give it to me for nothing. Enter the city, said the wise man, it is all yours.

Day 252

G. K. Chesterton tells the story of a young boy who was granted his choice of two wishes, to be huge, or tiny. As any small boy would choose, he chose huge. He was swayed by the appeal of being big and strong, and for the first couple of hours of his giant status he thoroughly enjoyed the sense of power.

After a while, though, the boy became bored. Because of his size, he was able to walk around the world in only a few steps, and he scaled the highest mountain ranges in one step. Like a child one half hour after the Christmas presents have been opened, he asked, "What is there to do now?"

"The young boy learned the lesson the hard way. Only "tiny" people can celebrate and enjoy life. They have nothing to prove, no score to settle, no one to impress. To tiny people, even the single flower growing from the side of a rocky hillside is an object of curiosity, beauty, and pleasure. Only tiny people can be truly humble people: unpretentious, approaching life not from power—and the need to defeat or dominate—but from respect. Only they are powerless, freed to receive."

Day 253

Consider the humorous tale of an efficiency expert critiquing a performance of Franz Schubert's "Unfinished Symphony":

For considerable periods the four oboe players had nothing to do. Therefore, the number of oboe players should be reduced and their work spread over the whole orchestra, thus eliminating peaks of activity.

All twelve violins were playing identical notes. This seemed like unnecessary duplication. The staff of this section should be drastically cut. If a large volume of violin sound is really required, this could be obtained through an electronic amplifier.

Much effort was absorbed in the playing of demisemiquavers. This seems an excessive refinement, and it is recommended that all notes should be rounded up to the nearest semiquaver. If this were done, it should be possible to use trainees and lower grade operators.

No useful purpose is served by repeating with horns the passage that has already been played by the strings. If all such redundant passages were eliminated, the concert could be reduced from two hours to twenty minutes.

If Schubert had attended to these simple matters, he would probably have been able to finish his symphony long before his death.

Day 254

Once while Knute Rockne was the football coach at Notre Dame, the team was facing a critical game against a vastly superior Southern California team. So in order to give his team a psychological edge,

Rockne recruited every brawny "hulk" he could find at Notre Dame and put them in the school uniform. On the day of the game, the Southern California team ran out on to the field first and awaited the visiting Fighting Irish. Suddenly, an army of green giants began pouring out of the Notre Dame dressing room. Their numbers seemed endless, and their sizes were huge. The USC team balked. Their coach tried to remind them that Rockne could only play eleven men at a time, but the damage had already been done. USC lost, beaten by their own fear.

For Reflection

One frigid winter night a boy and his mother were struggling to stay warm in their drafty one-room shack. The mother was unable to afford a blanket to shelter her son from the extreme cold and snow which drifted in through the cracks in the wall, so instead she covered him with boards and driftwood.

As they lay there shivering, the boy wrapped his arms around her and asked her, "Mom, what do poor people do on cold nights like this, who have no boards or driftwood to put over their children?"

There is always someone you can turn to who is worse off than yourself. Keep this in mind, and your problems won't seem quite as bad as they were.

1) How do differences in personal perception create difficulties or misunderstandings among the members of your team? How could you acknowledge the validity of others' perceptions while at the same time gently persuade them toward your point of view?

2) Could a breach in your relationship with a friend or loved one be caused by simply a difference in the perception of roles? How might you initiate a conversation where you and the other party calmly express your points of view?

3) In going about your daily life, do you search for weeds or flowers? What rewards would you receive if you focused on the positive aspects of life?

PERSUASION

You can get much farther with a kind word and a gun than you can with a kind word alone. — Al Capone

Day 255

Mr. Jones sat moist-eyed over his beer in the bar, and the man next to him said, "You look troubled, my friend. What is it?"

Jones signed deeply. "I married a girl and I've had an unhappy marriage ever since. You have no idea how miserable my life is. I would never have married that girl, either, if I had not been advised to do so in the strongest terms."

"Who advised you?"

And Jones said, "The girl."

How many times we let others make decisions for us—then live to regret it. Sometimes the most important word in the world is a two-letter one—No!

Day 256

Someone tells of a large company where the president set a goal that everyone would contribute to the United Fund. So everybody in the company gave, except one man. The other employees tried their best to convince the man to give. They appealed to his philanthropic nature; they told him about the great needs in the community; they told him how important it was to be a part of the team. He still refused to give.

The president of the company finally called the man into his office and said, "Sam, it is my desire that this company be a part of the United Fund, and it is my desire that our participation be 100 percent. There are two ways we will reach that level of giving. If you give, we will meet my goal, or if you don't give, I will fire you and we will meet my goal."

"Of course, I will give," the man responded. "It's just that nobody ever explained it that way to me before."

Day 257

If we come to view ourselves as working for an external reward, we will no longer find the activity worth doing in its own right. There is an old joke that illustrates this. An elderly man, harassed by the taunts of the neighborhood children, devised a scheme. He offered to pay them a dollar each if they would return on Tuesday and yell their insults again. The children did so eagerly and received the money. Then he told them he would pay only 25 cents on Wednesday. When they returned, insulted him again and collected their quarters, he informed them that Thursday's rate would be just a penny. "Forget it," they said—and never taunted him again.

Day 258

Joseph Duveen, the famed art dealer, was frustrated because although he had some of the world's richest and most important collectors among his clients, he hadn't been able to add to his portfolio the very knowledgeable and discriminating Andrew Mellon.

In order to secure Mellon's business, Duveen put together a fabulous collection of valuable pieces of art, leased an apartment directly beneath Mellon's, and covered the walls with these masterpieces. Then, before returning to New York, Duveen offered Mellon the key to the apartment and invited him to drop in whenever he wanted to look at the pictures.

After only one visit Mellon was hooked. He came back night after night and remained for hours staring at the paintings. Finally he called Duveen, ready to cut a deal. He bought the entire collection for $12 million.

Duveen took the time he needed to create a need for Mellon, and then fill it.

Day 259

There was once a very successful fisherman: he would take his small boat out on the lake every morning, and within a few hours he would return to shore with his boat full of fish. People wondered how he did it.

One day a stranger showed up and asked the man if he could go along the next time the man went out fishing. The man agreed. So the next morning the two of them took the fisherman's boat through the early morning mist to a small cove where the fisherman stopped the boat and cut off the motor. He seemed to be very unprepared for a fishing trip: he had no rod or reel, just a small net and a rusty old tackle box.

The man pulled the tackle box over to himself, opened it, and took out a red stick of dynamite. Taking a match, he lit the fuse, held it for a moment, and heaved it into the water. There was a terrific blast, and soon he was dipping dead fish out of the water with his small net and filling up the boat. After watching this for a few moments, the stranger reached into his pocket, pulled out his wallet, flashed his game warden badge, and told the fisherman that he was under arrest.

The fisherman seemed undisturbed by this, however. He reached into the tackle box, pulled out another stick of dynamite, lit it, held it for a moment while the fuse burned down, and then handed it to the game warden. "Now," he said, "Are you just going to sit there, or are you going to fish?"

Day 260

One lesser known characteristic of Thomas Edison was his penchant for engineering dazzling public-relations stunts. In an attempt to convince the New York City council to allow its streets to be torn up for the laying of electrical cables, Edison invited the entire group out to Menlo Park at dusk. He led them up a narrow staircase in the dark, and while they were fumbling their way and grumbling about the inconvenience, he suddenly clapped his hands. A flood of lights came on, illuminating a lavishly set dining hall complete with a sumptuous feast catered by New York's premier restaurant, Delmonico's.

It never hurts to add an element of show-biz to your presentation. More presentations are crippled by boredom that by dazzle.

Day 261

Dale Galloway tells the story of a ten-year-old retarded boy who goes shopping with his sister. He bumps up against the shoe rack and knocks it over. An irate salesman who has had his fill of Christmas shoppers, grabs the boy, applied pressure and starts yelling at him to pick up every shoe, not noticing that the boy is retarded. The boy shakes his head and yells, "No, no, I'm not going to do it."

The wise older sister sizes up the situation quickly, kneels down and begins to pick up the shoes. As she smiles at him, loving him, he soon begins to respond by helping to pick up the shoes.

When the shoes are all picked up and they rise to leave, the sister looks at the clerk and says, "Mister, you got to love him into doing it."

Day 262

Advertising guru David Ogilvy once told a story about Max Hart, the men's clothing tycoon. Hart complained to his advertising manager about his latest campaign. It had too much copy. "Nobody reads that much copy," he asserted.

The ad manager held his ground. "I'll bet you ten dollars, Mr. Hart, that I can write a whole newspaper page of solid type and you will read every word of it."

That was one challenge Hart was eager to take.

"I won't have to write even a paragraph to prove my point," the ad man continued. "I'll just give you the heading:
THIS PAGE IS ALL ABOUT MAX HART."

For Reflection

One day the great sea looked up at a pure, fleecy cloud in the sky and sighed. "That is not for me. I could never be like that. But yet I will try." And she hurled herself against the rocks, leaping up in a tall spray which fell back to the earth, baffled and beaten. At last the sea lay quiet and still, and cried out to the sun: "Isn't there something you can do to help me?" The sun replied, "Yes, I can. If you will let me." Then the sun sent down a soft and gentle ray upon the quiet water. Slowly the water from the sea became a mist, and then developed into a fluffy, white cloud. What the sea could not do by leaping and dancing and battering itself against the rocks, was accomplished by yielding to the quiet warmth of the sun.

If you can't accomplish something by battering away at it, try a little gentle persuasion instead.

1) Have you been "battering away" at someone with minimal results? What other persuasive techniques might be more effective in dealing with this person?

2) In order to successfully accomplish your goals, you may have to persuade other people to "buy into" your vision. Try brainstorming some creative ways for convincing them (remember Edison).

3) Effective persuasion requires knowledge of the audience you are trying to persuade. How might you get to know your audience better?

4) "Win/win" deals are inherently persuasive. What can you do to make your next "sell" satisfying for everyone involved?

POTENTIAL

"Get up in the mornings and look in the mirror. You're your own job security."
— H. Ross Perot

Day 263

Luetta C. Milledge, Head, Department of English, Savannah State College, delivered a commencement address some years ago and began with this classic dillustration:

"I wish to speak today of eagles. May I begin by relating the parable of the eagle as told by James Aggrey of West Africa. A certain man went through a forest seeking any bird of interest he might find. He caught a young eagle, brought it home and put it among his fowls and ducks and turkeys, and gave it chicken's food to eat even though it was an eagle, the king of birds.

"Five years later, a naturalist came to see him and, after passing through his garden said: "That bird is an eagle, not a chicken.' 'Yes,' said the owner, 'but I have trained it to be a chicken. It is no longer an eagle, it is a chicken, even though it measures fifteen feet from tip to tip of its wings.'

"'No,' said the naturalist, 'it is an eagle still; it has the heart of an eagle, and I will make it soar high up to the heavens.'

"'No,' said the owner, 'it is a chicken, and it will never fly.'

"They agreed to test it. The naturalist picked up the eagle, held it up and said with great intensity: 'Eagle, Thou art an eagle; thou dost belong to the sky and not to this earth; stretch forth thy wings and fly.'

"The eagle turned this way and that, and then looking down, saw the chickens eating their food, and down he jumped.

"The owner said: 'I told you it was a chicken.'

"'No,' said the naturalist, 'it is an eagle. Give it another chance tomorrow.'

"So the next day, he took it to the top of the house and said: 'Eagle, thou art an eagle; stretch forth thy wings and fly.' But again the eagle, seeing the chickens feeding, jumped down and fed with them.

"Then the owner said: 'I told you it was a chicken.' 'No,' asserted the naturalist, 'it is an eagle, and it has the heart of an eagle; only give it one more chance, and I will make it fly tomorrow.'

"The next morning he rose early and took the eagle outside the city away from the house, to the foot of a high mountain. The sun was just rising, gilding the top of the mountain with gold, and every crag was glistening in the joy of the beautiful morning.

"He picked up the eagle and said to it: 'Eagle, thou art an eagle; thou dost belong to the sky and not to the earth; stretch forth thy wings and fly.'

"The eagle looked around and trembled as if new life were coming to it. Yet it did not fly. The naturalist then made it look straight at the sun. Suddenly it stretched out its wings and, with the screech of an eagle, it mounted higher and higher and never returned. It was an eagle, though it had been kept and tamed as a chicken.'

"My people of Africa, we have been created in the image of God, but men have made us think that we are chickens, and so we think we are: But we are eagles, stretch forth your wings and fly. Don't be content with food of chickens!!"

James Aggrey's words could be applied to all of us. Many of us have been content to feed with the chickens and have forgotten that God has called us to be eagles.

Day 264

It is said that the famous French author Balzac fancied himself to be an expert at interpreting handwriting. He believed that he could determine the character of a person simply by analyzing their script. One day an old lady brought him a little boy's homework book and asked this great writer and handwriting expert to give his opinion of the child's potential. Balzac studied the irregular, untidy script very carefully and then asked, "Are you the boy's mother?"

"No," replied the old lady.

"Perhaps you are related?" he asked.

"Not at all," she answered.

"Then I will tell you frankly," he said, "the youth is slovenly, probably stupid. He will never amount to much."

"Ha!" said the woman, "It might surprise you to know that this notebook was your own when you were a little boy at school."

Potential can only be measured by accomplishment. No other system is as accurate.

Day 265

Several years ago, when the U.S.S. Forrestal caught fire, a 120-pound computer specialist bodily picked up and heaved a 250-pound bomb overboard, because he saw that it was about to explode.

We all have potential that we never realize. Putting that potential to work is the greatest challenge in life.

William Shakespeare put it best in *Twelfth Night*:
"Be not afraid of greatness.
Some are born great,
some achieve greatness,
and some have greatness thrust upon them."

Day 266

Many years ago the manager of the New York Giants, John J. McGraw, found himself with a teenage ballplayer on his team. This young man had a great natural ability to hit, but with a completely unorthodox batting style: he lifted his front foot into the air before hitting the ball.

McGraw was an expert at helping people develop their talents, and he knew that if he tried to tinker with the boy's batting style, the boy might lose his natural swing. So instead of sending the boy back down to minor leagues where some other managers might try to tinker with his batting, McGraw kept the young man on the bench with the Giants, sending him into games here and there, in situations where his inexperience was unlikely to hurt the team.

That young man, Mel Ott, went on to become one of the great sluggers of all time, a star right fielder, and ultimately a member of the Baseball Hall of Fame. And he always lifted his right foot into the air before hitting the ball.

Day 267

Albert Einstein could not speak until he was four years old, and did not learn to read until he was seven.

Beethoven's music teacher said that, "As a composer he is hopeless."

When Thomas Edison was a young boy, his teachers said he was so stupid that he could never learn anything.

When F. W. Woolworth was 21, he got a job in a store, but was not allowed to wait on customers because he "didn't have enough sense."

Walt Disney was once fired by a newspaper editor because he was thought to have "no good ideas."

Sometimes we have to look very hard to see potential in others or ourselves. Each of us is uniquely gifted, though. We all have something to contribute to the world.

Day 268

Soren Kierkegaard once described a make-believe town where only ducks lived. It was Sunday morning in Duckville and, as was the custom, all the ducks waddled out of their houses and down the streets to the First Duckist Church. They waddled down the aisle of the church, waddled into their pews, and squatted.

Shortly afterward, the duck minister took his place in the pulpit and the church service was under way. The scripture text for the morning was taken from the duck Bible and it read:

> Ducks, God has given you
>   wings—you can fly.
> Ducks, because you have wings
>   you can fly like eagles.
> Because God has given you wings
>   no fences can confine you,
>   no land animals can trap you.

Ducks! God has given you wings! And all the ducks said, "Amen!" And they all waddled home.

Day 269

All but forgotten today, Bertoldo de Giovanni was in his own time an important sculptor. In fact, his name might have been lost from memory forever, except for the fact that he had a pupil whose name was Michelangelo.

Michelangelo was only fourteen years old when he came to Bertoldo. It was apparent to Bertoldo, however, that his young pupil was enormously gifted. Bertoldo knew that gifted people are often tempted to coast rather than to grow, and he was therefore persistent in seeking to instill a desire in Michelangelo to give himself completely to his work.

On one occasion he came into the studio and found Michelangelo toying with a piece of sculpture far beneath his abilities. Bertoldo grabbed a hammer, stomped across the room and smashed the work into tiny pieces, saying, "Michelangelo, talent is cheap; dedication is costly."

Day 270

One of the world's largest diamonds, about the size of a small lemon, was found in a famous South African mine. After the diamond was found, the manager of the mine needed to get it safely to the company's office in London, but he was concerned that someone might hear of it and try to steal it. So he hired a small team of guards, and told them that four of them would take it in a steel box to the ship that was to transport it, and that two men needed to guard it at all times while it was in the ship's safe.

The package arrived in London safely, but when it was opened at the company's office, it was found to contain an ordinary lump of coal instead of the diamond. The diamond arrived three days later by ordinary parcel post in a plain package.

Now if someone had wanted to steal the diamond, which package do you think they would have gone for? And what would have been their reward for the effort? The owner had assumed correctly that most people would not pay attention to an ordinary cardboard box.

Are you overlooking untapped potential in the people around you?

Day 271

According to the UCLA Brain Research Institute, the potential of the human brain to create, store, and learn may be virtually unlimited. The prominent Soviet scholar, Ivan Yefremov, has told the Soviet people: "Throughout our lives we use only a fraction of our thinking ability. We could, without any difficulty whatever, learn forty languages, memorize a set of encyclopedias from A to Z, and complete the required courses of dozens of colleges." If this is true (and it is), why don't most people learn more and accomplish more in their lifetime?

Maybe the answer is to be found in something Andrew Carnegie once said, " The average person puts 25 percent of his energy and ability into his work. The world takes its hat off to those who put in more than 50 percent of their capacity, and stands on its head for the few and far between souls who devote 100 percent."

For Reflection

On the trip home from the Nobel ceremonies in Stockholm, prize-winning physicist Richard Feynman stopped in Queens, N.Y. and looked up his high-school records. "My grades were not as good as I remembered," he said, "and my I.Q. was 124, considered just above average."

"He was delighted," reported his wife, Gweneth. "He said to win a Nobel Prize was no big deal. But to win it with an I.Q. of 124–that was something."

1) Have you allowed other peoples' assessments of your potential to limit you? Look at your life honestly. In what areas of your life have people misjudged or underestimated your abilities?

2) Take some time to list your strengths and gifts. Look at this list when you need a confidence-booster.

3) How would your treatment of others change if you thought of every person as having unlimited, untapped potential?

4) What are some concrete ways you could encourage those around you to discover and live up to their personal potential?

PREPARATION

When Daniel Webster was asked to make a speech on some question at the close of a congressional session, he replied: "I never allow myself to speak on any subject until I have made it my own. I haven't time to do that in this case, hence, I must refuse to speak on the subject."

Day 272

In 1976, Indiana University's basketball team won the NCAA National Championship, led by the controversial Bobby Knight. A short time later, Coach Knight was interviewed on the television show "60 Minutes." The commentator asked him, "Why is it, Bobby, that your basketball teams at Indiana are always so successful? Is it the will to succeed?"

"The will to succeed is important," replied Bobby Knight, "but I'll tell you what's more important—it's the will to prepare. It's the will to go out there every day, training and building those muscles and sharpening those skills!"

Whether we are talking about sports, or education or science or business or any worthwhile endeavor in life, success goes to the person who has the will to prepare.

Day 273

A Pennsylvania executive once took his family on vacation. He had booked reservations in a hotel for them long in advance, sight unseen, to be sure of having a room. After a long day of sightseeing, the family arrived at the hotel late at night and went straight to bed.

Waking up in the hotel on the morning after their arrival, they heard several loud thuds and heavy crashes very close to them which seemed to be getting closer. Curious, and a little concerned, they went out into the hall and looked out a window. They saw that the noise they were hearing was caused by a wrecking ball smashing into their building! Their hotel was being torn down around them.

Obviously, this is not likely to happen to you (although I've stayed at a couple of hotels of a well-known national chain that should have been demolished). It might serve as a reminder, though, to make sure that your appointment calendar is up to date. Try to confirm reservations and meetings if they were set some time ago. While this may seem somewhat troublesome now, it can save you a lot of hassle later.

Day 274

Motivational speaker Billy Zeoli defines being ready as "the right person in the right place at the right time with the right thing to do and to say, and doing it and saying it." In one playoff game with the Dallas Cowboys at San Francisco, the Cowboys were trailing by 15 or 16 points going into the last two minutes. Cowboys coach Tom Landry turned to a young quarterback not too long out of the Navy named Roger Staubach. Staubach was not yet Dallas' starting quarterback.

In a critical situation with Dallas trailing in a playoff game, Landry turned to Roger Staubach and said simply, "Roger, go in." Many people might have questioned a move like that. Anyone who knew Landry would not imagine that he was throwing in the towel this soon. Still he said, "Roger, Go in." And Staubach replied, "I'm ready." And he was. In the next one minute and 57 seconds, Staubach led Dallas to two touchdowns and a field goal. Dallas won the playoff game because this young man fresh out of the Navy was ready.

Are you ready?

For Reflection

One spring not too long ago, a 42-year-old Ohio secretary found herself running a marathon, thinking that she had entered a much shorter race. The two races were to begin minutes apart from one another, and when the woman saw a crowd of runners all lined up for the start, she simply joined them and started running.

She finished the marathon, but her tears and swollen knees will remind her to do more checking before she sets out the next time to run a race.

1) Are you trying to run the race without planning for it? How has poor preparation in your past interfered with your potential for success?

2) What could you do on a daily, ongoing basis to keep yourself mentally, emotionally and physically prepared for life's events? Exercise? Pray or meditate? Read outside your field?

3) How might advance preparation help you better cope with an upcoming event you dread?

4) What could you do to help those with whom you work be prepared for personal growth and advancement?

PRIORITIES

One should want only one thing and want it constantly. Then one is sure of getting it. But I desire everything and consequently get nothing. Each time I discover, and too late, that one thing had come to me while I was running after another. — Andre Gide

Day 275

While he was president of Bethlehem Steel, Charles Schwab granted an interview with a management consultant named Ivy Lee. Lee told Schwab that his consulting firm could help Schwab's company become more efficient.

Schwab said, "If you can do that, I'll be glad to listen to your suggestions. And if they work, I will pay you whatever you ask within reason."

Lee said, "All right, I will give you a method right now that will increase your efficiency by 50 percent." He handed Schwab a sheet of paper and told him to list the most important things he had to do the next day. "Now number them in the order of their true importance," and he waited while Schwab did so. "Now, tomorrow morning," Lee continued, "you begin with number 1 on your list. After it is taken care of completely, move on to number 2 and complete it. Don't worry if you don't get all the way through the list. At least you will have completed the most important tasks. Do this every working day. After you have convinced yourself of this system, have your employees try it. Try it as long as you like, and then send me your check for whatever you think the idea is worth."

A few weeks later Charles Schwab sent Ivy Lee a check for $25,000.

Day 276

When Alexander the Great's soldiers took over the Persian Empire, they took for themselves anything they could find of value. At one point, they stormed the palace of King Darius. One soldier snatched up the bag containing the crown jewels of Persia, and, not realizing what they were, he dumped the jewels on the ground and kept the bag that had held them. He then ran around showing off the fancy new food bag that he had been clever enough to find.

We find value where we are trained to find it. The soldier spent much of his time wondering where his next meal would come from as the army tramped through strange lands. He had probably never even seen a jewel before. Therefore he saw what he wanted: something in which to store food.

Day 277

There is an ancient Scottish legend that tells the story of a shepherd boy tending a few sheep on the side of the mountain. One day as he cared for his sheep he saw a beautiful flower at his feet—one that was more beautiful than any he had ever seen in his life. He knelt down, scooped up the flower and held it close to his eyes, drinking in its beauty. As he held the flower close to his face, he suddenly heard a noise and looked up. There in front of him he saw the great stone mountain was opening itself to him. When the sun's rays pierced the interior of the mountain, he saw the sparkling of beautiful gems and precious metals.

With the flower forgotten in his hands, he walked inside. Laying it down, he began to gather all the gold and silver and precious gems in his arms. Finally, with all that his arms could carry, he turned and began to walk out of that great cavern. But suddenly a voice came from the cavern's depths and said to him, "Don't forget the best."

Thinking that he had perhaps overlooked some choice piece of treasure, he turned around again and picked up additional pieces of priceless jewelry. And with this arms literally overflowing with wealth, he turned to walk back out of the great mountainous vault. And again the voice said, "Don't forget the best."

But his arms were too full to take any more, so he walked outside. Instantly, all the precious metals and stones turned to dust. He looked around just in time to see the great stone mountain closing its doors again. For a third time he heard the voice, and this time it said, "You forgot the best. For the beautiful flower is the key to the vault of the mountain."

Too many people throw away the key when they get inside the door.

Day 278

A family gathered together on the boardwalk. They whispered and giggled together as they eagerly awaited the explosive event of Old Faithful's eruption. They were ready and waiting, the first ones to claim a spot for good viewing. Laughter and excitement filled the air.

As they began to feel the first sprays of moisture, the family became euphoric. Leaping to their feet, they all bunched together and turned to face the father of the family. For the next ten minutes, they smiled, giggled, and laughed as the father peered through the view finder of each camera in turn to take pictures of them, to capture the highlight of their first trip to Yellowstone on film.

By the time the picture taking was over, however, so was Old Faithful's appearance. They were ready, but when the moment came to witness the spectacle, the whole family had turned and looked in the wrong direction!

That can happen. We can be so engrossed in the peripherals that we miss what is really important.

Day 279

When Joseph Haydn worked for years as a composer for Prince Paul in Germany, the Prince's advisors constantly told him that the money could better be spent on fortifications and arms—what good was music? However, Prince Paul has long been forgotten, and his advisors are even more obscure. Germany has had many wars since those days. But the music of Joseph Haydn will live on for quite some time.

It's like one of Charles Schultz's *Peanuts* comic strips, Schroeder is playing the piano and announces to Lucy that he is learning all of Beethoven's sonatas. Lucy, leaning on the piano, says, "If you learn to play them all, what will you win?" Schroeder is upset and says, "I won't win anything." Lucy walks away and says, "What's the use of learning the sonatas if you don't win a prize?"

Some people have no feeling for that which lasts forever—only for that which gratifies for a moment.

Day 280

One of the most unusual stories to emerge from the famous 1889 Johnstown Flood involved two young women. Jennie Paulson and her friend Elizabeth Bryan were fashionably dressed and sitting in a train, waiting for it to take them to Philadelphia for the weekend. When the news came that the South Fork Dam had broken, the two girls were told to head for the hillside. They got off the train and had made it to safety when they turned back to get Jennie's overshoes, because her new shoes were getting wet and muddy. Both girls died.

Mis-placed priorities are always costly.

Day 281

A great line appeared recently in *The Jokesmith*: "It is a beautiful summer in corporate America. The sales people aren't back from lunch yet. The programmers are playing *Doom*. The executives are on the golf links. The secretaries are scheduling their weekends. And the Human Resources people are in another all day meeting, asking each other, 'What is our Mission?'"

Ooh, that shoe fits so tightly that it pinches. All kidding aside, we need to keep our primary mission in mind at all times.

A salesman always kept his hat on while working at his office desk. When kidded about it, he shot back, "That's to remind me I have no business being here."

Day 282

A number of years ago a story appeared in the newspapers about a young man who picked up a beautiful rock from a North Carolina stream bed and used it as his cabin's doorstop. Several years after he had picked up the rock a geologist was hiking in the area, and stopped at the cabin to ask for a glass of cold water. He saw the doorstop and immediately recognized it as a huge lump of gold. In fact, it proved to be the largest gold nugget ever found east of the Rocky Mountains.

Don't become so busy with "other things" that you miss the lump of gold that you are using for a doorstop. Take the time every now and then to examine your resources for hidden value.

Day 283

Not long ago a college professor in California assigned his freshman English class a 1,000 word essay on why they had come to college. He told his students to be honest—he wasn't going to mail them back to their parents.

Most of the essays declared they were going to college to be able to purchase a BMW, a fancy condo, to get big salaries; and in general they desired a fast track to an easy life with status and security.

However, there were two papers that reflected a different set of priorities for their education and eventual careers. These two students said they "wanted to make a difference in the world." They wanted to do something to improve the quality of life—especially among those who were oppressed and poor. Neither of the two students were from the United States. One was from Lebanon and the other was from Angola.

Big salaries are fine as far as they go, but the people who are the most remembered are those people who try to make a difference.

Day 284

Eastern Airlines Flight 401 was bound from New York to Miami with a heavy load of holiday passengers. As the plane approached the Miami airport for its landing, a light designed to indicate proper deployment of the landing gear failed to come on. The plane was forced to fly in a large, looping circle over the swamps of the Everglades while the cockpit crew checked to see if the gear actually had not deployed, or if the bulb in the signal light was merely defective.

When the flight engineer attempted to remove the light bulb, it wouldn't budge, so the other members of the crew tried to help him. As they struggled with the bulb, no one noticed that the aircraft was losing altitude. It subsequently flew right into the swamp, and dozens of people were killed in the crash.

While an experienced crew of high-priced pilots fiddled with a seventy-five-cent light bulb, the plane and its passengers flew right into the ground.

Attention to detail is important, but don't lose sight of your ultimate goal, or the details will overwhelm you.

Day 285

Bruce Larsen tells of an interesting discovery one of his sons made while crossing the Sahara Desert. The son found that there were two kinds of travelers making the trek: those who were intent on getting across the desert at any cost, and those who were more concerned with saving their vehicles.

He ran into two Swiss students whose Land Rover developed some small but potentially serious problem, and they started back to Switzerland immediately. He tells of traveling part of the time with a group of Germans who abandoned their fairly new Peugeot car in the desert and continued on their way, hitchhiking a ride on a truck. The most important thing to them was getting across the desert. The vehicle was just a means for getting there.

Of course, there is something to admire in both mind-sets. Those people who headed back were certainly doing the prudent, responsible thing. The real difference is in terms of goals. Is the goal to preserve the vehicle, or to cross the desert?

For Reflection

President Calvin Coolidge once said that people often accused him of harping on the obvious. Yet, he said, if we would all do the few simple things that we know we ought to do every day, most of our big problems would take care of themselves.

1) What are your true priorities in life? What actions taken now will give you the greatest sense of peace and happiness in your old age?

2) Are you spending more time on your true priorities or on other people's priorities? What percentage of your time are you spending on the important things in life? How might you re-schedule your life so that more of your time is spent on your true priorities?

3) In what ways do your personal priorities and your work priorities overlap? In what ways do they conflict? What might you do to bring your work and personal priorities in line with your mission in life?

4) What could you do to better communicate your company's or team's priorities in a way that all involved could understand?

PURPOSE

More men fail through lack of purpose than through lack of talent. — Billy Sunday

Day 286

Thomas S. Haggai tells about an old man who, year after year, had a line waiting for him to shine shoes at the Peabody Hotel in Memphis. When asked how he could shine shoe after shoe with such vigor and determination, he smiled with a warm, wide grin and said simply, "I'm not just shining your shoes, I'm working to make you proud of how you look."

There's a man with a mission. No wonder people are lined up at his stand.

Day 287

Once a man jumped into the river to drown himself. A friend saw him jump and immediately jumped in to save him. It so happened that the man who wanted to drown himself was an expert swimmer, but the man who was trying to save him could not swim at all. Though the first man wanted to die, he did not want to see his friend drown. So he set out to save the man who had jumped in to help him. In saving his friend, life took on new meaning for him—so much so that he decided he wanted to live.

Having a reason for living helps us do more than carry on—it helps us be victorious.

Day 288

One summer a group of college students was hired to work for a power company digging ditches. Mostly, their job consisted of digging a trench between a street and a home, laying a pipe, and then refilling the trench. And although it was hard work, they didn't mind it, for the pay was good and they were improving houses in the process.

Then one day the foreman told them to dig a number of holes in a certain yard, and when they were finished he told them to fill them up again. Then he told them to start digging holes again, and to fill them up again. And again. Well, it wasn't long before they got tired of this random hole-digging. They were used to digging holes, but what they were doing now didn't make any sense. They decided that they had enough, and they refused to lift another spadeful of dirt until the foreman gave them an explanation. It turned out that their digging was not purposeless after all: they were looking for an old gas line. After it was explained to them they were able to continue with the work, because once they realized that there was purpose in it, they had no problem doing it.

Everyone needs a purpose for doing something. Action without purpose is maddening. In leading others, be sure to make them aware of your goals.

For Reflection

Robert Schuller once asked Coretta Scott King where she got the dream that kept her going. She told him, "It was while I was attending Antioch College. . . I heard (a) quotation that deeply motivated me. Horace Mann said to his first graduating class at Antioch in the late 1850s, 'Be ashamed to die until you've won some victory for humanity.'"

1) What do you believe to be the grand purpose of your life?

2) Which "victory for humanity" are you uniquely suited to achieve?

3) What could you do to hone your strengths in preparation for achieving your purpose?

4) How might you utilize the talents of other people in achieving your purpose while simultaneously assisting them in their personal growth?

RISK

What is more mortifying than to feel you've missed the plum for want of courage to shake the tree? — Logan Pearsall Smith

Day 289

Barbara Wiedner is the mother of ten and the grandmother of twenty-three. Until 1981, she claims to have been so busy with her own personal life that she barely even knew who was president. But one day it suddenly struck her that if she didn't get involved in stopping the nuclear arms race, her wonderful grandchildren would never reach adulthood.

Barbara moved into action. She called a group of a dozen or so other grandmothers she knew to a meeting in her living room and asked them to help her do something. They founded Grandmothers for Peace, which now has hundreds of international members including Raisa Gorbachev who is a grandmother. Barbara now travels all over the world to talk about peace, and she has grandmas all over the world working for peace.

Instead of sitting around waiting for the government to act, one woman has chosen to act out of love with the courage of her convictions, and the world is a better place for her efforts.

Day 290

Dr. David Livingstone, author, medical missionary and explorer, spent most of his adult life living in primitive conditions in Africa during the 1800's.

While exploring in Africa, Dr. Livingstone received a letter from some friends which read, "We would like to send other men to you. Have you found a good road into your area yet?"

Dr. Livingstone sent this message in reply: "If you have men who will only come if they know there is a good road, I don't want them. I want strong and courageous men who will come if there is no road at all."

There is really nothing wrong with following a previously blazed trail to success. Just remember that the trailblazers will always get there first.

In the capitol building in Iowa is a large mural depicting the brave pioneers who settled the West. Beneath the picture is this inscription: "The coward never started, and the weakling fell by the way."

Day 291

In 1912, Carl Graham Fisher proposed raising $10 million for a graveled two-lane road from New York to San Francisco through donations. Thousands of people sent money in. By 1915 the pot was sufficiently full to make a start, but there still wasn't nearly enough money to build the necessary 3,389 miles of highway.

Fisher hit on the idea of constructing what came to be called "seedling miles." Here was the strategy. He would find a section of dirt road roughly midway between two towns and pave it. The idea of building a mile of good road in the middle of nowhere may seem odd, but Fisher rightly reasoned that once people got a taste of smooth highway they would want the whole concrete feast. Soon towns all along the route were raising funds to connect themselves to that tantalizing seedling mile.

Day 292

One Western reporter interviewing Boris Yeltsin asked him what gave him the courage to stand firm and help insure the fall of communism in the former U.S.S.R. Yeltsin credited reading the story of Lech Walesa, the electrician who helped bring democracy to Poland several years ago.

Similarly, Walesa has said that he was inspired by reading accounts of the civil rights movement in this country, led by the late Dr. Martin Luther King.

Dr. King indicated that he was spurred to action when he learned of the courage of one woman, Rosa Parks, who refused to sit in the back of the bus because of her skin color.

Now is it possible that the fall of communism began with one African-American woman who refused to sit in the back of a bus?

Day 293

Hanley Paige flew planes back in the early days of aviation. Once while he was taking a test flight in India, he became very sleepy and decided to land the plane in a field and take a nap. A few minutes after he took off again, he began to hear a gnawing sound in the plane behind him. He was pretty sure he knew what had happened: a rat must have gotten on board while he was grounded, and was now chewing on something in the plane. This could be a problem, because if the rat gnawed through some of the airplane's controls, Paige's plane could crash. He nervously wracked his brain for a solution.

Suddenly he had an idea: he remembered hearing somewhere that rats can only live in low altitudes. So he began to ease the plane upward and climbed until the air became so thin that he could hardly breathe. At the point that he knew he couldn't go any higher without blacking out, he leveled off and continued to fly at that altitude. After a short while he didn't hear the rat anymore, but he didn't want to take any chances. He continued to fly at the same altitude until he neared his next stop. When he did come down, he looked in the back of the plane, and sure enough, there was a dead rat.

Taking a chance and acting on a hunch may sometimes be the best way to get out of a bad situation.

Day 294

Kenneth Wydro in his book, *Think On Your Feet*, tells about an ambitious executive who was getting a bit exasperated. He had signed up to attend the seminar so that he could learn some practical ways to be more successful in his work. Instead, he ended up in a class where the facilitator simply challenged the attendees to expand their horizons and view life from a higher plain. How practical is that!? By the end of the second day, he was ready to pack it in and chalk up the experience as an unfortunate waste of time.

But before he left, he decided to go jogging to help work out the tension. As he was trotting along a back road near his motel, he suddenly heard a deep growl right next to him that made his heart pound. There, behind a thin wire fence about three feet high, was a huge, young and hyper Doberman Pinscher with its eyes blazing and teeth bared! The dog was as tall as the fence, and could have jumped it easily. The man knew he was petrified and stood still for a moment looking around desperately for a way out.

But much to the man's surprise, the dog didn't jump the fence. It barked loudly, jumped up and down, growled, ran back and forth, but it did not jump over the skimpy fence. Suddenly the man realized that he was safe: the dog had been conditioned to stay within the boundaries of the fence. In spite of its capacity to escape its confinement, the dog stayed where it was, gnashing its teeth and running around in angry circles.

The next day, the man returned to the seminar and asked to say a few words. He told the story of the dog, and his insight as to how it was trapped. "In that moment," he reported, "I knew I was just like that dog." He had come to see that he was living behind self-imposed fences, and he hadn't even realized he was trapped.

The great salesman and motivational speaker Earl Nightingale said, "It is easier to adjust ourselves to the hardships of a poor living than it is to adjust ourselves to the hardships of making a better one."

Day 295

Years ago a party of visitors at the national mint were told by a worker in the smelting works that if you first dipped your hand in water, a ladle of molten metal might be poured over the palm of the hand without burning it. Then the worker turned to a man who was there with his wife. "Perhaps you would like to try it?" he asked.

The husband drew back sharply. "No, thanks," he said, "I'll take your word for it."

Then the workman turned to the wife, "Perhaps you would like to try it?"

"Certainly," she replied. She then pulled up her sleeve, thrust her hand into a bucket of water, and calmly held it out while the metal was poured over it.

It is very difficult to overcome prejudices, especially ones involving physical danger. But sometimes challenging a prejudice is the best way to learn.

Day 296

Hans Babblinger of Ulm, Germany, wanted to fly. He wanted to break the bond of gravity. He wanted to soar like a bird. Problem: He lived in the 16th century. There were no planes, no helicopters, no flying machines.

He was a dreamer born too soon. What he wanted was impossible.

Hans Babblinger, however, made a career out of helping people overcome the impossible. He made artificial limbs. In his day amputation was a common cure for disease and injury, so he kept busy. His task was to help the handicapped overcome circumstance.

Babblinger sought to do the same for himself. With time, he used his skills to construct a set of wings. The day soon came to try them out, and he tested his wings in the foothills of the Bavarian Alps. Good choice. Lucky choice. Up currents are common in the region. On a memorable day with friends watching and sun shining, he jumped off an embankment and soared safely down.

His heart raced. His friends applauded. And God rejoiced.

How do I know God rejoiced? Because God always rejoices when we dare to dream. In fact, we are much like God when we dream. The Master exults in newness. He delights in stretching the old. He wrote the book on making the impossible possible.

—Excerpted from the book *And the Angels Were Silent* by Max Lucado, Multnomah Books, Questar Publishing; copyright 1992 by Max Lucado.

Day 297

During World War I, Sir Winston Churchill recommended that the British, with the greatest fleet in the world at the time, sail up the Dardanelles, take Constantinople, and attempt to end the war. So on March 18, 1915, the fleet began to move up the strait towards Constantinople. The first day of the invasion went as planned, but at the end of the day the admirals decided against Churchill's recommendation, because they were unsure of the dangers that lay ahead of them. Most historians agree that if the invasion fleet had continued, the war would soon have been over.

Ten years after the aborted invasion, Admiral Roger Keys again sailed up the narrows into Constantinople. When he arrived he was heard to say, "My God, it would have been even easier than I thought! We simply couldn't have failed . . . and because we didn't try, another million lives were thrown away and the war went on for another three years."

More projects fail from lack of trying than from an inability to complete them.

William Barclay once said there are three things which cannot come back: the spent arrow, the spoken word, and the lost opportunity.

Day 298

Lee Roberson in his book, *The Man In Cell No. 1*, tells an old legend about Aaron, the fisherman, who lived on the banks of a river. Walking home one evening after a hard day's toil, he was dreaming of what he would do when he became rich. Suddenly his foot stuck against a leather pouch, filled with what seemed to him small stones. Absentmindedly he picked up the pouch and began throwing the pebbles into the water.

"When I am rich," he said to himself, "I'll have a large house." And he threw a stone. "And I'll have servants and rich food." He threw another.

This went on until only one stone was left. As Aaron held it in his hand, a ray of light caught it and made it sparkle. It was then he realized that it was a valuable gem and that he had been throwing away the real riches in his hand, while he dreamed idly of unreal riches in the future.

For Reflection

"Don't wait for your ship to come in; swim out to it."

1) Try to define the fears that keep you from taking risks: fear of failure or success? Fear of what others might think? Fear of change? Fear of physical pain? From an objective standpoint, how valid are these fears?

2) What risk or risks could you take that, if successfully achieved, would improve your quality of life?

3) Risk-taking often involves personal vulnerability and openness. In what way does your need to project a certain image interfere with your ability to take risks?

4) What could you do to help encourage others to take needed risks?

SACRIFICE

No person was ever honored for what he received. Honor has been the reward for what he gave. — Calvin Coolidge

Everyone wants to be somebody; nobody wants to grow. — Goethe

Day 299

Abraham Lincoln used to remark that he could always find any number of men who were willing to shed their last drop of blood, but he found it quite difficult to get them to shed their FIRST drop of blood.

Albert Schweitzer once spoke to a graduating class in an English boys' school back in 1935. He said, "I do not know what your destiny will be. Some of you will perhaps occupy remarkable positions. Perhaps some of you will become famous by your pens, or as artists. But I know one thing: the only ones among you who will be really happy are those who have sought and found how to serve."

Day 300

Tolstoy once told a story of a Czar and Czarina who wished to honor the members of their court with a banquet. They sent out invitations and requested that the guests come with the invitations in their hands. When the guests arrived at the banquet, though, the guards did not look at their invitations at all, but they examined their hands. The guests wondered about this, but they were also curious to see who the Czar and Czarina would choose as the guest of honor to sit between them at the banquet. Imagine their shock when they found that it was the old scrub woman who had cleaned the palace for years. The guards, having examined her hands, declared, "You have the proper credentials to be the guest of honor. We can see your love and loyalty in your hands."

Wealth and power are not the true ingredients for earning respect, although many people think that they are, and they can substitute for a while. What earns true respect is hard work and loyalty.

Day 301

Author Robert Fulghum tells about an international chess competition many years ago in which a man named Frank Marshall made what is often called the most beautiful move ever made on a chessboard. Playing against an equally skilled Russian master, and Marshall sacrificed his queen—an unthinkable move, to be made only in the most desperate of circumstances. But it turned out to be a brilliant move—so brilliant that the Russian conceded the game.

When spectators recovered from the shock of Marshall's unusual tactic, they showered the chessboard with money. Marshall had achieved victory in a rare and daring fashion—he had won by sacrificing the queen.

Sometimes we must sacrifice something that is important to achieve a goal that is even more important. Don't get so attached to something that you will be unable to give it up when the moment comes.

For Reflection

The Athenian orator Demosthenes had difficulties in disciplining himself to tend to his studies instead of going out on the town. His solution was to shave one side of his head, leaving the hair long on the other; he looked so ridiculous that he was ashamed to be seen in public.

Demosthenes knew how to make a sacrifice in order to tap his potential.

1) How have the past sacrifices you have made or endured led to growth and reward?

2) How would your style of leadership change if service to others became your top priority? What benefits would you receive from this service mindset?

3) The ability to delay immediate gratification is essential to success in life. What might you sacrifice today in order to achieve a better tomorrow?

SELF-CENTERED

"All the world's a stage—but nobody wants to be a stagehand."

Day 302

A sailor was leaning on the deck rail when a shipmate stuck his head up through a nearby hatch. "The ship is sinking!" his friend cried. The sailor shrugged. "So what? It's not my ship."
I'm certain that he learned very quickly that it was indeed his ship. We are all in this together. If the world goes up in flames, so do we. Many people don't give their best, because they don't feel that they are working for their own benefit. They don't care that the ship is sinking under them.
A gravestone in an English cemetery carries this epitaph:
Here lies a fellow who lived for himself
And cared for nothing but gathering pelf.
Now where he is or how he fares,
Nobody knows and nobody cares!

Day 303

Recently a billboard was rented in downtown Hollywood where thousands of cars pass it each day. The only thing on the billboard was a painting of a relatively unknown young woman named Angelyne.
And why was Angelyne on this billboard? It's because she wants to be famous. As one interviewer noted, she is "untalented by her own admission." She really doesn't do anything, she just wants people to notice her. "I'm the first person in the history of this town to become famous for doing nothing," she says. "I can feel myself getting more and more famous every day."
Few people ever become known for doing nothing, as Angelyne herself noted.
Margaret Mitchell, the author of *Gone With the Wind*, is said to have personified many of the characteristics which she ascribed to Scarlett O'Hara. Namely, she was a neurotic and immature egotist. One biographer wrote that Margaret Mitchell could never endure a

conversation of which she was not the subject. Perhaps that is why she never produced another novel. When you are totally absorbed in yourself, you do not grow.

Day 304

The August 12, 1991, issue of *Time* magazine carried a story on the phenomenon of special interest groups and nuisance litigation. It included an interview that Peter Hart had with several teenagers. He asked, "What is it that makes America special?" There was silence for a long time, and then someone suggested, "Cable television." When they were asked, "How can we energize more young people to vote?" the answer was "Pay them."

Am I missing something here? Is this the best that our young can do? Have we really become so cynical and so self-serving that we might have to think in terms of paying people to vote? Maybe it's time for a new emphasis on values in our society.

Day 305

Author Stephen Covey writes about the time he was a faculty member at the Marriott School of Management. A student in one of his classes once approached him to find out how he was doing. They talked for a while, and then Covey confronted the student directly: "You didn't really come here to find out how you are doing in class," he said. "You came in to find out how I think you are doing. You know how you are doing in the class far better than I do, don't you?"

The student admitted that he did indeed know how he was doing in class: he was just trying to get by. Then he gave a host of reasons and excuses for why he was cramming and taking short cuts. He had come in to see if it was working. Covey, reflecting on this incident, writes, "If people play roles and pretend long enough, giving in to their vanity and pride, they will gradually deceive themselves."

Day 306

Bob Zuppke, a famous football coach, once asked the question "What makes a man fight?" He answered his own question by saying: "Two forces are at war in every fighter, the ego and the goal. An over-dose of self-love, coddling of the ego, makes bums of men who ought to be champions. Forgetfulness of self, complete absorption in the goal, often makes champions out of bums."

For Reflection

USA Today once printed a list of demands made to prospective employers by people looking for jobs. Here are a few from the files of a professional employment counselor:
A three week paid vacation before starting work.
A paid membership to the city zoo.
Elvis' birthday off.
Medical benefits for faith healer visits.
Italian and Chinese restaurants close to the office.
Extra pay for time thinking about work on nights and weekends.
And finally, a promise from the mail room to collect all foreign stamps for the stamp collection of the potential employee's child.

1) Many people are trapped by unrealistic expectations because they believe they "deserve" certain things in life. They become disappointed when they don't get what they "deserve." What exactly does the world "owe" mean to you? How has your perception of what the world owes you interfered with your personal happiness in the past?

2) How are the negative effects of selfishness made apparent in our world today?

3) What are you doing to model selflessness for the benefit of others? What else could you do?

4) What steps could you take to promote a more sharing, self-giving atmosphere at your place of work?

SKILL

Never try to teach a pig to sing. It just wastes your time and annoys the pig.

Day 307

The great violinist Niccolo Paginini willed his violin to the city of his birth, Genoa, Italy, on the condition that the violin never again be played. However, in the absence of use and handling, the wood in the instrument began to decay, and it became worthless. Whereas a violin that is constantly used can be preserved for hundreds of years, and in some cases even grow richer in tone, Paginini's wish had resulted in the crumbling of his precious violin in its case.

Thus it is with any of our skills and abilities. They tend to crumble and decay when they are not used.

Day 308

Do people get fired for lack of skill or a bad attitude? Add it up: A recent survey indicates that the most common reason for being fired is incompetence—37 percent. Incompatibility, the inability to get along with others, came in second—17 percent. Then came dishonesty—12 percent; negative attitudes—10 percent; lack of motivation—7 percent; failure to follow instructions—7 percent; and other—8 percent.

Day 309

There is a popular story about a group of animals who decided that they needed to expand their abilities. So they set up a curriculum for themselves that required everyone to master each of the activities of running, hopping, jumping, swimming, and flying. The experiment, however, was a disaster. A rabbit, an expert in hopping, spent so much time in his weak areas—swimming, climbing, and flying—that he nearly forgot how to hop. The eagle, who was a superb flier, got waterlogged and nearly drowned in swimming class. The squirrel, a superior climber, only thought he could master flying, much to his chagrin and discomfort. The turtle, an excellent swimmer, was a miserable failure in the jumping contest. The duck looked absurd trying to climb a tree. Soon it was evident that it was far more profitable for them to make use of the gifts they did have, rather than to seek gifts that they could not have.

Make use of your own gifts. Find what they are, apply them, and specialize in them. To do otherwise is a waste of both your time and your talent.

Day 310

In John Sanford's book, *The Kingdom Within*, he recounts the story of a well that his family once used. The Sanfords spent every summer at a farm house where all of their water was supplied by a well. However, they stopped using it when community water pipes were put in. A few years after the new water system was installed, someone tried to get water from the old well, but it was bone dry. This was strange, because the well had always had an abundant flow of water in the past. What they discovered was that hundreds of tiny streams had flowed into the well and kept the water supply steady: each time the well was used, water was sucked through the tiny streams. But when no one used the well, no water was brought into the streams, and they dried up. It had become useless simply because no one had been using it.

That well is a lot like a skill. When we don't use our skills, we forget how to use them: our brain dries up and no longer carries the information. Use your skills, or they will not be there when you need them.

For Reflection

Shelley Winters was asked to try out for a part in a Robert De Niro movie. When she arrived at the audition, she pulled an Oscar out of her purse and put it on the table. She opened her purse again and put a second Oscar on the table. "Some people think I can act," purred Ms. Winters. "Do I still have to audition?"

She got the part.

1) What are some things you could do each week to improve your skills?

2) Are there skills you could acquire which would make you more competitive in today's job market?

3) Which of your skills might you share to improve other people's lives?

4) What opportunities could you offer to your employees or team members in order to help them hone their skills?

SUCCESS

Success is to be measured not by wealth, power, or fame, but by the ratio between what a man is and what he might be.
— H. G. Wells

Don't confuse fame with success. Madonna is one; Helen Keller is the other.
— Erma Bombeck

Day 311

After serving 22 months in prison and paying over a billion dollars in fines for securities law violations, junk bond king Michael Milken was set to become a free man. On March 2, 1993, Milken, feeling as though he had survived the worst, was released from prison to start his life over again.

But on that very afternoon, he learned he had prostate cancer, a disease which afflicts an estimated 165,000 American men a year, resulting in 35,000 deaths.

For a 46-year-old man used to controlling his fate, Milken was devastated by the diagnosis. Still, true to his nature, he refused to let it defeat him. He became determined to find and finance a cure. In a matter of days after the diagnosis, he had contacted physicians all over the country. Within weeks he had met with leading researchers, and within two months he had created a foundation, Cap Cure (The Association for the Cure of Cancer of the Prostate), to which the Milken family's foundation has pledged $5 million for each of the next five years. The foundation has already financed 30 programs at 24 academic centers.

Day 312

There is a comic strip starring Scrooge McDuck, who is the richest duck in the world. In one story, the wind catches Scrooge's money and distributes it evenly among the population. And what do the newly rich do? Take a vacation, of course. Meanwhile Scrooge sets up a farm. In the end, everybody lines up to buy ears of corn from him, because they couldn't be bothered to work at such a menial task as growing food while rich. Spreading the wealth failed, and Scrooge is the richest duck around again.

What Carl Barks, the creator of Uncle Scrooge, seems to be saying is that Uncle Scrooge attracts wealth by his very nature. Even if his circumstances change, he will still end up at the top financially because of who he is, the things he values, and the work he is willing to do to obtain his goals.

Day 313

In 1963, at age twenty-four, CB Vaughan set a downhill skiing world record by speeding down a mountain in Portillo, Chile, at 106 miles per hour. But the next year, he did not even make the Olympic ski team. For the fastest downhill racer in the world, that was a major defeat.

CB planned his comeback, though, and it wasn't in downhill racing. Although he spent the next four years on the pro racing circuit in Europe, and worked for AMF Sports for a short while, CB's comeback actually began when he decided to create his own ski wear company.

In 1969, he read a book on pattern making, drew some ski pant designs, and approached contractors about making high-performance warm-up pants for skiers.

"They looked at me like I was really bizarre," says Vaughan.

Unable to work out a satisfactory contract with any of the established companies, Vaughan decided to begin manufacturing himself. He invested $5,000 in supplies, hired three part-time seamstresses in Bennington, Vermont, and began cutting and stitching. He knocked on the doors of ski shops and sports stores throughout New England and sold out of the trunk of his car. Gross sales in the first year were $67,000. In '70, he got $50,000 from a banker and introduced three new garments—a knitted ski hat, a racing shell jacket, and a ski parka.

CB Sports was on its way.

Today, CB Sports is a $40-million sports apparel company. Headquartered on a twenty-five-acre site in Glens Falls, New York, CB Sports also has manufacturing facilities in Bennington, Vermont; North Adams, Massachusetts; and Salem, New York, employing approximately 465 people.

Over the years, CB Sports has encountered all the problems of a rapidly growing company—under-capitalization, problems of meeting demand, headaches of constantly introducing new products while keeping up inventory. But the guiding principle of CB's career has become the guiding principle of his company: always come back. That attitude is infectious. When you're dealing with CB Sports, every problem is solvable, every demand can be met—nothing is too difficult!

Day 314

Bob W. Ireland crossed the finish line for the New York City marathon on Thursday, November 6, 1986, as 19,413th and final finisher—and as the first person to run a marathon with his arms instead of his legs. He had lost his legs in Vietnam seventeen years before. He recorded the slowest time in the marathon's history: 4 days, 2 hours, 48 minutes, 17 seconds. When asked why he ran the race, he gave these three reasons: to show he was a born-again Christian, to test his conditioning, and to promote physical fitness for others. He said, "Success is not based on where you start, it's where you finish, and I finished."

Olympic champion Jesse Owens once put it like this: "There is something that can happen to every athlete, every human being —it's the instinct to slack off, to give in to the pain, to give less than your best . . . the instinct to hope to win through luck or your opponents not doing their best, instead of going to the limit and past your limit, where victory is always to be found. Defeating those negative instincts that are out to defeat us is the difference between winning and losing, and we face that battle every day of our lives."

Day 315

A schoolmaster in France was once very discouraged with one of his students, and wrote of him: "He is the smallest, the meekest, the most unpromising boy in my class." Half a century later, an election was held in France to select the greatest Frenchman. By popular vote, that smallest, meekest, most unpromising boy was chosen. His name was Louis Pasteur, the founder of modern medicine. At the age of seventy-three, a national holiday was declared in his honor. Being too old and weak to attend the ceremony in Paris, he sent a message to be read by his son. It said: "The future belongs not to the conquerors, but to the saviors of the world."

Size and disposition are not requisites for being successful or unsuccessful. Success comes from confidence and a willingness to work for what you believe in.

Day 316

It would have been difficult to have been a plain man amidst all the finery and glamour of Louis XIV's court, but such was the case with poor prince Eugene. In fact, he was not only plain, but even ugly—and pale, and sickly, and he had a hunched back. He was ignored by everyone in the castle.

One day Eugene decided that he wanted to be a soldier, so he went to King Louis and asked for a commission in his army. Louis refused even to look at him.

A short time later Eugene sneaked out of the palace dressed as a woman and ran away to Vienna where the Turks were invading Europe. There he joined the Austrian army, where he turned out to be an excellent soldier. At 20 he was a commander; by 29 he had become Field Marshall; and at 40 he was appointed the Commander in Chief of all of Austria. He was a thorn in the side of Louis XIV for many years, and he was eventually recognized by Napoleon as one of the greatest generals of all time.

Success is made by determination and effort, both of which are inner virtues. The outer virtues—beauty, height, strength—have very little impact on how far we take ourselves through life.

Day 317

Years ago, when Archbishop Rembert G. Weakland was head of the Benedictine Order, he visited a high school in Lubumbashi, Zaire. The headmaster presented him to the students with a list of all his accomplishments. He told about the archbishop's degree in piano playing from the Julliard School of Music, but this did not seem to make an impression on the students; they had no point of reference. The number of languages the Archbishop spoke meant little to them as well, since they all spoke Kiswahili, French, and perhaps another dialect at home. And they had never even heard of Columbia University. Finally, one young man raised his hand.

"But, Father Headmaster," he asked, "you have not told us yet the most important thing: how many wives does he have?"

Success can be purely relative.

Day 318

When the Gallup organization polled Americans about their most important criteria for judging personal success, here is what they found:

Good health was cited most often, being listed by 58 percent of those polled. An enjoyable job was second, listed by 49 percent. These were followed by: a happy family (45 percent), a good education (39 percent), peace of mind (34 percent), and good friends (25 percent). Such materialistic factors as unlimited money, a luxury car, and an expensive home brought up the rear.

Day 319

Charles Schwab is one of the world's largest discount brokers. He seems to have been born with an entrepreneurial spirit:

He started out as a young boy by picking up walnuts around his neighborhood, putting them into sacks, and storing them at his house until he had enough to sell. Then, at age 12, he graduated to running a small chicken operation. He had a dozen chicks by the time he was 13, and he soon developed what he calls "a fully integrated operation" by offering eggs, fryers, and chicken fertilizer.

Imagine that the next time you see an image of this very polished, articulate stock broker—a young boy peddling chicken fertilizer.

The people who are the most successful are those who have been polishing their skill for a long time by working with them very hard.

Day 320

Success is more than power, wealth and fame.

Jessica Savitch was the first woman to anchor the network news. She was very driven and ambitious. Her success in her professional life did not mirror her miserable personal life. She died young in a car accident. Savitch never had a chance to reach a calm and peaceful plateau in her lifetime, and may have had inklings of such. She once copied a quote from the biography of a famous advertising executive that apparently struck a chord within her, and was posted on her office wall: "Success itself is sort of a failure. You reach the end of the rainbow and there is no pot of gold. You get your castle in Spain and there is no plumbing."

We lay the foundation for real success through our relationships—with our friends, with our family, with our God. Without those relationships there is no success.

Day 321

In his book *It Wasn't All Velvet*, Mel Torme tells a story that ought to give us all hope.

Torme had gotten an offer to go to Sydney, Australia, to play the Tivoli Theatre. It made great sense at that moment, and he grabbed the opportunity. In his words, he "went a little bananas in Sydney." Everywhere he looked, there went the most beautiful women imaginable. He began to realize how much he had missed being single. The Aussie audiences were enthusiastic and warm and he made some great new friends.

On his supporting bill was another American, a bird-like little red-haired woman with a perpetual quaver in her voice and fluttery, a Zasu Pitts sort of comic delivery. Torme thought she was wonderful, but the Australian audiences didn't react well to her brand of humor. The managing director of the Tivoli, David Martin, was a rather cold man with zero tolerance for failure. In Torme's estimation he was cruel and rude to this poor little comedienne and the reason soon became evident: he wanted to push her into quitting so he could save a few weeks' salary. During the first week they played the theater, this delicate and delightful performer came into Torme's dressing room on several occasions, crying her eyes out over the rotten treatment she was getting from Martin.

Why doesn't he like me, Mel?" she wailed pitifully. "What have I done to deserve such meanness?"

"Absolutely nothing," Torme tried comforting her. "Don't take it personally, dear. He's just a very irascible man. Tough it out."

She shook her head forlornly. "I can't. I simply can't." She quit, to David Martin's great satisfaction, and went back to the States, her tail between her legs. A couple of years later, Irene Ryan became world-famous on "The Beverly Hillbillies." The show ran and ran, and she made money hand over fist. When it was all over, says Torme, she could have bought and sold David Martin. Once, when Torme saw her at a press party, she came over to him and smiled. That's all, she just smiled. He knew what she was thinking: sometimes there is such a thing as justice.

For Reflection

Ex-soap star Ellen Dolan (who played Margo Hughes on "As the World Turns") was invited to deliver the '93 commencement address to her alma mater; Decorah High School, in Decorah, Iowa.

"Everything I needed to know about life I learned in high school driver's ed," said Dolan, "If you follow the Smith System's five rules of defensive driving—Aim High in Steering; Get the Big Picture; Keep Your Eyes Moving, Leave Yourself an Out; and Make Sure They See You—you'll always be on the right path."

1) How do you, personally, define success? What would a successful day for you look like?

2) What aspects of your life interfere with your ability to achieve success? Poor personal habits? Procrastination? Lack of a mission? Lack of discipline? Destructive relationships? What is one step you could take today to overcome one of these barriers?

3) Are you committed to your own vision of success, or do you allow yourself to become side-tracked by others' perceptions of success? How might your attitude toward your life change if you stopped comparing yourself to others?

4) What are some ways you might help others achieve success?

TEAMWORK

Nothing we do, however virtuous, can be accomplished alone. — Reinhold Niebuhr

A doctor conducting a physical examination noticed bad bruises on the patient's shins.

"Those from playing hockey or soccer?" asked the doctor.

"Neither," replied the patient. "Bridge."

Day 322

Russell Dalby worked on an assembly line for many years. The job was very monotonous. Work was long, sometimes boring, and often tiring. What made the difference was the people that he worked with every day: they became his friends.

Russell described many after-work activities that he and his co-workers participated in—pot lucks, Christmas and Thanksgiving dinners; there were times when the co-workers celebrated a new birth, and there were times when people were sick and in the hospital. When someone came to work who had experienced a tragedy in their life, everyone would pull together for them, offering help in many forms. Russell told of his personal tragedies and the time he was embarrassed to go back to work. When he returned to work, however, he discovered that his fellow employees were there for him. There was one special co-worker named Hazel who helped him through some difficult times in his life. She encouraged him when he was ready to give up.

Now that Russell has retired, he misses his co-workers a lot. He still remembers their names and birthdays. They are a very special part of his life.

Day 323

Elmer Booze is a professional page-turner for concert pianists. His job is to follow the score that a pianist is playing and turn the pages at the proper times. He is supposed to be as unobtrusive as possible, working quickly and without obscuring the performer's vision. Booze does his job so well that he has earned a nickname as "the ghost."

A good page-turner should help make the performer successful. The page-turner doesn't share the bows, nor is he listed in the program. He has done his job well if he has enabled the pianist to perform uninterrupted, and if he himself has remained unnoticed. Elmer Booze is important for the success of the concert, but he must be content to make an anonymous contribution.

There is a lot of anonymous help involved in any project (who answers the phone? delivers the project to others? actually ships out the order?). Be sure to thank these people somewhere along the way, even if they don't get any of the acclaim.

Day 324

Former Surgeon General C. Everett Koop is a man of conviction and insight. In his memoirs he tells of his desire to attend medical school. As he prepared for his career as a doctor, there was one thing he knew for sure. He would attend medical school at Columbia University's College of Physicians and Surgeons. When he went to Columbia for his admissions interview in the fall of his senior year at Dartmouth, he felt very much at home. In his own mind it was inconceivable that he would not be admitted. His discussion with the admissions panel seemed to go well until one of them asked him, "Do you ever expect to make any major discoveries in medicine?" "It was a stupid question then; it is a stupid question now," Dr. Koop writes. He answered the question like this, "Well sir, from what little experience I have in reading about discoveries in the field of medicine, I rather think that those who make them are building upon the efforts of many who preceded them, but did not do that final thing that achieved success and fame. I would like to be the one who makes a major discovery, but I will be content to contribute to the process."

"We don't think you've got the stuff we are looking for at the College of Physicians and Surgeons!" the admission interviewers said. Dr. Koop was devastated. But he still feels that he gave a good answer.

And it was a good answer. Most discoveries these days are made by teams, not individuals. Individuals today simply don't have the resources and the broad experience necessary to succeed in today's fast-paced society. Are you a contributing member of a team, or are you trying to struggle on your own?

Day 325

Lefty Gomez was a talented baseball player. When he was inducted into the Baseball Hall of Fame, a reporter asked him what his secret was. He smiled and replied, "Two things: Clean living and a fast infield." Lefty was acknowledging that he wasn't the only person responsible for his victories. His teammates helped. Very few, if any, successes are possible through the efforts of just one person.

A brawny man stood in front of a painting by Sargent in a New York art gallery. He kept muttering to himself, "I've been given a place at last. I have a place at last." Artist Robert Henri was standing nearby, and he was mystified by the man's words. "Are you in this line of work?" he asked the man. "Oh, yes," said the man, "but this is the first time I've been displayed like this." Now Henri was really confused. "But I thought that this work was by the great painter Sargent," he said. "That's right," said the man, "but it was me that made the frame."

Many contributions are necessary for a project to be done properly. All of them are significant. And all contributors deserve gratitude for the parts they play.

Day 326

Some psychologists tell us that most of us fit into one of four styles of personality behavior. Some of us are dominant. Dominant folks like to be in control. Nobody has to ask dominant people what they think: they are blunt, direct; fast to make judgments and ready to take action.

Then there are those for whom life is a party. These are "people" people, and they are very animated. They like to talk and meet new friends. Their nature is optimistic, and they are fun to be around.

Then there are the folks who are marked by their steadiness. They like situations that are dependable and predictable. They will never be the life of the party, but they're good listeners. They make others feel comfortable.

Finally, there are the detail people. They like to do things right. They take care of the little things and are highly conscientious. Some people call them perfectionists, and some of them are, but most of them simply take pride in a job well-done.

These four personality types are all valuable and necessary for our society to function. There is a clever story that helps illustrate these four types of personality.

Four of Napoleon's officers were found guilty of betrayal, and were sentenced to die on the guillotine. Somehow, though, as the blade was ready to drop, it jammed. Napoleon took this as a sign that he should show mercy and gave the men their freedom. The reaction of the four officers to this news shows us a lot about their personalities.

The dominant soldier growled, "I told you I was innocent. This execution should never have been planned in the first place!"

The people soldier shouted, "We're free! We're free! Let's go party!"

The steady soldier consoled the executioner: "I want you to know that I don't blame you. You were just doing your job."

Meanwhile, the detail-oriented soldier had been staring thoughtfully at the jammed blade on the guillotine. "Hmmm," he said aloud, "I think I see how this thing can be fixed!"

Figure our how your own personality works, and then apply it to your ventures. Use your strong areas to your advantage, and defer some of those duties which can be accomplished better by another personality type.

Day 327

Chuck Swindoll says that when he was in the Marines, they taught the troops to make a fox hole big enough for two when preparing for combat. There's nothing quite like fighting a battle all alone. Having a friend with you gives you both extra strength and keeps you from panic in battle.

And the buddy system works in every aspect of life, not just combat. Your responsibilities will eventually overwhelm you if you try to handle them by yourself. We all need someone to lean on.

Day 328

In a little town in the Swiss Alps, there is a monument with two figures in it. One is a cultured scientist, the author of many books. The other is a poor Swiss peasant, an Alpine guide. Together they had conquered a great mountain. The scientist's name made all of the newspapers, but the monument contains both figures because the great scientist could never have made the ascent without the humble guide.

Many people have their names put in lights for their accomplishments. But we must never forget that not one of them would have accomplished what they did without the aid of the so-called little people, who, in this light, aren't really so little at all.

George MacDonald once noted that one draft horse can move two tons of weight. Two draft horses in harness, working together, can move twenty-three tons of weight.

Working by ourselves, very little can be done. But when we work together, we can perform miracles.

Day 329

During the Nazi occupation of Paris, a husky storm trooper stepped into a subway car and tripped headlong over the umbrella of a little old lady sitting next to the door. After picking himself up, he launched into a tirade of abuse against the woman, and then bolted from the car at the next station. When he was gone, the passengers burst into spontaneous applause for the little old woman. "I know it isn't much," she said, graciously accepting the compliments, "but he's the sixth one I brought down today." Everyone has a part to play if goals are to be accomplished.

John Wooden was a great basketball coach. Called the wizard of Westwood, he brought ten national basketball championships to UCLA in a span of twelve years. Two back-to-back championships are almost unheard of in the competitive sports world, but he led the Bruins to <u>seven titles in a row</u>. It took a consistent level of superior play; it took good coaching; and it took hard practice. But the key to the Bruins' success was Coach Wooden's unyielding dedication to his concept of teamwork.

Day 330

A few years ago Snoopy, the beagle in the *Peanuts* cartoon, had broken his left leg. Hundreds of concerned readers wrote letters to Snoopy or sent him sympathy cards. Snoopy himself philosophized about his plight one day while perched on top of his doghouse, looking at the huge white cast on his leg. "My body blames my foot for not being able to go places. My foot says it was my head's fault, and my head blames my eyes. My eyes say my feet are clumsy, and my right foot says not to blame him for what my left foot did . . ." Snoopy looks towards the audience and confesses, "I don't say anything because I don't want to get involved."

Animal tamer Clyde Beatty said that the moment in his act that he dreaded most was the one in which the big cats who are natural enemies—lions, tigers, and leopards—discovered that they were close together in the same small cage.

Too often more time is spent on passing blame for causing a problem than on trying to fix it. And it's often everyone involved in the blame-passing who is actually at fault. Concentrate on working together so that the problem does not come up again.

Day 331

One of the turning points in World War II was the Battle of the Bulge. Historians point out that it was really not one big battle but a multitude of smaller battles, fought out along the Allied lines. In his book, *World War II*, James Jones describes these battles like this: "No one of these little road junction stands could have had a profound effect on the German drive. But hundreds of them, impromptu little battles at nameless bridges and unknown crossroads, had an effect of slowing enormously the German impetus... These little diehard 'one-man-stands,' alone in the snow and fog without communications, would prove enormously effective out of all proportion to their size."

So it is with any effort. The pieces never look like they will accomplish the set goal, but when they are all assembled, the goal is attained quite easily.

Day 332

Many years ago, there was a king of Burma whose potter and elephant keeper were bitter rivals.

One day the royal potter came up with a plan to be rid of the man who washed the king's elephant once and for all. He convinced the king that his black elephant would be worth much more if it were white, and that he should order the keeper to scrub it until all the black was washed away.

The elephant keeper laughed when he heard this, and said that the task would be simple enough, but that first he needed a basin large enough to hold the elephant. The king naturally assigned the task to the potter. Eagerly the potter made the basin as commanded; but it shattered as soon as the elephant stepped into it. The king ordered him to try again. The potter made a stronger bowl this time, but again it broke under the enormous weight. Several more times the potter tried to make a bowl strong enough to hold the elephant, but it broke each time. Finally the king grew weary of the man's incompetence, and had him sent into exile.

Envy and hatred of another is an excellent way of bringing yourself to ruin.

Day 333

Today we consider James Watt to be the inventor of the steam engine. But that is not quite true. Peter Drucker in one of his books notes that Thomas Newcomen built the first steam engine which actually performed useful work in 1712. It pumped the water out of an English coal mine. Watt's steam engine was simply a more refined version of Newcomen's machine. The true inventor of the combustion engine, however, and with it what we call modern technology, was neither Watt nor Newcomen. It was the great Anglo-Irish chemist Robert Boyle, who did so in a "flash of genius." Unfortunately, Boyle's engine did not work very well. Boyle used the explosion of gunpowder to drive the piston, which so fouled the cylinder that it had to be taken apart and cleaned after each stroke. Boyle's idea, however, enabled first Denis Papin (who had been Boyle's assistant in building the gunpowder engine), then Newcomen, and finally Watt, to develop a working combustion engine. Boyle had the idea, and the others built on that foundation, continuing to refine it.

For Reflection

Remember, people support that which they help create... Always get the commitment of others in any undertaking. Have them take a piece of the action so it's their action as well as yours. Involvement begets commitment. Commitment begets power.

— Herb Cohen

1) What are the unique strengths of each member of your work team? How do the members' strengths compliment your strengths?

2) What past successes have you achieved through teamwork?

3) What could you do to promote the values of respect, compassion and cooperation among your team members?

4) How might you show appreciation to people who work "behind the scenes"?

VISION

Soon after the completion of Disney World, someone said, "Isn't it too bad that Walt Disney didn't live to see this?"

Mike Vance, creative director of Disney Studios, replied, "He did see it—that's why it's here."

Sight is a faculty; seeing is an art.
— George Perkins Marsh

The world stands aside to let anyone pass who knows where he is going.
—David Starr Jordan

Day 334

Conrad Hilton had a rough time during the great depression. He had acquired several luxury hotels during the boom years of the 20s, but after the crash of 1929, few people could afford to stay in them. By 1931, Hilton was nearly bankrupt, and he was so short on cash that he was borrowing money from a bellboy in order to eat.

One day that same year, when things were at their lowest, he came upon a picture of the Waldorf Hotel, with its 6 kitchens, 200 cooks, 500 waiters, 2000 rooms, and its private hospital and private railroad siding in the basement. Hilton cut that photograph out of the magazine, and wrote across it, "The Greatest of Them All."

He kept that photo of the Waldorf in his pocket and looked at it daily to remind himself of his dream. In a couple of years, when he acquired a desk again, he placed the photo under the glass top. Eighteen years later, in October 1949, Conrad Hilton bought the Waldorf.

That picture focused his mind and gave substance to his dream.

Day 335

Hockey legend Wayne Gretzky once did an interview before the second game of the Stanley Cup playoffs. His team had lost the first game of the series, and the reporter asked him if their coach had shown them their mistakes from the last game.

Gretzky told the reporter that he had not. Instead he had shown them everything they had done right in the first game. He had wanted to show them how good they were, not how bad they had been. The interview ended, and Gretzky went to lead his team to victory in that game, and in the series.

Don't dwell on your mistakes, think about your successes and try to emulate and improve them in the future.

Day 336

Many years ago, a sculptor in Florence named Agostino d' Antonio worked for months trying to sculpt a huge block of marble. But no statue came. "I can do nothing with it!" he told his friends. Others tried, but the shape of the stone was wrong and its lines were awkward. It was finally declared hopeless, and they pushed the big block of marble outside and onto a rubbish heap. For forty years it lay there, big and bulky and useless. And then came Michelangelo. He was out for a stroll when the unsightly hunk of stone caught his eye. But he could see what the others missed. He examined the mass with great admiration and inspiration, and he said, "There is a spirit in there that I must free!" And today the world is captivated by the spectacular beauty of Michelangelo's *David*.

One mark of genius is the ability to see success where others have only been able to see failure.

Day 337

A track coach once had a pole vaulter on his team who tended to be overwhelmed by the crowds. He did okay at the practice sessions, but when the meets came he didn't seem to be able to lift his body high enough to clear the bar. So one day the coach took his camera out to the field, and he snapped a picture of the man just as he slid neatly over the bar during practice. Then the coach had the photograph enlarged, and he gave it to the athlete. He told him to post it in his room where he'd see it first thing every day. Do you know why he did that? He did it so that the man would get one single picture in his mind, the picture of what he could do. The picture of what he could manage. The picture of what he had the ability to be. The coach wanted to break the crowd's image in that man's mind, and he wanted to build a new image in its place.

If you constantly think about the things that might hinder you, you'll never accomplish anything. Concentrate on doing what needs to be done, and your ability to do it.

Day 338

This statement by Dr. Carl Bates reminds me to keep away from the comfortable and attempt something greater than my ability:
There came a time in my life when I earnestly prayed, "God I want Your power!"
Time wore on and the power did not come,
One day the burden was more than I could bear.
"God, why haven't You answered that prayer?"
God seemed to whisper back His simple reply.
"With plans no bigger than yours, you don't need My power."

Day 339

The same principles apply in churches as in business: A study was done by the Northwest Friends churches not long ago concerning the growth patterns of churches. The patterns of sixty churches were documented, showing statistics for attendance, age, and average income of each. Also, questions were asked to determine the attitudes of the various leaders.

Not surprisingly, there was a correlation shown between leadership style and church growth. The leaders in growth situations were characterized as positive, confident, cheerful, and goal-oriented. They always tried to involve as many people in the congregation as possible.

The static churches, on the other hand, had leaders with little vision and little creative imagination. Vision and goal setting, the report said, were unquestionably the most important ingredients needed for growth.

Day 340

There is an old Indian legend about a father and his three sons. One day the father pointed to a high mountain many miles away and ordered the youths to climb up the mountain as far as they could and to bring back a memento of their adventure. One returned with an unusual flower. The second came back with a rare rock. The third returned and said, "I climbed to the top and I brought back a vision of the sea."

"That is the most important of all," says Leroy Brownlow. "If you have the vision, you can cultivate the flowers and quarry the rocks. In this particular case, it led them to build canoes and sail to a more fruitful and habitable island. With no vision their lives were a restricted existence."

Day 341

There is a story that is told about Alexander the Great. A friend once gave Alexander two great hunting dogs—supposedly the greatest hunting dogs in the world. Alexander was quite a sportsman so he was anxious to get out and give these two famed dogs a try. He knew of a field where there were always rabbits. "Any good dog will chase rabbits," he said to himself. He couldn't wait to see what these two great dogs would do. They got to the field. They spotted some rabbits. He ordered the dogs to be unleashed. He waited expectantly to see what the dogs would do. What a surprise he got. Those two great hunting dogs—the greatest in the world—lay down on the ground and went fast asleep. Alexander couldn't believe it. "Maybe they are simply tired from the journey from their former master's house," he thought to himself. "I'll try again tomorrow."

The next day he took them to a field where there was a good chance they would spot some deer. Sure enough, there was a beautiful buck. The dogs were unleashed. This was an exciting moment. Exciting—except to those two dogs. They gave a great yawn, lay down and went back to sleep. This infuriated Alexander. In fact, he was so angry that he had those two dogs put to death right there on the spot.

A few days later his friend came to see him. "How are those two dogs that I gave you doing?" he asked. Alexander sadly told him the whole story. The friend shook his head. "Alexander," he said, "you showed those dogs some rabbits and some deer and they went to sleep. But if you had shown them a lion or a tiger you would have seen what great dogs these were."

For Reflection

Several years ago World Vision developed a wonderful poster which said in big bold letters across the top, "How Do You Feed a Hungry World?" In the bottom right-hand corner was a tiny picture of a child and these words in small type: "One at a Time."

1) Do you clearly understand your company's vision? What part do you play in making that vision real?

2) As a part of the broader company vision, what is your perception of your team's or department's vision?

3) What visual images could you use to help motivate you to reach your goals?

4) What could you do to effectively communicate your vision to your family and/or co-workers?

WINNING

For nothing can seem foul to those that win. — Shakespeare, *Henry IV*, Part 1, Act V, Scene l.

Winning Isn't Everything. It's the only thing. — Vince Lombardi

Show me a good loser, and I'll show you a loser. — Leo Durocher

Day 342

In one of his books, Jamie Buckingham tells about a group of women who started a movement to have all competitive sports—especially football—removed from public schools. Team sports, they complained, were too traumatic. Children, they argued, should not be led to believe their team could win, then suffer the trauma of losing. They should only play games where everyone wins.

They did not stop to think that there can be no victory where there is no possibility of defeat.

As psychologist Elliot Aronson says, "From the Little League ballplayer who bursts into tears after his team loses, to the college student in the football stadium chanting, 'We're number one!'; Lyndon Johnson, whose judgment was almost certainly distorted by his oft-stated desire not to be the first American president to lose a war, to the third grader who despises his classmate for a superior performance on an arithmetic test; we manifest a staggering cultural obsession with victory."

In a team-based business environment, we must learn that cooperation is as important to success as competition.

Day 343

"Who won?" That's the first question most parents ask after a game. Yet, winning isn't always so important to the kids themselves. In fact, according to a national survey of 10,000 boys and girls by the Youth Sports Institute of Michigan State University, pressure to win is one reason they said they quit team sports as teenagers. When asked to rank the experiences in sports that made them feel successful, "my performance made me feel good" came in first. "I won" didn't even make the top half.

There's a saying of Tranxu, a great Chinese sage: "When the archer shoots for no particular prize, he has all his skills; when he shoots to win a brass buckle, he is already nervous; when he shoots for a gold prize, he goes blind, sees two targets, and is out of his mind. His skill has not changed, but the prize divides him. He cares! He thinks more of winning than of shooting, and the need to win drains him of power."

Day 344

It used to be that companies banked on competition between their employees and between their company and others. However, in recent years businesses have begun to stress teamwork and cooperation among their employees and to think "win/win" in their dealings with other businesses.

A tragic consequence of the "win at any cost" mentality occurred at the Center for Disease Control. According to Rosabeth Moss Kanter in *When Giants Learn to Dance*, research professionals, in their zeal to find a cure for AIDS, actually sabotaged each others' experiments, thereby hindering their ability to reach their crucial goal.

It looks as though the new push toward cooperation in business is a step in the right direction.

Day 345

Mark Gottlieb of Tacoma, Washington, set a record for playing the violin under water, and a couple in Des Moines sat in tubs of vanilla pudding for 24 hours, 34 minutes, and 20 seconds. A plumber named Ronnie Farmer ate one hundred hot jalapeno peppers in fifteen minutes, beating the old record of 94 in 111 minutes. Lang Martin of North Carolina holds the record for balancing golf balls vertically (he stacked up six). Arden Chapman, at Northeast Louisiana University caught the grape in his mouth thrown from the farthest distance (259 feet). The Guinness Book of World Records shows that people are obsessed with beating others.

Day 346

The crowd who attended the Amateur Athletic Union's basketball contest thought they would be home by midnight. But instead they sat there mesmerized as Harold "Bunny" Levitt dunked his 499th consecutive free throw. They finally went home when he missed his 500th. Bunny, however, wasn't finished. He continued to make 371 perfect shots until 2:30 a.m., when the janitor finally persuaded him to leave so he could lock up the building.

Later, Bunny hooked up with the Harlem Globetrotters, who offered $1,000 to any man who could beat Levitt in a contest of 100 foul shots. The money was never claimed. The best any challenger ever scored was 86; the worst performance Levitt ever turned in was 96.

You may ask, if Levitt was such an incredible foul shooter, why did he never achieve fame as either a college player or a basketball pro? The reason: Bunny stood only five feet, four inches tall.

Day 347

As a leading contender in the seventies, Martina Navratilova traveled on the women's professional tennis circuit with Olga Morzova, Chris Evert, Betty Stove, Jeanie Brinkman, Jerry Diamond, and Frankie Durr. They were friends and traveling companions, but they were also intensely competitive.

After the tour, Navratilova observed: "Being on the court with an opponent is a strange business. You're totally out for yourself, to win a match, yet you're dependent on your opponent to some degrees for the type of match it is and how well you play. You need the opponent; without her you do not exist."

Day 348

Every politician has his favorite story about do-good citizens who show up with kind words and offers to help after elections are won, not before.

Representative Dan Kuykendal, Republican of Tennessee, has the topper.

A man walked up to Kuykendal on a Memphis street after his successful campaign, slapped him on the back, pumped his hand vigorously and said sincerely:

"If I'd know'd you was going to win, I'd of voted for you."

For Reflection

A winner is always part of the solution;
    a loser is always part of the problem.
A winner always has a program or response;
    a loser always has an excuse or explanation.
A winner always says "Let me do it for you,"
    a loser always says "That is not my job."
A winner sees an answer in every problem;
    a loser sees a problem in every answer.
A winner exclaims "It may be difficult, but it is possible;"
    a loser cries "It may be possible, but it's much too difficult."
A winner makes a commitment;
    a loser makes promises.

1) What is the difference between negative competition and healthy competition? How could you promote healthy competition at your place of work?

2) In your next business negotiation, how might you create an environment where both you and the other party "win"?

3) Are you "winning battles but losing the war"? Where do your priorities fit in when it comes to winning?

4) What could you do to affirm the winning qualities in other people?

WORK

As one author has pointed out, "Work you enjoy is the best guarantee you can find for a long, happy, and healthy life."

Sign in an aerospace research and development lab:
This Is A LABORATORY... Let's Have More LABOR, Less ORATORY

Day 349

Country comedian Jerry Clower tells about two old boys in this one town who hung out together all the time. One was called Hog, and the other one was known as "The Go-Gitter." This was because when anyone asked him what he did, he would say, "I'm a go-gitter. My wife works at the McComb Manufacturing Company, and every evening at 4:30 I go gitter."

Well, there's another man in that community, too: nosiest fellow in the world. He'd get up before daylight if he thought he could find out what chicken was going to get off the roost first. One day he was coming along and he saw the vehicles of old Hog and that "Go-Gitter" at the beer joint, so he stopped. He figured he would discuss these men's occupations with them. He sat down on the stool, and he looked at the "Go-Gitter" and said, "Sir, really now, what do you do?"

He said, "I am a go-gitter. Every evening at 4:30 I go get my wife. Every morning I take her to work. I'm a go-gitter. I don't do nothing."

Sitting over there by him was old Hog, and this fellow asked him "Hog, what do you do?" He said, "I help him."

Day 350

Once upon a time there was a wild duck who was a very fine flyer. But one day while flying around he got tired. So, he decided to visit his cousins in the barnyard below and rest awhile. He discovered that the ducks in the barnyard had a relatively easy life. It was a less exciting life than his, but that seemed to him to be a decent trade-off at the time. So he began to eat and live with the tame ducks and soon became fat and lazy. Eventually he forgot how to fly.

In the spring and fall, however, as the wild ducks flew overhead, he looked up and wistfully wished he could fly with them; but he couldn't,

because he had forgotten how. His old friends heard about what had happened, and wrote this poem about him.
He's a pretty good duck for the shape he's in,
But he isn't the duck that he might have been.
Taking the easy path may seem like the profitable choice to take, but in doing so you will never achieve your full potential.

Day 351

Bill Walsh became a TV commentator after retiring as coach of the San Francisco Forty-Niners, but he soon realized how much he missed coaching. So he decided to conduct a series of camps for NFL quarterbacks which emphasized the basics.

He had these football pros paying $10,000 for a week-long training session that focused on the kinds of simple techniques taught to children on peewee teams. But NFL coaches and quarterbacks knew it was worth it.

New York Jets coach, Bruce Coslet, was the first to enroll his quarterbacks. He commented, "The number one premise when a quarterback gets to the pro level is that he knows everything, but their technique can slip. They need drills to reinforce it over and over again, and I can't think of anyone who is a better teacher and technician than Bill Walsh."

If you feel your technique slipping, you may want to look again at the basics.

Day 352

If you look at old maps of the ocean currents, you will see large areas just north of the equator in the Atlantic, Pacific, and Indian oceans marked "doldrums." This is an area between the prevailing oceanic winds where the air is very still, warm and humid. Sea captains learned to avoid the doldrums early on.

However, every now and then an unfortunate sailing ship would wander into the center of the doldrums—or the doldrums would shift north or south to capture unwary ships.

The sails on such a ship would sag and droop lifelessly for days on end. The sun would beat down, creating a smelly, humid dungeon of the ship's interior. Sailors would get sick. Occasionally light, baffling winds would stir some excitement in the crew, but in the doldrums winds blow with little consistency.

The only hope of survival for a ship caught in the doldrums was a sustained breeze. But sustained breezes are so rare in the doldrums that some ships were actually caught for so long that their crews died, only to be found later when the ship finally drifted clear of the calm, killing waters.

Be aware of where your own doldrums are, and try to stay away from them. Few things can kill motivation better than a long period of sustained unproductiveness.

Day 353

Vilfredo Pareto, a mathematician, sociologist, and economist of the 1800s, gave us the 80/20 rule. Pareto theorized that in any given group there are relatively few "significant" items, and that attention must be placed on these if maximum results are to be expected. His conclusion was that 80 percent of the results will come from 20 percent of the events. For instance, an insurance company discovered that 80 percent of its income came from 20 percent of its clients. A manufacturing firm realized that 80 percent of its sales was coming from 20 percent of its product line. It would seem to follow from this that, in any organization, 20% of the people do 80% of the work. Resolve that you will be part of the productive 20%.

Day 354

Once there was an article on Tom Cruise in the *Washington Post*, which examined the method that he used to get him where he is today: hard work. Don Simpson, producer of *Top Gun*, learned about Cruise's dedication to work at a school for race car driving. "We were supposed to study a racing manual," Simpson recalled for the reporter, "but I preferred watching TV. Tom Cruise would come in the room and say, 'Hey, turn that thing off, we've gotta study.' Then he'd make me quiz him until midnight."

Simpson said to Cruise, "You go 100 percent at everything, don't you?"

Tom replied, "That's the only way I know how to do it. Full speed ahead at 100 percent!"

Day 355

Work is a gift: In 1937 songwriter Cole Porter was severely injured when he fell off a horse and both his legs were crushed. This led to long years of pain and more than 30 operations. Meanwhile, Porter immersed himself in his work. His best songs were written in the 10 years following the accident.

When asked by a reporter if he composed easily, Porter replied, "When this horse fell on me I was too stunned to be conscious of great pain, but until help came, I worked on the lyrics of the songs for 'You Never Know.'"

Porter, feeling this tremendous desire to work, kept his mind busy even in time of great physical agony.

Day 356

Dr. Benjamin Bloom of the University of Chicago conducted a five-year study of leading artists, athletes, and scholars based on anonymous interviews with the top twenty performers in various fields, as well as their friends, families and teachers. He wanted to discover the common characteristics possessed by these achievers which led to their tremendous successes.

"We expected to find tales of great natural gifts," Bloom commented, "We didn't find that at all. Their mothers often said it was another child who had the greater talents." What they did find were accounts of extreme hard work and dedication: the swimmer who performed laps for two hours every morning before school and the pianist who practiced several hours a day for seventeen years. Bloom's research determined conclusively that drive, determination, and hard work, not great natural talent, were what led these individuals to their extraordinary achievements.

Day 357

In May 1927, a secretary rushed into her boss's office shouting, "He did it! He did it! Lindbergh has landed in Paris!" The boss was unimpressed. "Don't you understand?" she asked. "Lindbergh has flown the Atlantic all by himself."

"A man can do anything by himself," the boss replied quietly. "Let me know when a committee has flown the Atlantic."

Investigators say perhaps a dozen people planned the World Trade Center bombing. Having worked on committees, we're amazed the explosion ever occurred.

Meeting: I came, I saw, I concurred.

305

Day 358

In a national study, top achievers were asked to rate the factors that they considered to be most important in contributing to their success. Hard work emerged as the highest-rated factor. Not talent or luck—hard work. This was true even for areas in which one would think talent would be the critical factor, such as music or drama or sports.

Another study of elite student violinists showed that the number of hours spent practicing was the only factor which separated potential music superstars from others who were merely good. Following the careers of violinists studying at the Music Academy of West Berlin, psychologists found that by the time the students were 18, the best musicians had already spent about 2,000 more hours in practice, on average, than their fellow students.

As some unknown writer once said:

"A loose wire gives out no musical note; but fasten the ends, and the piano, the harp or the violin is born. Free steam drives no machine, but hamper and confine it with piston and turbine and you have the great world of machinery made possible. The unhampered river drives no dynamos, but dam it up and we get power sufficient to light a great city. So our lives must be disciplined if we are to be of any real service in this world."

Day 359

A Japanese company and an American company had a boat race; the Japanese won by a mile. The Americans hired analysts to figure out what went wrong. They reported that the Japanese had one person managing and seven rowing, while the Americans had seven managing and only one rowing. The American company immediately restructured its team. Now they had one senior manager, six management consultants and one rower.

In the rematch the Japanese won by two miles. So the American company fired the rower.

Restructuring organizations will not revive them if there is not a determined effort to win the minds and the hearts of the workforce. Motivating employees to give their best is still the secret to successful business.

Day 360

I went to visit a Mountaineer in East Tennessee. He was the laziest man I have ever seen. I don't want to do him an injustice, but if it required any voluntary and sustained exertion on his part to digest his food, he would have died years ago from lack of nourishment. The father and son were sitting in front of the fireplace smoking their pipes.

Said the father, "Son, step outside and see if it's raining."

Said the son, "Aw Pa, why don't we jest call in the dog and see if he's wet!"

How can we motivate people? We can't. Motivation comes from within. In today's highly competitive business environment, though, motivation is more important than ever before. As someone has said, "Laziness travels so slowly that poverty soon overtakes it." Or as an old Chinese Proverb puts it, "Man stand for long time with mouth open before roast duck fly in."

Day 361

There once was a salesman who was stuck on an elevator between floors in an office building where he had some clients waiting for him. Nobody in the building knew he was there, but luckily there was a telephone in the elevator, which he used to call the fire department to report his predicament. While he was waiting for the fire department and an elevator service person to free him, he got on the telephone and called each of his accounts in the building, explaining what had happened and taking their orders by phone. By the time he was released, some two and a half hours later, he had finished all his business in the building and was on his way to the next appointment.

A wise use of available resources now may save you a lot of time and hassle later.

Day 362

In the 1930s, Duncan Hines traveled across the U.S. as a Public Relations man. He discovered, as he journeyed, that the different restaurants in which he dined were uneven in quality. He loved to eat, and he wanted to keep a record of the best places, so he began to take notes. He would ask locals for their recommendations, sometimes eat as many as six meals a day, and write vigorously about the best stops. Eventually he filled up several notebooks, and before long he published a book. People began to call him at home each day to find out where the best places were to eat on an upcoming trip.

It wasn't long before the name of Duncan Hines became associated with good eating all across America. And that's why when a certain businessman wanted to introduce a new line of food products, he linked up with Duncan Hines.

Work with your abilities and interests to enhance your work environment. Who knows where it might lead you.

Day 363

There was once a great Quaker leader by the name of Rufus Jones. Jones wrote and published one book a year for over fifty years. He did this while attending countless meetings, making frequent speeches, editing a magazine and taking care of countless other chores that his position required. Someone once asked him how under these circumstances he found the time to write so many books. He answered, "I wrote my books on Tuesdays." Throughout his career he set aside Tuesdays as his one "free" day—accepting no appointments that could be avoided. He began after breakfast and wrote until dark. He might think about his next project all week long, but he did not put it on paper until Tuesday. By following that simple plan he left behind a great body of work.

Day 364

E. Paul Hovey tells about an eager young person who was employed during his summer vacation in a shirt factory. A bonus was offered to workers in this factory who produced the most shirts, so the young man worked very quickly. Unfortunately, however, he destroyed a lot of good cloth in his haste.

When the superintendent came to reprimand him for his haste, the boy said that only a few shirts were poorly cut out: eighty-five per cent of them were fine. And in school 85 percent is good.

His boss retorted, "A grade of 85 per cent may be good enough in school, but I'd soon go out of business if 15 percent of my material was spoiled. When you work quickly, you must also work skillfully."

Day 365

Charlie Moore has set a football record that, like George Blanda's and Walter Payton's, may never be broken: Moore recently made his 14 millionth football. He went to work at Wilson Sporting Goods Company's factory in Ada, Ohio, at the age of 21, and has churned out pigskins ever since with such zeal his photo already graces the Pro Football Hall of

Fame in Canton, Ohio. "This ain't a job," he says, recalling the nights and weekends he's given to his craft. "It's a passion."

For Reflection

Arthur Gordon, in his book *A Touch of Wonder*, talks about "The Power of Purposeful Pausing." Robert Louis Stevenson once said that, "Extreme busyness, whether at school, work or market, is a symptom of deficient energy." In other words, staying busy is not the sign of a person with a high energy level. It is rather the sign of a lazy person. The overly busy person has not put enough energy into the really hard work of thinking and setting priorities first. Arthur Gordon discusses this and concludes that if we took more time to pause, we would increase our efficiency, and the work we do would be of a better quality.

1) Are you busy working on life's non-essentials? How might you invest time and thought now to make your work more efficient and worthwhile later?

2) What is it about your work that energizes and motivates you? How could you spend more time on these aspects of your career?

3) What could you do to make your meetings more efficient and productive?

4) How might you motivate your team members to view their work more positively?

NOTES

Introduction: (New York: Harper & Row). Story attributed to Gregory Bateson.
Day 2: Douglas M. Lawson, *Give To Live* (California: ALTI Publishing, 1991), pp.109-110.
Day 3: James Hewett, *How to Live Confidently in a Hostile World*, (Wheaton, IL: Word Publishing, 1989), pp. 115-116.
Day 5: Sarah Brown, quoted by H. Jackson Brown, Jr., in *P.S. I Love You* (Rutledge Hill).
Day 6: Gerard L. Nierenberg, *You're the Expert: How You Can Solve Your Problems In Business and in Life*, (New York: Berkley Books, 1986), pp. 61-62.
Day 12: John Madden, *One Knee Equals Two Feet*, (New York: Jove Books), 1987.
Day 13: Martin Thielen, *Getting Ready For Sunday's Sermon*, (Nashville: Broadman Press. 1990).
Day 14: Denis Waitley, *Personal Selling Power*
Day 16: Joe Franklin, *A Gift For People*, (New York: M. Evans and Company, Inc.,1971).
Day 20: Don Emmitte
Day 21: George Shinn, *The Miracle Of Motivation* (Wheaton, Illinois: Tyndale House Publishers, Inc., 1981), p.293, p. 141.
Day 23: Milch, Robert J. "Work Horse of the Skies," *American History Illustrated*. June, 1967, p. 23-30.
Day 24: Timothy C. Walker, *The Stained Glass Gospel*.
Day 25: From a sermon by Eric Ritz
Day 26: Richard L. Weaver II. "Attitude, Not Aptitude, Determines Attitude." in *Vital Speeches of the Day*.
Day 30: Dolly Parton, *Dolly* (HarperCollins).
Day 31: *Bits & Pieces*, January 6, 1994, p. 17.
Attitude: John C. Maxwell, *The Winning Attitude*, (Nashville: Thomas Nelson Publishers, 1993).
Day 32: Benjamin Hoff, *The Tao of Pooh*, (New York: E.P. Dutton, Inc., 1982).
Day 35: Dr. David J. Schwartz. *The Magic of Thinking Success, Your Personal Guide to Financial Independence*, (North Hollywood: Wilshire Book Company, 1987).
Day 36: "Reflections on Retirement," by Warren Bennis, *Vital Speeches of the Day*, Oct.1, 1995, p. 754.

Day 37: Elaine M. Ward, *Once Upon a Parable* . . . (Educational Ministries, Inc., 1994), p. 122.
Day 38: Dennis Conner, *The Art of Winning*, (New York: St. Martin's Press, 1988), pp. 177-178.
Reflection (after Day 38): Maurice Boyd, *A Lover's Quarrel With the World*, (Philadelphia, Pennsylvania: The Westminster Press, 1985).
Day 39: David W. Richardson
Day 41: Philip Holzman and George S. Klein, "Motive and Style in Reality Contact," *Bulletin of the Menninger Clinic 20* (1956): 181-91. Cited in Dr. Nelson Boswell, *Inner Peace, Inner Power* (New York: Ballantine, 1985).
Day 42: Newt Gingrich, Renewing American Civilization video; "Master of the House, Nancy Gibbs and Karen Tumulty, *Time*, December 25, 1995-January 1, 1996.
Charles R. Swindoll, *The Bride* (Grand Rapids, Michigan: Zondervan Publishing House, 1994), p. 114.
Day 43: *The Executive Speechwriter Newsletter*
Reflection (after Day 44): S.H. Simmon, *New Speaker's Handbook*, (New York: The Dial Press, 1972).
Day 45: Tim Bowden, *One Crowded Hour* in Jon Noble, "To Illustrate . . ." *Leadership* (Spring, 1990), p. 48.
Day 47: Dr. Eugene Brice
Day 48: "Show Dog Flees, Misses Flight," *The Knoxville News-Sentinel* (June 17, 1989), Section A, p. 5.
Day 49: Edward B. Lambeth, "Gene Roberts," *The Quill*, June 1991, p. 22, p. 111.
Day 51: Josh McDowell, *The Secret of Loving*, (San Bernardino, CA: Here's Life Publishers, 1985).
Day 52: *More Beautiful Than Diamonds*, (Nashville, TN; Thomas Nelson Publishers, 1991).
Reflection (after Day 52): Sir Thomas More, *Utopia*, (Penguin Classics, 1965), p. 75.
Day 53: Earl F. Palmer, *Love Has Its Reasons* (Waco: Word, 1977).
Day 54: S. Baum, "The Gifted Preschooler: An Awesome Delight," *Gifted Child Today*, 9(4)(1986), 42-43.
Day 55: Thomas Butts, *Tigers in the Dark*, (Nashville: Abingdon, 1974).
Day 56: Richard Wokomir, "Mounties Forever, But These Days Rarely on Horseback." *Smithsonian*. Feb, 1989, p. 82.
Day 57: William W. Purkey, *Self Concept and School Achievement*, (Englewood Cliffs, N.J: Prentice-Hall, 1970), p. 1-2.
Day 60: (New York: Warner Books, 1983).

Day 63: Bill G. Bruster and Robert Dale, *How to Encourage Others*, (Nashville: Broadman Press. 1983).
Creativity: B. Eugene Griessman, *Time Tactics Of Very Successful People*, (New York: McGraw-Hill, Inc., 1994), pp. 47-48.
Day 66: From a speech by Robert McVicker, senior vice president of Kraft General Foods, Speaker's Idea File.
Day 67: James W. Moore, *Some Things Are Too Good Not To Be True*, (Nashville: Dimensions for Living, 1994).
Day 68: Marcia B. Cherney and Susan A. Tynan, *Communicoding*, (New York: Donald I. Fine, Inc., 1989), p. 36.
Day 69: Gerard L. Nierenberg, *You're The Expert: How You Can Solve Your Problems In Business And In Life*, (New York: Berkley Books, 1986), pp. 87-88.
Day 71: Betty Goodwin, "How Far Actors Will Go to Land a Role," April 23, 1988.
Day 72: Alex Osborn, L.H.D., *Your Creative Power*, (New York: N.Y.: Dell Publishing Co., Inc., 1948).
Reflection (after Day 72): Joel Arthur Baker, *Paradigms*, (New York: HarperCollins Publishers, Inc., 1992).
Customer Service: Bruce Nash and Allan Zullo, *The Misfortune* (New York: Simon & Schuster, Inc., 1988), p. 114.
Day 73: *Training & Development*, July 1994, pp. 2-3.
Day 76: Esther Blumenfeld and Lynne Alpern, *The Smile Connection* (New York: Prentice Hall Press, 1986), p. 58.
Day 78: John C. Maxwell, *The Winning Attitude*, (Nashville: Thomas Nelson Publishers, 1993). Reprinted with permission.
Day 80: J.B. Fowler, Jr., *Illustrated Sermons For Special Occasions*, Nashville, Tennessee: Broadman Press, 1988.
Day 81: Don Emmitte
Day 82: Michael Crichton, "Travels," *Esquire*, May 1988.
Reflection (after Day 82): Peter Hay, *The Book Of Business Anecdotes* (New York, NY: Facts On File Publications, 1988).
Day 86: David Frost. *Book Of World's Worst Decisions*. New York: Prince Paperbacks-Crown Publishers, Inc. 1983.
Determination: Norman Vincent Peale, *The Power Of Positive Living* (New York: Doubleday, 1990).
Day 87: Gary Inrigh, *A Call To Excellence*, (Wheaton: Victor, 1985).
Day 88: Mark O. Wilson. Hayward, WI. Moreno Valley Butterfield Express. p. A-14, 3/8/89.
Day 89: (New York: Berkley Books, 1990).

Day 90: Herman L. Masin, *For Laughing Out Loud* (New York: Scholastic Book Services, 1954).
Day 91: Keith A. White "Spirit of the Olympics" *Reader's Digest* Jul.1992 pp.133-136.
Day 92: Hubert E. Dobson, *Power To Excel* (Houston: Rich Publishing Co., 1982).
Day 93: H.S. Vigeveno, *How To Live The Good Life* (Eugene, Ore: Harvest House Publishers, 1982).
Day 94: Sufrin, Mark. "Saga of the U.S.S. England," *American History Illustrated* (June, 1970), pp. 13-23.
Day 95: James W. Moore, *Is There Life After Stress?* Nashville: Dimensions for Living, 1992, p. 63.
Day 99: William R. Lampkin, *Minute Devotions*, (Lima, Ohio: Fairway Press, 1990).
Day 100: (New York: Harper and Row, 1967), p. 57. Reprinted with permission.
Day 101: Henry Gariepy, *Wisdom To Live By*, (Wheaton, Illinois: Victor Books, 1991), p. 57.
Day 103: Laura A. Liswood, *Serving Them Right*, (HarperCollins Publishers, 1990).
    Howard G. Hendricks, William D. Hendricks, *Living By The Book* (Chicago: Moody Press, 1991), p. 17.
Day 104: Harvey MacKay, *Swim With The Sharks*, (New York: William Morrow and Company, Inc., 1988).
Day 106: Cecil G. Osborne, *The Art Of Getting Along With People*, (Grand Rapids: Zondervan, 1980), pp. 176-77.
Day 107: Lee Buck, *Tapping Your Secret Source Of Power*, (Old Tappan, NJ: Fleming H. Revell Co. 1985).
Day 109: Bruce Barton, *The Man Nobody Knows*, (New York: Macmillan Publishing Company, 1952).
Day 111: *News of the Weird* (Plume Book: 1989), *Campus Life*, October 1994, p. 39.
Day 113: Dennis Conner, *The Art Of Winning*, (New York: St. Martin's Press, 1988), p. 41. Reprinted with permission.
Day 114: Al Ries and Jack Trout, *Horse Sense*, (New York: McGraw-Hill, Inc., 1991).
Day 115: (New York: Avon Books, 1971).
Day 116: Jack Canfield and Mark Victor Hansen, *A 2nd Helping Of Chicken Soup For The Soul*, (Deerfield Beach, FL: Health Communications, Inc., 1995), pp. 85-86. Reprinted with permission.
Day 118: "What's So Good About Failure?" condensed from *Fortune* by

Patricia Sellers, *Reader's Digest*, August 1995, p. 110.
Day 119: Warren Bennis, *On Becoming a Leader*.
Day 120: Quote from historian Paul Israel, "The Undiscovered World of Thomas Edison," by Kathleeen McAuliffe, *Atlantic Monthly*, December 1995, p. 88.
Day 122: "Fathers of Invention," (research by Eric Nash), *The New York Times Magazine*, January 1, 1995, p. 28.
Day 124: F. W. Woolsey. *Louisville Courier-Journal Magazine*.
Day 129: Ronald F. Bridges, *Disciplines of the Devoted Heart*, (San Bernardino, CA: Here's Life Publishers, 1991).
Illustration Digest, Dec-Jan-Feb 1992/3, p.15.
Day 130: "Remember the Risen Christ," by Maurice R. Irvin, *Alliance Life*, March 27, 1996, p. 8.
Day 132: Source unknown.
Reflection (after Day 133): "Just Showing Up," by Martha Manning, *Salt of the Earth*, Nov./Dec. 1995, p. 38.
Day 138: Tim Hansel, *Holy Sweat*, (Waco: Word Books. 1987).
Day 139: John Madden, *One Knee Equals Two Feet*, (New York: Jove Books, 1986).
Day 140: *A Celebration of American Folklore*, (New York: Pantheon Books, 1982).
Day 141: Robert Conklin, *Think Yourself to the Riches of Life* (Chicago: Contemporary Books, Inc., 1992), pp. 19-20.
Day 142: Skip Ross, *Say Yes To Your Potential*, (Waco: Word, 1983).
Day 143: Doug Parker, "Energy is derived from a goal."
Day 144: (Colorado Springs, Colorado: NavPress, 1989), p. 102.
Day 145: Jack Canfield and Mark Victor Hansen, *Chicken Soup for the Soul*,(Deerfield Beach, FL: Health Communications, Inc., 1994), pp. 173-176. Reprinted with permission.
Day 146: Don J. McMinn, *Strategic Living*, (Grand Rapids, Michigan: Baker Book House, 1988).
Day 147: Richard Koffarnus in Eileen H. Wilmoth, *365 Devotions*, (Cincinnati, Ohio: The Standard Publishing Company, 1993).
Day 148: Robert McGarvey, "Get What You Want Out of Life," *Reader's Digest*, June '92, p. 106.
Day 152: Billy Graham
Day 153: James L. Lundy, *Teams*, (Chicago, IL: The Dartnell Corporation, 1994).
"Frank & Ernest," *The Knoxville News-Sentinel* (Aug. 10, 1990), Section B, p. 5.
Day 154: "Silver Medalist KO's Imposter But Not Middleweight

Champ," *The Knoxville News-Sentinel* (July 18, 1990).
Day 155: Don Martin, *Team Think* (New York: Penguin Books Ltd: 1993), pp. 88-89.
Day 156: Paul Tournier, *A Listening Ear*, (Minneapolis: Augsburg Publishing House, 1986). Reprinted with permission.
Day 157: Albert L. Hock in *Augsburg Sermons 2*, Gospel Series A. (Minneapolis: Augsburg Publishing House, 1983).
Day 158:"The Speaker's Digest," *Quote*, May-June 1993, p. 171.
Day 159: James McDermott, *Daily Guideposts*. (New York: Guideposts, 1983), pp. 227-228.
Day 162: Bruce Larson, *My Creator, My Friend*, (Waco: Word, 1986).
Day 163: Don Martin, *Team Think* (New York: Penguin Books Ltd: 1993), p. 91.
Day 164: Bob Ward, *The Light Stuff*, (Huntsville, Alabama: Jester Books, 1982).
Day 166: Lee Iacocca, *Talking Straight*, (New York: Bantam Books, 1988). Reprinted with permission.
Day 167: Cullen, Joseph P. "James' Towne,"*American History Illustrated*. October, 1972. p. 33.
Day 168: Chuck and Anne Murphy, *When the Saints Go Marching Out*, (New Jersey: Chosen Books, 1986), pp. 121-122.
Day 171: Adrian P. Rogers, *God's Way to Health Wealth and Wisdom*, (Nashville, Tennessee: Broadman Press, 1987).
Day 173: *The Winning Attitude*, (Nashville: Thomas Nelson, 1993).
Reflection (after Day 173): Philip Markanna, "Ghosts," *American History Illustrated, XXIII* (May, 1988), p. 25.
Day 174: Gerald and Patricia Del Re, *The Only Book* (New York: Ballantine Books, 1994), pp. 172-173.
Day 175: Lloyd Dobyns and Clare Crawford-Mason, *Quality Or Else*, (New York: Houghton Mifflin Company, 1991).
Day 176: William E. Diehl, *Thank God, It's Monday*, (Philadelphia: Fortress Press, 1982).
Day 177: Earl C. David, First Baptist Pulpit, Memphis, TN, March 31, 1991.
Day 179: Karl Albrecht, *At America's Service*, (NewYork: Warner Books, 1992) p. 92.
Day 180: Tom Finley. *The World Is Not Enough*. (Ventura, Ca.: Regal Books, 1986).
The Jokesmith, Vol. VIII, No. 3, p. 4.
Day 181: Jerry D. Twentier, *The Positive Power Of Praising People*, (Nashville: Thomas Nelson Publishers, 1994).
Day 182: Thomas S. Haggai, *Today*, (Nashville, Tennessee: Thomas

Nelson Publishers, 1989).
Day 183: Bill Leavins, Troy AL
Day 184: Fran Tarkenton, *Playing to Win*, (Toronto, New York: Bantam Books, 1984).
Day 187: Gary Collins, *You Can Make A Difference*, (Grand Rapids, MI: Zondervan Publishing House, 1992), p. 57.
Day 188: Jamie Buckingham, *Parables*, (Lake Mary, Florida: Creation House, 1991).
Day 189: Dennis Conner, *The Art Of Winning*, (New York: St. Martin's Press, 1988), pp. 141-142. Reprinted with permission.
Reflection (after day 189): "Lessons in Leadership," Vol. 12 No. 5, *Personal Selling Power*, 15th Anniv. Issue 1995, p. 86.
Day 190: John W. Drakeford, *The Awesome Power Of The Listening Heart*, (Grand Rapids: Zondervan Corporation, 1982).
Day 191: (New York: Harper & Row, 1985).
Day 192: Tony Campolo, *Who Switched the Price Tags?* (Waco: Word Books, 1986).
Day 193: Eileen Dempsey, Scripps Howard News Service.
Day 195: (*Odyssey*) --Gordon MacDonald, *Rebuilding Your Broken World*, (Nashville: Oliver-Nelson Books, 1988).
Day 196: "Soviets Assured Cigarette Shortage Won't Last," *The Knoxville News-Sentinel* (Aug. 26, 1990).
Day 197: William E. Hulme, *Managing Stress In Ministry*, (San Francisco: Harper and Row Publishers, 1985).
Day 199: Ruby Dee, *Modern Maturity*, Jul.-Aug. 1994, p. 85.
Day 200: Neil Eskelin, *Yes Yes Living In A No NoWorld*, (New Jersey: Logos International, 1980), p. 144.
Day 202: In the "Letters" section of the *Lexington Herald-Leader* by H. D. Uriel Smith, March 14, 1995, p. A 8.
Day 206: Joseph L. Felix, *It's Easier For A Rich Man To Enter Heaven*, (Nashville: Thomas Nelson Publishers, 1981).
Day 209: Anthony de Mello, *Taking Flight* (New York: Bantam Doubleday Dell Publishing Group, Inc., 1990), p. 173.
Day 210: Denis Waitley in *The Winner's Edge* (Berkley Books).
Day 212: (New York: Bantom Books, 1980). Reprinted with permission.
Day 213: M.W.Cohn (Phoenix Ariz.) *Reader's Digest*, Feb. '84.
Day 214: Mortimer R. Feinberg, Ph.D., *Effective Psychology for Managers*, (Englewood Cliffs, N.J.: Prentice-Hall, Inc.).
Day 216: Claire Poole "Once you're hungry, you're different," *Forbes 400* Oct. 19, 1992 p. 44.
Day 217: Richard Lamparski, *Whatever Became Of . . . ?*, (New York: Crown Publishers, Inc., 1967), p. 60-61.

Day 218: Charles R. Swindoll, *Stress Fractures* (Multnomah Press, 1990), pp. 267-268. Reprinted with permission.
Day 219: *Laugh Connections*, Vol. 3, Summer, 1991, p.4.
Bits & Pieces, July 21, 1994, p. 19.
Day 220: Don Jacobs, "Robbery Suspect Thanks Man Who Captured Him," *The Knoxville News-Sentinel* (June 26, 1990).
Day 221: Bruce Larson, *Wind and Fire*, (Waco: Word Books, 1984).
Day 222: Brian Adams, *Sales Cybernetics*, (California: Wilshire Book Company, 1985), p. 137.
Reflection (after day 222): Lloyd Dobyns and Clare Crawford-Mason, *Quality Or Else*, (New York:Houghton Mifflin Company, 1991).
Day 223: Dr. Denis Waitley, *The Double Win*, (New York: Berkley Book, 1985).
Day 227: Michael Hodgin, *1001 Humorous Illustrations For Public Speaking* (Michigan: Zondervan Publishing House, 1994), p. 248.
Context, 21:3, February 1, 1989, p. 1. Cited in Mark Trotter, *What Are You Waiting For?* (Nashville, Tennessee: Abingdon Press, 1992), p. 93.
Day 228: Leslie Parrott, *The Habit Of Happiness* (Waco, TX: Word Books Publisher, 1987), pp. 184-185.
Day 229: *The Emmanuel Factor*, (Nashville: Broadman Press, 1987).
Day 230: Charles Kuralt, *A Life on the Road*, (New York: G.P. Putnam's Sons), 1990, pp. 177-178.
Day 231: *The Detroit News. USA Week-End.* 10-21/23-88, p. 5.
Reflection (after Day 232): Bernice Kanner, *Are You Normal?* (New York: St. Martin's Press, 1995), p. 82.
Day 233: Carol Hyatt and Linda Gottlieb, *When Smart People Fail*, (New York: Simon and Schuster, 1987).
Day 234: Thanks to Reverend Robert Harding of Omaha, Nebraska.
Day 236: J. Kenyon Rainer, M.D., *First Do No Harm: The Making of a Neurosurgeon*, (New York: Random House, 1987).
Day 239: *Parade Magazine*, April 21, 1996.
Day 240: Norman Vincent Peale, *The Power of Positive Living* (New York: Doubleday, 1990).
Day 243: Christopher Dickey, "The Princes of Tides" *Newsweek*, Aug. 10, 1992, p. 26.
Day 245: C. W. Bess, *Sermons for the Seasons*, (Nashville: Broadman Press, 1985).

Perspective: Arnold Willis, *Sense and Nonsense*, contributed by David Karges, Hydro, OK.
Day 246: Haddon B. Robinson, *The Christian Salt and Light Company*, (Discovery House Publishers, 1988), p 34.
Day 248: Paul Tournier, *The Listening Ear*, (Minneapolis: Augsburg Publishing House), 1986.
Day 250: Carl Lomen, the reindeer king of Alaska, *Keep Open the Window of Your Mind* by Merle Crowell in the *The American Magazine*.
Day 251: *The Desert Fathers*
Day 252: Terry Hershey, *Go Away, Come Closer*, (Dallas: Word Books, 1990).
Day 253: Tony Campolo, *Everything You've Heard Is Wrong*, (Dallas: Word Publishing, 1992), pp. 157-158. Reprinted with permission.
Day 254: A. Philip Parham. *Letting God*. New York: Harper & Row.
Reflection (after Day 254): Bennett Cerf, *The Sound Of Laughter* (New York: Bantam Books, 1970).
Day 257: *Boston Globe*
Day 258: *Funny, Funny World*, July, 1985.
Day 260: From historian Paul Israel, "The Undiscovered World of Thomas Edison," by Kathleen McAuliffe, *Atlantic Monthly*, December 1995, p. 93.
Day 261: Ronald K. Brooks, *A Flint, A Sponge, Or A Honeycomb*, (Lima, OH: Fairway Press, 1993).
Day 263: *Vital Speeches*
Day 266: *Forbes*, April 26, 1993, p. 64.
Day 268: Tony Campolo, *Everything You've Heard Is Wrong*, (Dallas: Word Publishing, 1992), p. 185. Reprinted with permission.
Day 269: Gary Inrig, *A Call To Excellence* (Wheaton, IL: Victor Books, 1985).
Day 270: Dr. William P. Barker, *Tarbell's Teacher's Guide*, (Elgin, Illinois: David C. Cook Publishing Co., 1988).
Day 272: John R. Noe, *Peak Performance Principles For High Achievers*, (New York: Berkley Books, 1984).
Day 273: Herb Miller, *Actions Speak Louder Than Verbs*, (Nashville: Abingdon Press, 1989).
Day 275: As told by Charlie "Tremendous" Jones in *Life Is Tremendous*, (Wheaton, IL: Living Books, 1982).
Day 277: Thanks to Rev. Rodney J. Miller, Church of the Nazarene, Potomac IL for this illustration.
Day 278: *Augsburg Sermons 3*, (Augsburg, Minneapolis: Gospels,

Series C, 1994), by Loren J. Gustafon, p. 64.
Day 284: Charles Paul Conn, *Making It Happen*, (New York: Berkeley Books, 1983).
Day 285: Bruce Larson, *The Presence*, (HarperCollins Publishers, 1988), pp. 40-41.
Day 286: *Today*, (Nashville, Tennessee: Thomas Nelson, 1989).
Day 287: Charles L. Allen, *Powerless But Not Helpless*, (Tarrytown, New York: Fleming H. Revell Company, 1954/1992), p. 93.
Day 288: Robert H. Schuller, *Success Is Never Ending--Failure Is Never Final* (Nashville: Thomas Nelson, 1988).
Day 289: David Albert Farmer and Edwina Hunter, *And Blessed Is She* (San Francisco: Harper & Row, Publishers, 1990).
Day 291: Bill Bryson, *Made In America*, (New York: William Morrow and Company, Inc., 1994), pp. 169-170.
Day 292: Jerry McQuay, Christian Life Center, Tinley Pack, IL.
Day 293: Attributed to Dr. William Barclay of Scotland.
Day 294: (New York: Prentice-Hall Press).
Day 296: *And the Angels Were Silent*, Max Lucado, Multnomah Books, Chapter 9, "Courage to Dream Again," pp. 67-68. Reprinted with permission.
Day 297: William Manchester, *The Last Lion: Winston Spencer Churchill*, Vol. I (Boston: Little, Brown & Company), 1989.
Day 298: (Murfreesboro, TN: Sword of the Lord Publishers, 1993).
Day 301: Robert Fulghum, "Time to Sacrifice the Queen," *Reader's Digest*, August 1993, p. 136.
Reflection (after Day 301): Bruce Felton and Mark Fowler, *Best, Worst*, (New York: Gramercy Publishing Company, 1975).
Day 303: *People* magazine
Day 305: Stephen R. Covey, *Principle Centered Leadership*, (New York: Summit Books, 1990), p. 53. Reprinted with permission.
Day 306: Charles L. Allen, *Joyful Living In The Fourth Dimension*, (Old Tappan, New Jersey: Fleming H. Revell Company, 1983).
Reflection (after Day 306): Anthony Robbins, *Unlimited Power*, (New York: Simon and Schuster), 1986.
Reflection (after Day 310): Al Ries and Jack Trout, *Horse Sense*, (New York: McGraw-Hill, Inc., 1991).
Day 311: By Tom Teicholz, *The New York Times Magazine*, June 5, 1994, p. 34.

Day 312: N. Scott Vance, "Donald Duck Helps Professor." The Detroit News for Scripps Howard News Service.
Day 313: Dennis Conner, *The Art Of Winning*, (New York: St. Martin's Press, 1988), pp. 39-40.
Day 315: Edward Chinn, *Wonder Of Words*, (Lima, Ohio: C.S.S. Publishing Co. Inc, 1987), p 18.
Day 316: *Smithsonian*. January, 1985, p 55ff..
Day 317: "How to Tell If You're Successful," *Catholic Digest*, Oct. 1992.
Day 319: Earl F. Palmer, *Love Has Its Reasons*, (Waco: Word, 1977).
Day 320: Stephen M. Silverman, *Where There's A Will* . . . (New York: Harper-Collins Publishers, 1991), p. 191.
Day 321: (New York: Kensington Publishing Company, 1988). Reflection (after Day 321): *USA Today*, May 10, 1993, p. 3D.
Day 324: C. Everett Koop, *Koop: The Memoirs Of America's Family Doctor*, (New York: Random House, 1991), p. 52.
Day 329: John C. Maxwell, *Developing The Leaders Around You*, p. 1. Reprinted with permission.
Day 331: James A. Harnish, *What Will You Do With King Jesus?*, (Nashville: The Upper Room, 1987).
Day 334: B. Eugene Griessman, *Time Tactics Of Very Successful People*, (New York: McGraw-Hill, Inc., 1994), p.8.
Day 338: Bill Glass, *Expect to Win* (Waco: Word, 1981), p. 52.
Day 339: "Friends in the Soaring '70's: A Church Growth Era, Oregon Yearly Meeting of Friends Churches" (Newberg, OR, August 1969), p. 121.
Ted Engstrom, *High Performance*, (San Bernardino, CA: Here's Life Publishers, 1988), p. 256.
Day 340: *Making The Most Of Life*, (Brownlow, 1988), p. 109.
Day 343: Jamie Buckingham, *Look Out, World*, (Altamonte Springs, FL: Strang Communications Company, 1993).
Good Housekeeping, May 1995, p. 163.
Day 344: "The Competitive Edge," February 1992, pp. 30-31.
Day 345: Dr. William P. Barker, *Tarbell's*, (Elgin, Illinois: David C. Cook Church Ministries, 1994).
Day 346: Richard B. Manchester, *Incredible Facts* (New York, New York: Bristol Books, 1990).
Day 347: Dennis Conner, *The Art Of Winning*, (New York: St. Martin's Press, 1988), p. 170. Reprinted with permission.
Day 348: Dick Hyman, *Washington Wind & Wisdom*, (Lexington, Massachusetts: The Stephen Greene Press, 1988).
Work: Bob Ward, *The Light Stuff*, (Huntsville, Alabama: Jester, 1982).

Day 349: *Stories from Home*, (Jackson, Mississippi: University Press of Mississippi, 1992). Reprinted with permission.
Day 350: Charles L. Allen, *In Quest Of God's Power*, (Old Tappan, N.J: Fleming H. Revell Co), 1952.
Day 351: Dr. John Ed Mathison, "The Weekly Frazer Memorial Messenger," (August, 1990), p 1.
Day 354: Denis Waitley, *Timing Is Everything*, (Nashville: Thomas Nelson Publishers, 1992), p. 178.
Day 355: Mortimer R. Feinberg, Ph.D. *Effective Psychology For Managers*, (Englewood Cliffs, N.J: Prentice-Hall, 1987).
Day 356: Dr. Denis E. Waitley, *Winning the Innovation Game*, (New York: Berkley Books, 1986).
Day 362: *Smithsonian*, November 1984, p. 87.
Day 361: *Sales Upbeat*.
Day 365: Doug Spitzer, "Having a Ball," *Modern Maturity*, May/June 1996, p. 18.

INDEX OF NAMES

Alcott, Louisa May, hd. 27
Aleichem, Shalom, day 232
Alexander the Great, day 180, 276
Ali, Muhammed, day 238
Allen, Woody, day 110
Angelyne, day 303
Anthony, Susan B., day 89
d'Antonio, Agostino, day 336
Atlas, Charles, day 217
Augustine, St., ref. 245

Babblinger, Hans, day 296
Baeyer, Johann von, day 66
Banister, Roger, day 125
Barclay, William, day 297
Bell, Alexander Graham, day 8, 35, 235
Bench, Johnny, day 92
Berlin, Irving, day 72
Birzler, Mrs. Joseph, day 338
Bjork, Amy, day 191
Blanda, George, day 365
Bloom, Benjamin, day 356
Booze, Elmer, day 323
Brahms, Johannes, day 194
Braun, Wernher Von, ref. 44
Brown, Les, day 27
Briggs, LeBaron, day 237
Bristol, Dave, day 353
Buckingham, Jamie, day 342
Burns, James Francis, day 106

Caen, Herb, day 365
Cafego, George, day 90
Campolo, Anthony, day 192
Capone, Al, hd. 255
Carlson, Curtis, day 148
Carnegie, Andrew, day 271
Carroll, Lewis, day 137

Caruso, Enrico, day 110
Cato, Marcus, day 114
Cher, day 26
Chesterton, G.K., day 252
Christie, Agatha, day 37
Churchill, Winston, hd. 174, day 244, 297
Cid, El, 176
Clery, Howard & Connie, day 2
Cohen, Herb, ref. 333
Cohen, Myron, hd. 39
Columbus, Christopher, ref. 64, day 341
Confucius, day 280
Coolidge, Calvin, day 62, 198, ref. 285
Coppersmith, Joshua, Day 39
Corbett, Jim, day 244
Coslet, Bill, day 351
Cousins, Norman, day 76
Covey, Stephen, day 305
Crichton, Michael, day 81
Custer, George, day 56, 168

Darius, day 276
Darwin, Charles, day 26
Davis, Eric, day 153
Davis, Jim, day 37
Demosthenes, ref. 301
Dewey, John, day 5
Diebel, Nelson, day 243
Dietrich, Marlene, day 181
Disney, Walt, day 110
Disraeli, Benjamin, day 26
Dolan, Ellen, ref. 321
Duveen, Joseph, day 258

Eastman, George, day 158
Edison, Thomas, day 26, 35, 64,

70, 120, 135, 201, 260
Einstein, Albert, day 108
Eisenhower, Dwight, day 96, 185
Esterlin, Walter of, day 102
Euclid, Day 364

Fabre, Jean Henri, day 59
Feldman, Ben, day 141
Fisher, Carl Graham, day 291
Fitzgerald, F. Scott, day 26, hd. 162
Ford, Henry, day 70, 108, 169
Fosdick, Harry Emerson, day 61
Franklin, Ben, day 163, 172
Frost, Robert, day 110
Fujimoto, Shun, day 87
Fulghum, Robert, day 301
Galloway, Dale, day 261
Gebel-Williams, G., day 133
Getty, Estell, day 71
Gide, Andre, hd. 275
Gingrich, Newt, day 42
Giovanni, Bertoldo de, day 269
Goddard, John, day 142
Goethe, day 299
Goldwyn, Sam, day 336
Gomez, Lefty, day 325
Gould, Shane, day 210
Grant, Ulysses S., ref. 197
Gray, Thomas, day 245
Grellet, Stephen, hd. 153
Gretzky, Wayne, day 335
Griessman, B. Eugene, hd. 65
Griffin, Merv, day 138

Haggai, Thomas S., day 286
Halsey, Admiral, day 94
Hanks, Nancy, day 97
Hansen, Mark Victor, day 145
Harris, Tom, day 191
Hart, Peter, day 304
Havlicek, John (Hondo), day 15

Haydn, Joseph, day 279
Henry, Joseph, day 84
Hilton, Conrad, day 334
Hines, Duncan, day 362
Hoff, Benjamin, day 32
Holmes, Oliver Wendell, day 50
Holtz, Lou, day 104
Hoover, J. Edgar, day 46
Hopkins, Arthur, day 237
Hovey, E. Paul, day 364
Hugo, Victor, day 204
Hunt, J.B., day 216

Iacocca, Lee, day 148
Ibsen, Henrik, day 150
Ireland, Bob W., day 314

Jackson, Edgar, day 12
Johnson, Lyndon, day 342
Jolson, Al, day 16
Jones, James Earl, day 18
Jones, Rufus, day 363
Jordan, David Starr, hd. 334
Juran, Joseph, ref. 220

Keller, Helen, day 26, 315
Kettering, Charles, hd. 223
Keys, Roger, day 297
King, Billie Jean, day 92
King, Coretta Scott, ref. 288
King, Martin Luther, day 292
Klutznik, Mendel, day 202
Knight, Bobby, day 272
Koop, C. Everett, day 324
Kramer, Jerry, day 221
Kuralt, Charles, day 230
Kuykendal, Dan, day 348

Landry, Tom, day 205, 274
Lasorda, Tommy, day 161
Lee, Ivy, day 275
Lee, Robert E., hd. 45

Leigh-Mallory, George, day 88
Lincoln, Abraham, day 112, 126, 299
Lindbergh, Charles, day 357
Livingstone, David, day 290
Lombardi, Vince, ref. 96
Lotito, Michel, day 146
Louis XIV, day 316

MacDonald, George, day 328
Madden, John, day 11, 139
Madonna, day 315
Mann, Horace, ref. 288
Mantle, Mickey, day 113
Marconi, Guglielmo, day 115
Marriott, John W., day 21
Marshall, Frank, day 301
Marx, Harpo, day 50
Maslow, Abraham, day 307
Maxwell, John C., day 78
McFerrin, Bobby, day 231
McGraw, John J., 266
McMahon, Ed, day 53
Meir, Golda, hd. 32
Mellon, Andrew, day 258
Metzger, Bruce, day 282
Michelangelo, hd. 87, day 97, 105, 240, 269, 336
Milken, Michael, day 311
Miller, Arthur, day 28
Milne, A.A., day 32
Mitchell, Margaret, day 303
Monk, Art, day 180
Montana, Joe, day 11
Moody, Dwight L., day 130
Moore, Bishop Arthur, day 183
Moore, Colleen, day 33
More, Sir Thomas, ref. 52
Morita, Akio, day 103
Morley, Christopher, hd. 233
Moses, Grandma, day 10

Napoleon, day 205, 316, 326
Navratilova, Martina, day 347
Newton, Sir Isaac, day 26, 163
Niebuhr, Reinhold, hd. 322
Nightingale, Earl, day 294, 298

O'Brien, Pat, day 107
Ogilvy, David, day 262
Ormandy, Eugene, ref. 38
Ott, Mel, day 266
Owens, Jesse, day 314

Paderewski, Ignace, day 222
Paganini, Niccolo, day 307
Paige, Hanley, day 293
Pareto, Vilfredo, day 353
Parks, Rosa, day 292
Parton, Dolly, day 30
Pasteur, Louis, day 315
Patton, Gen. George, day 4
Pavarotti, Luciano, ref. 86
Payton, Walter, day 365
Peale, Norman Vincent, day 223
Pearl, Minnie, day 124
Perot, H. Ross, hd. 263
Peters, Tom, Introduction, day 8
Peterson, Bill, day 335
Phelps, Karen, day 241
Picasso, Pablo, day 95
Pickens, T. Boone, hd. 83
Plunkett, Roy, day 122
Porter, Cole, day 355

Quijano, Meg, day 31

Reagan, Ronald, day 36
Redding, Dave, day 24
Reis, Philip, day 235
Rice, Grantland, day 121
Roberts, Gene, day 49
Rockne, Knute, day 208, 254
Rogers, Kenny, hd. 97

Roberson, Lee, day 298
Roosevelt, Eleanor, day 187
Rossini, Day 123
Rubinstein, Anton, day 204
Rubinstein, Arthur, ref. 92, day 101
Ruth, Babe, day 109, 228
Ryan, Irene, day 321

Sandberg, Ryne, ref. 152
Sanford, John, day 310
Savitch, Jessica, day 320
Schubert, Franz, day 253
Schuller, Robert, day 212, 238
Schwab, Charles, day 275, 319
Schwarzkopf, Norman, ref. 189
Schweitzer, Albert, day 299
Seligman, Martin, day 225
Shakespeare, William, day 265, hd. 342
Shirer, William, day 233
Smith, Logan Pearsall, hd. 289
Spitz, Mark, day 186
Staubach, Roger, day 274
Stone, W. Clement, day 29
Stradivari, Antonio, day 101
Sunday, Billy, hd. 286
Swindoll, Chuck, ref. 26, day 42, 327
Syrius, Publius, hd. 137

Tacitus, hd. 59
Tamerlane, Emperor, day 242
Tarkenton, Fran day 184
Teresa, Mother, ref. 136
Thatcher, Margaret, ref. 148
Tiberius, hd. 59
Toffler, Alvin, day 138
Tolstoy, Leo, day 300
Torme, Mel, day 321
Tournier, Paul, day 248

Tranxu, day 343
Truman, Harry, day 175

Uris, Leon, day 110

Van Gogh, Vincent, day 114
Vaughan, Charles, Jr., day 313

Waitley, Dennis, day 13
Walesa, Lech, day 292
Walgreen, Charles R., day 80
Walsh, Bill, day 351
Walton, Sam, day 181
Warfield, Paul, day 147
Washington, George, day 7
Waterman, Robert H., Intro.
Weakland, Rembert G., day 317
Webster, Daniel, hd. 272
Weidner, Barbara, day 289
Welles, Orson, day 181
Wells, H. G., hd. 311
Wersching, Ray, day 139
Westy, Captain William, ref. 64
Wilson, Woodrow, ref. 31
Winters, Shelley, ref. 310
Wirthlin, Richard, day 36
Wood, Robert Elkton, day 200
Wooden, John, day 329
Wright, Frank Lloyd, day 148
Wright, Orville & Wilbur, day 8, ref. 64

Yamaguchi, Kristi, day 91
Yeager, Chuck, day 38
Yeltsin, Boris, day 292
Young, Kevin, day 146

Zeharias, Babe D., day 244
Ziegler, Edward, day 12
Ziglar, Zig, ref. 9, day 224
Zuppke, Bob, day 306

TOPIC INDEX

Ability, day 162
Action, days 1-9; day 30, 85, 144, 234, 241, 268, 349, 365
Adversity, day 2, days 10-26, day 36, 37, 42, 53, 55, 69, 87, 88, 90, 91, 107, 127, 140, 157, 201, 217, 222, 223, 224, 233, 265, 267, 298, 314, 321, 327, 331, 334, 362
Aim, day 132
Anonymity, day 302
Apathy, 268, 302
Appearance, day 57, 67, day 104, 270
Arrogance, day 58, 170, 171, 176
Aspiration, days 27-31, day 63, 263, 341
Attention, day 128
Attitude, day 14, days 32-38, day 44, 78, 80, 120, 123, 126, 148, 160, day 210, 223, 224, 227, 229, 308, 326
Attributes, day 23
Audacity, day 230

Blame, 330
Boredom, day 252

Calm, 32, 34, 282
Challenge, day 143
Change, days 39-44, 111, 220
Choice, day 31, 42
Commitment, day 7, 240
Communication, days 45-52, 153, 288

Compassion, day 218, 322, 338
Competence, day 308
Competition, day 195, 344, 345, 346, 347, 348
Complaint, day 12, 17
Concentration, day 133
Confidence, days 53-58, 210, 212, 228, 230
Conformity, days 59-64, 131, 268, 294
Contribution, 324, 325, 329
Cooperation, day 344
Courage, day 4, 289, 290, 292, 295
Courtesy, day 172
Creativity, day 10, 12, 16, 21, 40, 52, 64, days 66-72, 122, 140, 145, 152, 163, 204, 293, 301, 312, 336, 345, 362
Criticism, day 95
Curiosity, day 125
Customer Service, days 73-82, 100, 103, 106

Deadline, day 208
Deceit, day 305
Decision, days 83-86, 119, 175, 198
Dedication, day 269, 329, 356, 358
Demand, day 17
Depression, 352
Desire, day 196
Detail, day 105, 184, 221, 284
Determination, day 3, 14, 15, 18, 26, 38, 42, 54, 71, days 87-92, 130, 140, 142, 145, 146, 157, 164,

199, 201, 216, 217, 222, 233, 234, 242, 239, 243, 245, 291, 311, 314, 319, 334, 354
Discipline, day 178, 320, 358
Distraction, 128, 278, 337, 355
Dream, day 28, 29, 142, 296

Education, day 164
Efficiency, day 253, 275, 309, 357, 361, 363
Emotion, day 196, 231
Encouragement, day 11, days 93-96, 116
Energy, day 231, 271
Enthusiasm, day 22
Ethics, day 151
Example, day 150
Excellence, day 61, 78, 79, 80, 81, 87, days 97-107, 245, 269, 286
Excuse, day 10, 237
Expectation, day 104, 270
Experience, day 167, 170, 173, 236, 248, 266
Experimentation, day 8
Expert, day 165

Failure, day 71, 72, 73, 86, days 108-124, 136, 266, 267, 311, 313
Fame, day 303
Fear, day 124, 126, 254, 294, 297, 330
Flaw, day 11
Flexibility, day 339
Focus, day 32, 105, days 125-136, 137, 139, 142, 194, 226, 247, 248, 306, 335, 337, 355
Friendliness, day 156

Future, day 39, 150, 166, 229, 232, 315

Genius, day 72, 97, 336
Goals, day 27, 31, 91, 129, days 137-148, 221, 285, 287, 288, 306, 331, 338
Gratitude, day 9, 323, 325, 328
Greed, day 277, 283
Growth, day 13, 299, 303

Happiness, day 37, 161, 320
Health, day 35, 318
Helpfulness, day, 74
Hobby, day 10
Honesty, day 152
Humility, day 252

Idea, day 275, 333
Identity, day 263
Ignorance, day 62, 168, 276, 280
Image, day 183
Incentive, day 200, 206, 215
Indifference, day 75
Influence, day 18, 99, 292, 333
Innovation, day 65, 66, 68, 70
Inspiration, day 205, 212, 242
Instruction, day 83
Integrity, day 77, days 149-152, 206
Intimidation, day 254
Invention, day 66
Involvement, day 174, 187

Jealousy, day 169, 332

Kindness, day 76, 79, 95, 96, 116, days 153-161
Knowledge, day 47, 118, 214, 293, 348, 364, 162-173

Laziness, day 70, 237, 271, 305, 349, 350, 353, 360
Leadership, day 4, 59, 119, 149, 161, days 175-189, 198, 205, 339
Leisure, day 190
Lifestyle, days 192-197
Limitation, day 12
Listening, day 49, 50, 51, 118, 127, 171
Longevity, day 279
Loyalty, day 180, 188, 300

Misguided, day 135, 253
Mission, day 281, 289
Mistake, day 33, 81, 86, 103, 114, 121, 125, 131, 134, 136, 153, 165, 169, 176, 186, 188, 193, 202, 207, 235, 236, 264, 273, 276, 277, 284, 297, 307, 332, 359
Misunderstanding, days 45-47
Money, 209
Motivation, day 93, 94, 95, 143, 177, 184, 185, days 198-222, 256, 259, 352, 353, 354, 360

Name, day 262
Networking, day 3
Nonconformity, day 6, 89, 92, 282

Oblivious, day 24
Obsession, day 342
Obstinacy, day 298, 54
Offense, day 51
Optimism, day 36, days 223-232, 238, 246, 249, 335
Option, day 24, 31

Ownership, day 214

Passion, day 365
Perception, day 114, 135, 139, 178, 318, 340,
Perseverance, day 15, 19, 26, 81, 109, 110, 112, 113, 117, 120, days 233-245, 272, 321
Persistence, day 88, 89, 115
Personality, day 326
Perspective, day 41, 55, 77, 154, 159, days 246-255, 261, 317
Persuasion, day 213, 246, days 256-291, 291
Planning, day 108, 232, 273, 363
Possibility, day 29
Potential, days 264-271, 315, 316, 350
Practice, day 244
Preparation, days 272-274
Pride, 148, 207, 208, 219
Priority, day 138, 146, 151, 154, 157, 158, 165, 179, 189, 192, 202, 211, 226, days 275-285, 343
Problem, day 280
Productivity, day 200
Progress, day 203
Promise, day 186
Protocol, 33
Purpose, day 1, 28, 63, 287, 288

Real, day 34
Relationship, day 50, 51, 76, 322, 327, 347
Resources, day 162, 173, 282, 298
Respect, day 96, 160, 219

329

Results, day 5
Rigid, day 83
Risk, day 3, 4, 6, 30, 40, 56, 59, 109, 113, 115, 117, 118, 124, 258, 274, 285, days 289-297, 301, 313, 316

Sacrifice, days 299-301
Security, day 218
Self-Centered, day 102, 203, 264, 287, days 302-306
Service, day 185, 199, 299, 300
Significance, day 219
Skill, day 167, days 307-310, 319, 346, 351, 364
Status Quo, day 39
Strength, day 20, 290, 310
Stress, day 197
Success, day 3, 5, 21, 38, 110, 122, 137, 142, 144, 148, 149, 158, 164, 180, 181, 189, 195, 272, 274, days 311-321, 328, 343, 356
Suffering, day 238
Support, day 323, 324, 348
Sympathy, day 179

Talent, day 110, 138, 309
Teamwork, days 322-333, 357
Threat, day 256, 259
Time, day 97, 191, 249, 258, 359, 361
Tradition, day 60
Training, day 351
Trapped, day 19
Trust, day 295
Truth, day 250

Unity, day 286
Utility, day 307, 310

Values, day 312
Vision, day 225, 228, 247, days 334-341

Win, day 225, 235, 241, days 342-348
Work, day 35, 197, 281, days 349-365
Worry, day 32, 44

Youth, day 304